# A TRANSLATION OF JEROME'S *CHRONICON*
# WITH HISTORICAL COMMENTARY

# A TRANSLATION OF JEROME'S *CHRONICON* WITH HISTORICAL COMMENTARY

Malcolm Drew Donalson

Mellen University Press
Lewiston/Queenston/Lampeter

**Library of Congress Cataloging-in-Publication Data**

Jerome, Saint, d. 419 or 20.
  [Chronicon. English]
  A translation of Jerome's Chronicon with historical commentary /
Malcolm Drew Donalson.
     p.          cm.
  Includes bibliographical references.
  ISBN 0-7734-2258-7
  1. Church history--Primitive and early church, ca. 30-600.
2. Rome--History--Empire, 284-476.  I. Donalson, Malcolm Drew.
II. Title.
BR65.J473C4713  1996
270.2--dc20

                                            95-35398
                                              CIP

A CIP catalog record for this book is available from the British Library.

    The Edwin Mellen Press                  The Edwin Mellen Press
           Box 450                              Box 67
      Lewiston, New York                 Queenston, Ontario
      USA  14092-0450                   CANADA  L0S 1L0

The Edwin Mellen Press, Ltd.
Lampeter, Dyfed, Wales
UNITED KINGDOM  SA48 7DY

Printed in the United States of America

For Simon Zachary

"And who except you could work such wonders? But You have taken him from this world early in his life, and now I remember him without apprehension, since there was not anything in his boyhood, his youth, or in any portion of his life that should cause me to fear for him."

Augustine,

*Contra secundam Juliani responsionem opus imperfectum*

# TABLE OF CONTENTS

# FOREWORD

When Malcolm Donalson began work in the late 1980's on Jerome's continuation of Eusebius' *Chronicon*, the Latin, Greek and "Oriental" Christian chronicles covering late antiquity presented formidable obstacles to the interpreter. The Latin texts were generally untranslated and hence deprived of the minimal interpretation a translation and translation notes can provide. When translations did exist, they were almost always in Latin and without annotation. The complex and confusing interrelationships among the various chronicles was often recognized, but frequently ignored in practice, as lists citing multiple sources for an event often appeared without any indication of how or even that the notices were related to each other. Independent authority could easily be assumed for clearly dependent sources. Of course, the direction of dependence was not a simple matter. Some later chronicles could be demonstrated to have preserved lost early sources, but a century of Quellenforschung had seemed to many to have been far to speculative. Many source-critical problems appeared intractable and some doubted the value of the entire enterprise. Hence even clear cases of dependence were often left unnoted.

Donalson's dissertation makes Jerome's important work much more accessible, not only providing an English translation and references to ancient sources and modern scholarly literature, but also by demonstrating the value of careful source criticism. The extensive introduction and rich source-critical notes in Helms' magisterial edition (and in the other volumes of the griechischen christlichen Schriftsteller series devoted to historians covering the fourth century) are fully exploited and carefully evaluated. Donalson provides a clear discussion of source-critical controversies and indicates for each notice cases of certain and probable relationships among the sources. This has value, of course, not only for those wishing to use Jerome's work properly, but also for those working with the other sources used by or using the *Chronicon*.

Already while Donalson was in the final stages of his work, interest in the historians and chronicles of late antiquity had begun to experience a dramatic rise. The pace of work has increased considerably. The past six years have witnessed the publication of an astounding number of scholarly monographs, research tools and annotated English translations, the latter especially demonstrating how timely Donalson's project was. While the present series is not intended to provide revisions or up-dated bibliography, readers might find the following highly selective bibliographical notes helpful.

The on-going series of annotated translations in the series Translated Texts for Historians, published by Liverpool University Press, includes a number of published and projected volumes of particular interest for the present work. Most important among these are the *Chronicon Paschale 284-628 AD* by M. and M. Whitby (1989), which came to Donalson only as he was completing his work and is therefore only sporadically mentioned in the commentary, H.W. Bird, *Eutropius: Breviarium* (1993) and *Aurelius Victor: De Caesaribus* (1994), and A. Palmer, S. Brock, R. Hoyland, *The Seventh Century in the West-Syrian Chronicles* (1993).

Among monographs and editions dealing with chronicles related to Jerome's, see especially R.W. Burgess, *The Chronicle of Hydatius and the Consularia Constantinopolitana* (Oxford, 1993), S. Muhlberger, *The Fifth-Century Chroniclers: Prosper, Hydatius, and the Gallic Chronicler of 452* (Leeds: Francis Cairns, 1990), and W. Witakowski, *The Syriac Chronicle of Pseudo-Dionysius of Tel-Mahre: A Study in the History of Historiography* (Uppsala, 1987). Of fundamental importance for the so-called Anonymous Arian Historian, according to Donalson, one of Jerome's chief sources, is H.C. Brennecke, *Studien zur Geschichte der Homöer: Der Osten bis zum Ende der homöischen Reichskirche*. Beiträge zur historischen Theologie 73 (Tübingen: J.C.B. Mohr, 1988).

For an important collection of essays on historiography, see G. Clarke (ed.), *Reading the Past in Late Antiquity* (Australian National University Press, 1990). A recent guide to the sources can be found in F. Winkelmann and W. Brandes (eds.), *Quellen zur Geschichte des frühen Byzanz (4.-9. Jahrhundert): Bestande und Probleme* (Amsterdam: J.G. Gieben, 1990). Particularly important for sources and chronology is T.D. Barnes, *Athanasius and Constantius: Theology and Politics in the Constantinian Empire* (Cambridge: Harvard University Press, 1993). Finally, John Matthews' monumental *The Roman Empire of Ammianus* (Baltimore: John Hopkins, 1989) provides a vast amount of information for anyone interested in the history and historiography of the fourth century.

David Levenson
Associate Professor of Religion
Florida State University

# ACKNOWLEDGMENTS

I would like to thank the members of my committee for their help and support throughout the entire period of my work in the Humanities Program and especially while I was writing my dissertation. I am also happy to thank Althea Ashe, Scott Goins, Florian Saille and Maureen Tilley for their help and suggestions concerning specific points of the dissertation. I am grateful to Dr. Bernhard Tesche of Akademie-Verlag, Berlin, for permission to reproduce Rudolf Helm's critical text of the section of Jerome's *Chronicon* that forms the subject of this dissertation.

# CHAPTER 1

## INTRODUCTION

Around 380 or 381, Jerome of Stridon composed in Constantinople a Latin chronicle of sacred and secular history extending from the birth of Abraham to his own day. As he explains in his preface, the work is a translation and expansion of the second part of Eusebius' well known *Chronological Canons with an Epitome of Universal History, both Greek and Barbarian.*[1]

> For it must be known that I performed in part both the function of a translator and an author, because I both expressed the Greek very faithfully and added some things which seemed to me omitted, especially in the Roman history, of which Eusebius, the original author of this book, was not as uninformed as he was knowledgeable, but it seems to me that since he was writing in Greek, he found it necessary to provide only a cursory treatment for his own countrymen. Therefore from Ninus and Abraham up to the capture of Troy it is a pure Greek translation. From Troy up to the twentieth year of Constantine there are many things, now added and now mixed in, which I have very carefully excerpted from Tranquillus and other illustrious historians. However, from the year of Constantine cited to the sixth consulship of the Emperors Valens and the second of Valentinian it is all mine. Content with this ending I have reserved my pen for a broader history of the remainder of the period of Gratian and Theodosius, not because I feared to write freely and truly about the living -- for the fear of

---

[1]Eusebius gives the full title of the work in *ecl.* 1, 1 and *h.e.* 1, 1, 6. The first part of the work consisted of epitomes of the histories of various peoples; e.g., that of the Hebrews as based upon the Old Testament, Josephus and Clement of Alexandria. The second part, that translated by Jerome, was composed of synchronous tables with notices indicating historic events. In *p.e.* 10, 9 Eusebius calls this portion the *Chronicon canones*. In the following pages I shall refer to this as the *Chronicon*, or *Chron.* For the date of Eusebius' original work, see T.D. Barnes, *Constantine and Eusebius* (Cambridge: Harvard University Press), 1981, 113 and n. 66. For more on the question of various editions by Eusebius, see R. Helm, "Eusebius' Chronik und ihr Tabellenform," *Abhandlungen der Berliner Akademie,* phil.-hist. kl. no. 4 (1923) (Berlin: 1924): 42; D. Wallace-Hadrill, "The Eusebian Chronicle: The Extent and Date of Composition of its Early Editions," *JTS* n.s. 6 (1955): 248-53; R. M. Grant, *Eusebius as Church Historian* (Oxford, 1980), 7-9.

God drives out the fear of men--, but since, up till now, everything is uncertain while the barbarians are wandering madly through our land.[2]

Jerome's work therefore had a three-fold character: the translation of Eusebius' Greek text; supplementary notices added to the translation, primarily about Roman affairs;[3] and an original chronicle of events continuing Eusebius' work to 378.

Eusebius' Greek is no longer extant. The chief witnesses to it are Jerome's translation and a sixth-century Armenian translation.[4] In addition, substantial

---

[2]Sciendum etenim est me et interpretis et scriptoris ex parte officio usum, quia et Graeca fidelissime expressi et nonnulla, quae mihi intermissa videbantur, adieci, in Romana maxime historia, quam Eusebius huius conditor libri non tam ignorasse ut eruditus, sed ut Graece scribens parum suis necessariam perstrinxisse mihi videtur. Itaque a Nino et Abraham usque ad Troiae captivitatem pura translatio est. A Troia usque ad vicessimum Constantini annum nunc addita, nunc admixta sunt plurima, quae de Tranquillo et ceteris inlustribus historicis curiosissime excerpsi. A Constantini autem supra dicto anno usque ad consulatum Augustorum Valentis sexies et Valentiniani iterum totum meum est. Quo fine contentus reliquum temporis Gratiani et Theodosii latioris historiae stilo reservavi, non quo de viventibus timuerim libere et vere scribere, timor enim Dei hominum timorem expellit, sed quoniam debacchantibus adhuc in terra nostra barbaris incerta sunt omnia.

In the *vita Malchi* 1 (*PL* 23, 53 BC) Jerome also cites his interest in writing a fuller history--specifically, of the Church--beginning with the advent of Christ and continuing to his own time; see P. Jay, *Jérôme et sa exégèse* (Paris: 1985), 43 n. 128.

[3]See Helm, "Hieronymus' Zusatze in Eusebius' Chronik und ihr Wert für Literaturgeschichte," *PS* 21 no. 2 (1929). One of Jerome's chief sources for his additions was the *vir. ill.* of Suetonius, cited in the *Chron.* preface as "Tranquillus" (above); for a discussion of Jerome's use of Suetonius including several errors by the former see J. W. Duff and A. M. Duff, *A Literary History of Rome from the Origins to the Close of the Golden Age* (New York: Barnes and Noble, 1960), 88, 94, 117 and 163.

[4]A. Mosshammer, *The Chronicle of Eusebius and Greek Chronographic Tradition* (Lewisburg: Bucknell University Press, 1979), 75ff.; Helm, *Chron.*, intro.; and T. Barnes, *Constantine and Eusebius*. 340 n. 58. For an example of the discrepancies between the Armenian version and Jerome, see Duff and Duff, *A Literary History*, 464 on Livy's dates. For the Armenian version see the editions of A. Schoene, *Eusebii Chronicorum Canonum Quae Supersunt* (Berlin: Wiedmann, 1866) and J. Karst, *Die Chronik des Eusebius aus dem armenischen ubersetz*, (*Eusebius Werke* 5, *GCS* 20; Leipzig: Akademie-Verlag, 1911); also Mommsen's "Die armenischen Handschriften, der Chronik des Eusebius," *Hermes* 30 (1895): 321-38.

fragments are preserved by later Byzantine and Syriac chroniclers.[5] Because of its importance for establishing the chronology of much of ancient history, considerable scholarly attention has been devoted to the reconstruction and evaluation of Eusebius' work.[6] Surprisingly little work, however, has been done on Jerome's continuation, which represents the first extant Christian history of the fourth century and which formed the basis for virtually all later late antique and medieval Christian Latin chronicles.[7] The present study consists of the first translation and critical analysis of Jerome's entirely original contribution, i.e., the portion covering the years 327 to 378.

---

[5]The Byzantine works include Georgius Syncellus' *Chronicon* (ed. E. Weber, Bonn: Academia Litterarum Regiae Borussicae, 1829), Georgius Monachus' *Chronicon Syntomon* (ed. C. de Boor, Leipzig: Teubner, 1904), the *Chronographia Syntomos* (also known as *Anonymous Matritensis*) (ed. A. Bauer, Leipzig: Teubner, 1909), and Georgius Cedrenus' *Synopsis Historion* (ed. I. Bekker, *CSHB*; Bonn: Weber, 1838). All are works of the ninth century except Cedrenus, which dates from the end of the eleventh. Schoene's ed. of the *Chron.* (Berlin: Wiedmann, 1866) prints the Greek fragments beside Jerome's Latin. See T. Barnes, *Constantine and Eusebius*, 340 n. 58. For the Syriac witnesses to the *Chron.*, refer to the following editions: *Chronicon Miscellaneum ad a. D. 724 Pertinens*, ed. E.-W. Brooks, *CSCO* 4, 2, 3; *Chronicon Iacobi Edesseni*, ed. E.-W. Brooks, *CSCO* 4, 3, 2; *Chronicon Civile et Ecclesiasticum Anonymi Auctoris*, ed. I. E. Il Rahmani Scharfeh (Lebanon: 1904); and *Chronique de Michel le Syrien*, ed. J.-B. Chabot (Paris: 1900). See Keseling, "Die 'Chronik' des Eusebius in der syrischen Überlieferung," *Oriens Christianus* 1 (1926/7): 23-48, 223-41; 2 (1927): 33-56; also Mosshammer, *The Chronicle*, 322 n. 23.

[6]See Mosshammer, *The Chronicle*, 29ff. and Helm, *Chron.*, intro. esp. XXX-XXXI.

[7]The nearest pagan equivalents were the *breviaria* of Festus and Eutropius (ed. J. W. Eadie, London: The Athlone Press, 1967 and ed. C. Santini, Leipzig: Teubner, 1979), and the *De Caesaribus* of Aurelius Victor (ed. P. Dufraigne, Paris: Societe d'edition, Les belles lettres, 1975). Of these, Jerome appears to have used at least Eutropius for his *Chron.* (see below on sources). On the use of Jerome's *Chron.* by later chroniclers, see A.-D. van den Brincken, *Studien zur lateinischen Weltchronistik bis in das Zeitalter Ottos von Freising* (Dusseldorf: Michael Triltsch Verlag, 1957).

Date, Place and Circumstances of the Composition of the *Chronicon*

Although several alternative hypotheses have occasionally been offered, [8] the
overwhelming consensus of scholarship assigns the composition of the *Chron.* to
380 or 381, while Jerome was living in Constantinople. [9] A number of factors lead
to this conclusion.

The preface to the *Chron.*, cited above, states that it was written during the
reign of Gratian and Theodosius. This would place the composition between
Theodosius' accession in January, 379, and Gratians' death in August, 383. That
the *Chron.* was written toward the beginning rather than the end of this period can
probably be established by a reference to it in a letter Jerome wrote to Damasus
which consists of a detailed exegesis of Isaiah 6:

> Now Ozias reigned fifty-two years, at the time when Amulius reigned
> among the Latins and Agamestor the eleventh king among the Athenians.
> After his death the prophet Isaias saw the vision which we are now
> endeavoring to explain; that is, in the year in which Romulus, the founder

---

[8]A. Grisart cites Jerome's interest in Hilary's *de syn.* at Trier, ca. 368-370, and
suggests that the *Chron.* was begun there; "La Chronique de S. Jerome. Le lieu et
la date de sa composition," *Helikon* 1 (1962): 251-52 n. 16. A. di Berardino suggests
that the concordance between Jerome and Eusebius' *h.e.* against the Armenian
translation of the *Chron.* may be explained by Jerome's revision of Eusebius,
perhaps at Trier (*Patrology*, vol. 4, *The Golden Age of Latin Patristic Literature
From the Council of Nicea to the Council of Chalcedon* [trans. P. Solari;
Westminster, MD.: Christian Classics, Inc., 1986], 227). J. Ziegler and W.
Sontheimer suggest that the work may have been written during the period in the
Chalcis desert, ca. 374-376 ( *Der Kleine Pauly. Lexikon der Antike auf der Grundlage
von Pauly's Realenencyclopaedie der classischen Wissenschaft* [Stuttgart: Alfred
Druckenmuller Verlag, 1964], 2:460 and 1138). For Jerome's scholarly activity in
this period, see J.N.D. Kelly, *Jerome. His Life, Writings, and Controversies* (New
York: Harper and Row, 1975), 49.

[9]For a date in 380, see *PL* 22, 571; H. W. Peter, *Die geschichtliche Litteratur über
die römische Kaiserzeit bis Theodosius I und ihre Quelle* (Hildesheim: G. Olms, 1967
[repr. of 1897 ed.], 374; for 380-381, Kelly, *Jerome*, 144; and Barnes, *Constantine
and Eusebius*, 112; for 381, Jay, *Jérôme et sa exégèse*, 178 n. 245; for a date prior to
382, Fotheringham, *The Bodleian Manuscript*, XXV-XXVI and 12; and for the
question of a "Roman edition," see below.

of the Roman empire, was born, as will be evident to those who shall be willing to read the book of the *Chronicles* which we have translated from the Greek speech into the Latin tongue. *Ep.* 18A. 1,4 (Mierow trans., p. 22).[10]

If, as most scholars have suggested, this letter is to be identified with the small treatise on *Isaiah* 6 Jerome refers to in his *Commentary on Isaiah* (6, 1) written thirty years later, it must have been written at the latest in 381, since Jerome states he composed the treatise while in Constantinople studying with Gregory of Nazianzus, and Gregory left the city in June of that year.[11] This would mean that the *Chron.* would have to have been written in early 381 at the latest. The fact that in his preface Jerome refers to "the remainder of the time of Gratian and Theodosius" (*reliquum temporis Gratiani et Theodosii*) indicates that some time has passed since Theodosius' accession on January 379. It therefore seems best to place the composition of the *Chron.* in 380 or early 381.

There is also a reference to the *Chron.* in a list of Jerome's writings in his *De vir ill.*, 135, which supports a date of composition during Jerome's stay in Constantinople:

> I have written the following: *The Life of Paul the Monk*, a book of letters to different people, *An Exhortation to Heliodorus*, *Controversy of a Luciferian and an Orthodox*, a chronicle of universal history, twenty-eight homilies on

---

[10]Regnavit autem Ozias annis quinquaginta duobus (2 *Reg.* 17), quo tempore apud Latinos Amulius, apud Athenienses Agamestor undecimus imperabat. Post cuius mortem Isaias Propheta hanc visionem, quam explanare nunc nitimur, vidit, id est, eo anno quo Romulus Romani imperii conditor natus est: sicut manifestum esse poterit his, qui voluerint legere Temporum librum quem nos in Latinam linguam, ex Graeco sermone transtulimus.

[11]Jay, *Jérôme et sa exégèse*, 178 n. 245, points to the association of this letter with Jerome's study under Gregory, and accordingly dates it to early 381; see also G. Gruetzmacher, *Hieronymus. Eine biographische Studie zur alten Kirchengeschichte*. 3 vols. 1. *Sein Leben und seine Schriften bis zum Jahre 395* (Berlin: Scientia Verlag Aalen, 1969 [repr. of 1901 ed.]), 55.

*Jeremiah* and *Ezekiel* by Origen, which I have translated from Greek into Latin . . .[12]

The translations of Origen's homilies were also written in Constantinople, and like the *Chron.*, were dedicated to Vincentius. [13] Finally it is worth noting that many of the notices in the *Chron.* concern Constantinople, adding to the probability that it was composed there.[14]

---

[12]Haec scripsi: *Vitam Pauli monachi, Epistularum ad diversos librum unum, Ad Heliodorum exhortatoriam, Altercationem Luciferiani et Orthodoxi, Chronicon omnimodae historiae, In Ieremiam et Ezechiel homilias Origenis* viginti octo quas de Graeco in Latinam verti, . . .

[13]See Kelly, *Jerome*, 60-63 and Berardino, *Patrology*, 237-38. Vincentius was an aristocratic friend who at times was Jerome's travel companion as well as patron of his scholarly activity; see Kelly, *Jerome*, 114 and 116. It was at his urging that Jerome translated Origen's homilies *(Comm. on Ezekiel [GCS* 33, 318]). The *Chron.* is also dedicated to Gennadius, another friend of whom nothing more is known (not to be confused with Gennadius of Marseilles, who wrote a continuation of Jerome's *vir. ill.*). For more on Jerome's translations at Constantinople, see Jay, *Jérôme et sa exégèse*, 72 and n. 21, and below on the *Chron.* in Jerome's career.

[14]Jerome also refers to his translation of the *Chron.* in *Ep.* 57 (to Pammachius) as written about twenty years earlier. The context is the defense of his translation of Epiphanius' letter to John, bishop of Jerusalem (Jerome, *Ep.* 51):
> Whence I also was taught by such things and then deceived also by similar error, while certainly not knowing that you would object to this, about twenty years before when I was translating Eusebius of Caesarea's *Chronicle*, among other things I used such a preface: (a quotation of the Chron. preface follows).
> *(Unde et ego doctus a talibus ante annos circiter viginti, et simili tunc quoque errore deceptus, certe hoc mihi a vobis objiciendum nesciens, cum Eusebii Caesariensis Chronicon in Latinum verterem tali inter caetera usus sum praefatione).*

The lapse of twenty years has been the subject of speculation by scholars. Since the letter in question is usually dated to 393, this creates a difficulty with the commonly accepted date for the *Chron.* (above). It has been suggested that *viginti* is an error for *quindecim*; see Migne, *PL* 22, 571, 309 n. d. It is likely that Jerome simply rounded out the number.

For the chronology that points to Sept., 393, for the date of Epiphanius' letter, see P. Nautin, "La date du *De viris inlustribus* de Jerome," *RHE* (1961): 33-35; Nautin, "Études de chronologie hieronymienne," *REAug* (1972): 209-18; and "Hieronymus," *Theologische Realenzyklopädie* (Berlin: Walter de Gruyter): 1986, Band XV, 306-7.

## The *Chronicon* in Jerome's Career

As we have seen, Jerome composed the *Chron.* at Constantinople in 380 or 381, and this was one of his several translations of Greek fathers in the period. During the same period he was refining an already excellent classical education with biblical and patristic studies under Gregory of Nazianzus (newly appointed as bishop of Constantinople by Theodosius) and others, including Gregory of Nyssa.[15]

Born at Stridon in Dalmatia, ca. 331,[16] Jerome was educated at Rome beginning some time in the 340's,[17] in part under the famous master Aelius Donatus, whom he cites in the *Chron.* (239e). His early interest in history, as in heresy, may be seen in his transcription of Hilary's *De synodis* at Trier, ca. 368. While at Trier, where he had probably gone seeking a secular career,[18] he was attracted to Christian asceticism. After some time in Italy and his native Dalmatia, he pursued his studies at Antioch under the patronage of the influential Evagrius, ca. 372-374. Subsequently he pursued a vocation as an ascetic in the Chalcis desert, ca. 374-376, followed by another period of study in Antioch. From 379 to 382 he

---

[15]Kelly, *Jerome*. 70-71.

[16]For support of this date, given in Prosper, see Kelly, *Jerome*, 337-39. For additional discussion see P. Hamblenne, "La longevité de Jerome. Prosper avait-il raison?" *Latomus* 28 (1969): 1081-1119; P. Jay, "Sur la date de naissance de s. Jerome," *RELA* 51 (1973): 262-80; A. Booth, "The Date of Jerome's Birth," *Phoenix* 33 (1971): 346-52; cf. F. Cavallera, *Saint Jerome: sa vie et son oeuvre*. 2 vols. Specilegium sacrum Lovaniense etudes et documents, fasc. 1 (Louvain: Specilegium sacrum Lovaniense, 1922), 2, 3-12 and Gruetzmacher, *Hieronymus*, 1, 45-50 for a date as late as 347.

[17]I have followed Kelly's chronology in *Jerome*. For Jerome's life and career, see the following entries in the *Bibliography*: Antin, Bartelink (in Greschat), Brochet, Cavallera, Chauffin, Collombet, Cutts, Favez, Gorce, Jay, Mierow, Monceaux, Murphy, Nolan, Palanque, Penna, Pernoud, Quain, Sugano, Steinmann, Testard, Zeiller, Zoeckler.

[18]Kelly, *Jerome*, 27.

resided in Constantinople after his ordination as a presbyter by his friend Paulinus, bishop of Antioch. While in Constantinople he translated not only the *Chron.* but also Origen's homilies on *Jeremiah* and those on *Ezekiel*. In 382 he accompanied Paulinus to Rome, and this journey may have afforded him the opportunity to offer Damasus a presentation copy of the *Chron.*[19] Thereafter he carried out his revision of the Latin New Testament[20] and enjoyed the height of his career as a papal secretary with delegated authority to handle synodical enquiries. Before his hasty withdrawal from the capital in 385, he himself may have been a serious candidate for the Roman see.[21] Thereafter he moved to Bethlehem where he was to spend the rest of his life in the monastery he had established there. He occupied himself with biblical translations[22] and exegetical studies.[23] In the 390s he became involved in the Origenist controversy, the occasion of a bitter break with Rufinus, heretofore his close friend, who had established a monastery on the Mount of Olives with Melania (see immediately below). Near the end of his life Jerome

---

[19]That Damasus was interested in ecclesiastical history, of which one-half of the *Chron.* is composed, is well-known. This is evident from his restorations of the catacombs, his composition of epigrams for the martyrs, and his reorganization of the papal archives, attested by his inscription commemorating the event; A. Ferrua, *Epigrammata Damasiana* (Rome: 1942, no. 57), 210-12. See L. Hertling and E. Kirschbaum, *The Roman Catacombs and Their Martyrs* (trans. M. J. Costelloe, Milwaukee: The Bruce Publishing Co., 1956), 33 and 57, and R. Krautheimer, *Three Christian Capitals. Topography and Politics* (Berkeley: University of California Press, 1983), 103. For further bibliography, Berardino, *Patrology*, 221-22.

[20]See Berardino, *Patrology*, 221-22 for bibliography.

[21]Kelly, *Jerome*, 90 and 111; see Jerome, *Ep.* 45, 3.

[22]*Ibid.*, 153ff. on the Old Testament; see Berardino, *Patrology*, 224-26 for bibliography.

[23]For bibliography on Jerome's exegesis, see Jay, *Jerome et sa exegese*, 435ff. and Berardino, *Patrology*, 232-36.

opposed the Pelagian heresy. He died at Bethlehem in 419 or 420.[24]

Jerome's Revisions and the Question of a "Roman Edition"

There is some evidence that Jerome himself revised his work. The most direct is

a passage in Rufinus' *Apology against Jerome* 2, 29, 1ff.:

> Nor should even that admirable deed of his be left unknown, lest we should strike shame into our hearers, that he had written in his very own Chronicle that the granddaughter of the consul Marcellus, who was first of the Roman nobility, after she had left her small son at Rome, had gone to Jerusalem and there on account of the distinguished merit of her virtue was called Thecla. Afterwards he scratched that out of his own copies *(exemplaria)*, when he had seen that his own actions were displeasing to a woman of stricter discipline.[25]

The deletion of Melania the Elder's name thus must have occurred before 401,

since that is the date of Rufinus' writing. The grounds for it are uncertain.[26] In any

case, Rufinus does not mention any other revisions of the *Chron.* This single

instance of a deletion attested by Rufinus may point merely to a correction of one

passage by Jerome rather than a general revision, since Rufinus expressly states

---

[24]Kelly, *Jerome*, 337-39 citing Prosper, *epit. chron.* 1274 *(MGH auct. ant.* ix, 469 and the anonymous Hieronymus noster *(PL* 22, 184).

[25]Etiam nec illud eius admirabile factum silendum est, ne pudorem incutiamus audientibus, quod Marcelli consulis neptem, quam Romanae nobilitatis primam, parvulo filio Romae derelicto, Ierosolymam petisse, et ibi ob insigne meritum virtutis Theclam nominatum, in ipsis Chronicis suis scripserat, post id de exemplaribus suis erasit, cum actus suos vidisset districtioris disciplinae feminae displicere.

[26]Melania was apparently involved in some controversy and seems to have left Jerusalem under pressure; F. X.Murphy, *Rufinus of Aquileia (345-411). His Life and Works* (Washington: Catholic University of America, 1945), 156 and n. 78 and E. Clark, *The Life of Melania the Younger. Introduction, Translation and Commentary* (New York: The Edwin Mellen Press, 1984), 148-51. Palladius refers to Melania the Elder's return to Rome for the purpose of rescuing her granddaughter from heresy; *hist. Laus.,* 54.

that Jerome made the change in his own copies. In fact, the notice on Melania has been retained in our mss.[27]

Aside from Rufinus' explicit reference to a change in the *Chron.*, several scholars have suggested that Jerome revised his work before presenting it to Damasus in 382 (on the occasion of the Roman synod). Thus there has been discussion of a hypothetical "Roman edition" of the *Chron.*[28] Considering the custom of offering one's book to a powerful patron, this is a possibility. However, there is no specific evidence supporting such an edition.

Some scholars have seen evidence in the manuscript tradition for a revision by Jerome. According to them, some textual variants show Jerome's own revisions rather than the work of later copyists.[29] The variants, however, originate at

---

[27]See Helm's ed., 247d.

[28]For more on the theory of a "Roman edition," prepared for presentation at the Roman synod in 382, see Schoene, *Die Weltchronik*, 173; Fotheringham, *The Bodleian Manuscript*, XXV-XXVI; Helm, *Chron.*, intro., XX; and Mosshammer, *The Chronicle of Eusebius*, 51ff. The importance of dedications/presentations of literary works in the period is well-attested. In the *Chron.* itself Jerome cites both Porphyry (232e) and Hilary (241g) as winning recall from exile following the presentation of their books to Constantine and Constantius, respectively. Augustine offered the *de civ. dei* to the *vicarius* Macedonius; see Aug., *Ep.* 154, 1-2, and Ep. 152, 3. For dedicatory remarks in prefaces, see Jerome, pref. to the Gospels, addressed to Damasus, and those of the anonymous *de rebus bellicis* and the *breviaria* of Eutropius and Festus--all addressed to emperors; see H. W. Bird, "A Reconstruction of the Life and Career of S. Aurelius Victor," *CJ* 70 (1975): 51; Bird, "Eutropius: His Life and Career," *Echos* 32 (1988): 60; and B. Baldwin, *Studies on Late Roman and Byzantine History, Literature and Language* (Amsterdam: J. C. Gieben, 1984), 205-6. For the importance of literary works for career advancement, see Bird, "A Reconstruction of the Life and Career," above, esp. 71, for the case of Eutropius.

[29]Kelly, 1975, 175: "he seems to have inserted a few more entries in later editions;" and A. Feder, *Studien zum Schriftstellerkatalog des hl. Hieronymus* (Freiburg: Herder and Co., 1927), 158-60. Examples of the variants seen as evidence include the phrase *Probus praefectus Illyrici*, at 246f in some mss., contrasted with *Illyrici Equitius comes* in others. Such changes as this one may represent some political sensitivity, whether on the part of Jerome or a later editor (see Schoene, *Die Weltchronik*, 96f.; Mommsen, "Uber die Quellen," 604f.; Mommsen, ed., *Chronica Minora* (Berlin: Wiedmann, 1961), I, 367-68; Fotheringham, *The Bodleian Manuscript*, 12f.; and Feder, ibid., X, 25, and 158-60). Helm includes this variant in

different stages in the development of the manuscript tradition.[30] In any case, even several variants in the early stage of the manuscript tradition hardly demonstrate a revision by the author.[31]

Style of the Continuation

Jerome is well-known for his skills as a Latinist.[32] However, the nature of the *Chron.* does not generally allow for Ciceronian elegance. Its notices are somewhat typical of a chronicle, i.e., many consist of the barest record of an event or person. Examples of this kind of entry include 245m--*Magna fama in Phrygia*--and 236k--*Solis facta defectio.* In addition, many of the notices are lifted directly from the sources.[33] It is true that Jerome discusses style at some length in the preface, but he is primarily concerned there with his approach to translating Eusebius'

---

his detailed discussion of the mss. tradition (*Chronicon*, Intro., XV and XIX), but in his conclusion (ibid., XLVI) he subscribes to the following opinion of Fotheringham (*The Bodleian Manuscript*, XXXIII): "I maintain that this is certain, . . .that Jerome continued, filled out, and interpreted Eusebius, and that he edited his canons only once."

[30]Fotheringham, *The Bodleian Manuscript*, 12f.

[31]Some changes in the text may be due not only to the usual kinds of copyists' errors, but to the preservation of mistakes in later versions of the *Chron.* by Marius of Aventicum *et al.*; Mosshammer, *The Chronicle of Eusebius*, 52.

[32]See esp. Gruetzmacher, *Hieronymus*, 1, 117 ; O. Zoeckler, *Hieronymus. Sein Leben und Wirken aus seinen Schriften dargestellt* (Gotha: Verlag von Friedrich Andreas Berthes, 1865), 323; and H. Goelzer, *Etude lexicographique et grammaticale de la latinite de saint Jerome* (Paris: Librairie Hachette et Cie, 1884).

[33]Here Jerome's *Chron.* is similar to other chronicles; for example, cf. M. Whitby and M. Whitby, *Chronicon Paschale 284-628 A.D.* (Liverpool: Liverpool University Press, 1989), xxvii on this problem in the *Chron. pasch.* For an introduction to the problems posed by the chronicle genre see K. Krumbacher, *Geschichte der byzantinischen Literatur von Justinian bis zum Ende des oströmischen Reiches (527-1453)* (Munich: 1897, 325-34, and H. Hunger, *Die hochsprachliche profane Literatur der Byzantion.* 2 vols. Band 1. Philosophie, Rhetorik, Epistolographie, Geschichte, Geographie (Munich: Beck, 1978).

original.[34] Nevertheless, several stylistic features are worth noting. First, the notices show the marked tendency to begin with the proper name most important to the notice. Examples include 232b--*Donatus agnoscitur, a quo per Africam Donatiani*--and 233d--*Constans, filius Constantini, provehitur ad regnum.* Occasionally, Jerome indulges in his own lengthier compositions, as is shown by the comparative study of his notices and the sources. For example, at the very outset of his continuation, he provides a Ciceronian period with six dependent constructions (231g) to relate the career and conversion of Arnobius, while providing a detail not found in any of the other extant sources (see commentary).[35] Further, some scholars have attempted to classify the *clausulae* of the notices.[36]

<u>Interests of the Chronicon</u>

Jerome has inherited several of his historical interests in the *Chron.* from Eusebius' original. Among these are his interests in (1) the Church, particularly as represented by the bishops; (2) the emperors and their reigns; and (3) the persecution of Christians. This last interest is modified in Jerome's continuation. In the period it covers, with the exception of the reign of the emperor Julian, the persecution is that of the orthodox by the Arians rather than that of Christians by pagans.

---

[34]For example, he is concerned to explain that the translator sometimes must avoid the literal (sect. 2).

[35]Other such notices which appear to be Jerome's compositions include 237a, b, c, and 238f; see Appendix B.

[36]Helm, *Chron.*, intro., XXI and K. Mras, "Nachwort zu den beiden letzten Ausgaben der Chronik des Hieronymus," *WS* 46 (1928): 200ff. See also M. C. Herron, *A Study of the Clausulae in the Writings of Saint Jerome* (Washington: The Catholic University of America, 1937).

## The Church

Like Eusebius, Jerome lists only the most distinguished bishops. Thirty-six notices cite bishops, while eight refer to lower clergy (e.g., 233n). There are eleven which refer to orthodoxy as the "right faith"–*fidem rectam* (247e), "our doctrine"–*nostro dogmate* (246e), "our religion"–*nostra religione* (240c), etc. Other ecclesiastical affairs include eight references to monks or asceticism (including the famous reference to Melania, discussed above) and nine to martyrs or relics (e.g., 240d).

## The Empire

Like Eusebius, Jerome is interested in the empire and its rulers. Forty-eight notices in the continuation recount the character or deeds of the emperors (e.g., 233i and 234e on the Caesar Dalmatius). In nine places the author records the deaths of the emperors, and in ten others, the rebellions of the usurpers. Fourteen times he names important secular officials such as prefects or consuls (e.g., 235i and 247d). As might be expected, he reports military conflicts. Fifteen notices refer to the continuing struggles with the barbarians (e.g., 235b and e on campaigns vs. the Franks)[37] while in seven instances he records Rome's relations with Persia (e.g., 234b).

## Persecution

Twenty-six notices relate the deeds of heretics, predominantly the Arians.[38] When Jerome wrote the Chron. at Constantinople the Arians were still a presence

---

[37]For Jerome and the barbarian invaders see J. R. Palanque, "St. Jerome and the Barbarians," in F. X. Murphy, *A Monument to St. Jerome. Essays on Some Aspects of His Life, Works and Influence* (New York: Sheed and Ward, 1952), 171-200.

[38]The others are the Donatists (232b, 239h), Audians (235d), Macedonians (235h, 241h), Eunomians (246g) and Photinians (248d).

in spite of Theodosius' legislation *(CTh* 16, 1, 2, dated Feb. 27, 380) and his replacement of the Arian Demophilus with Gregory of Nazianzus.[39] Eighteen notices describe the persecution of the orthodox by the Arians up to 378.

Jerome has added his own interests both in the translation and in the continuation. These may be summarized as follows:

Intellectual History

This includes literary history, for which, as we have seen, Jerome borrowed from Suetonius for the translation portion. In the continuation he has included ten notices on individual authors (e.g., 232d on Juvencus). Other subtopics include famous rhetors (e.g., 245g on Libanius) and philosophers (e.g., 248d on Photinus). As we have seen, Jerome cites his own famous teacher, Aelius Donatus.

Places, Buildings and Topography

Jerome is interested in Constantinople. In the preface the first person plural "on our land" may refer to the inhabitants of Constantinople, including himself, in the chaotic period following the battle of Adrianople.[40] In the continuation he includes famous events like the mob's abuse of the master of the soldiers Hermogenes (235f); natural events such as a great hailstorm (245c); and buildings, such as the great aqueduct erected by Clearchus (247b). Jerome is also interested in Antioch. He provides numerous references to persons, events and buildings there (e.g., 232c on the bishops, 243d on the synod, and both 231i and 235g on the "Golden

---

[39]C. Mango, *Le Development urbain de Constantinople (IVe--VIIe siècles)* (Travaux et Memoires Monographies 2; Paris: 1985), 47, and R. Janin, *Constantinople byzantine* (2nd ed.; Paris: 1964), 351-52.

[40]However it might instead refer to a broader Roman view; e.g. Jerome's own native Stridon was devastated by the Goths, probably in 379. See Kelly, *Jerome*, 3, citing first Ammianus 31, 16, 7, and then A. Mocsy, "Stridon," *PW* suppl. IX (1962): col. 578, and Cavallera, *Saint Jerome*, 2, 67.

Church"). Rome is named often in a number of different contexts. For example, there are the references to its bishops, including the fighting at the basilica of Sicininus which followed the election of Damasus (244e). Other notices include Rome as the site of the Montensian heresy (239h), famous individuals involved in conspiracies there (238a and b), important natural events like a three-day tremor (236f), and the careers of distinguished rhetoricians (239b).

## Natural Phenomena

Finally, something may be said of Jerome's interest in natural wonders, an interest true to the chronographical tradition.[41]  Eusebius preserved the earthquake and darkness of the crucifixion as he believed he found them in Phlegon of Tralles (174d in Jerome's translation), and he recorded the great eruption of Vesuvius (189b). Likewise Jerome recorded earthquakes, hail, etc., which hint at the operation of God in history.[42] For example, there is the destruction of Neocaesaria, save for the bishop and his congregation, who took refuge in the church during the earthquake (236d). Of other particular interests are the devastation of Nicaea (245f) and the earthquake with worldwide implications (244c), the former for its associations during a period of Arian persecution and the latter for its apocalyptic ring.

## Themes of the Chronicon

A close examination of the continuation reveals a striking balance between secular and ecclesiastical history. The author appears to have consciously given

---

[41]e.g., see Spinka and Downey, 1940, esp. 125-32, for the same interest in Malalas, and Whitby and Whitby, op. cit., xxv, for the same in the *Chron. Pasch*

[42]Jerome's notices may be termed "hints" when they are compared to those of other chroniclers; e.g., to Malalas: "Syrian Antioch the Great collapsed by the wrath of God," (17, 4).

equal attention to the affairs of church and state. The product is a "Christian Roman history," whose author is at once both Christian and Roman. Emerging from this balance of secular and ecclesiastical are several key themes: (1) the continuity of the Roman empire; (2) the Church preserved in the successions of the orthodox bishops; and (3) the empire as the guarantor of the "peace of the Church."

## Continuity of the Roman Empire

Jerome was a staunch defender of an idealized Rome, a personification of a "cultural and linguistic ideal." [43] In the *Chron.* he is concerned as a Roman citizen; this is revealed by such expressions as "our lands" (preface) and "we squandered certain victory" (2361).[44] His thematic treatment of Rome in terms of the empire is characteristic of contemporary historiography in the period. Aurelius Victor and Ammianus, for example, were committed to the idealization of Rome.[45] Jerome

---

[43]F. Paschoud, *Roma Aeterna. Études sur le patriotisme romain dans l'occident latin à l'epoque des grandes invasions* (Rome: Institut suisse de Rome, 1967), 211. As is well-known, this interest caused him significant anxiety, represented by his famous dream; Kelly, *Jerome*, 41-4. Cf. C. Favez, *Saint Jérome peint par lui-meme* (Brussels: *Revue des études latines*, 1958), 15-22, and P. Antin, "Jérôme, antique et chrétien," *REAug* 16 (1970): 35-46.

[44]On Roman patriotism in the period and Jerome in particular, see Paschoud, *Roma Aeterna*, 209-21. See also and M. Fuhrmann, "Die Romidee der Spatantike," *HZ* 207 (1968): 529-61. K. Sugano carefully describes Jerome's "Rombild" and traces its development from various precedents in *Das Rombild des Hieronymus* (Europäischen Hochschulschriften. Reihe 15. Klassischen Sprachen und Literaturen. Band 25; Franfurt-am-Main: Peter Lang, 1983).

[45]See P. Dufraigne, ed., *Aurelius Victor. Livre des Cesars* (Paris: Société d'édition, Les belles lettres, 1975), xxiv; Antin, "Jérôme," 36; Cavallera, *Saint Jerome*, 1, 314-17.

17

shares such pro-Roman sentiments, and his patriotism in the continuation is confirmed by later writings, especially after the disaster at Rome in 410.[46]

Perseverance of the Church

The order of the Church as represented by the bishops was, as we have seen, an interest inherited from Eusebius. Jerome likewise looks to the preservation of the Church in the succession of the orthodox bishops *per se*. Given the historic situation--the struggle between these and the Arians--Jerome considers it important to relate the orthodoxy or heterodoxy of a given emperor, or at least the emperor's actions in favor of or against either party's bishops. For example, we have Constantius' recall of Hilary from exile (241g) and Constantine's letter honoring Anthony (233h). The theme of the Church's perseverance through its bishops makes the *Chron.* an important document for the first period of the empire's sanction of the bishops. Following the precedents of such authors as Hegesippus, Irenaeus and Eusebius, Jerome matter-of-factly cites bishops in numerical succession. At 232c Vitalis is precisely the twentieth bishop of Antioch, and at 237b Liberius is the thirty-fourth of Rome. Further, the fact that the orthodox bishops are the mainstay of the Church explains the need to dismiss the Arian bishops as "adversaries of Christ" at 232c. Thereafter, the reader, whose orthodoxy is assumed, is to understand that all Arian bishops are illegitimate. The eventual collapse of the Arians and triumph of the orthodox may be seen as the clear direction in which Jerome points. Particularly poignant is the tardy recall of the orthodox bishops by Valens at 249b just before his doom.

Rome and the Peace of the Church

---

[46]See Paschoud, *Roma Aeterna*, 218-21, and C. Trieber, "Die Idee der vier Weltreiche," *Hermes* 27 (1892): 341.

It is clear in the continuation that it is under the aegis of the Roman empire that the Church will flourish in the world. The Roman emperor is not only responsible for the maintenance of secular peace but for ecclesiastical peace as well. Every undertaking for religious harmony may be interpreted as beneficial to the state, and vice versa.[47] This explains how Jerome's readers could be expected to see events as diverse as the lynching of a heretical bishop and a campaign against the Franks as equally pertinent. The chronicle of the Roman empire and that of the Church are one. Rome is that which preserves civilization from the chaos of barbarism; it is also the guardian of the Church in the world.[48]

---

[47]This concept continued to be refined under Roman Christian leadership; see esp. Leo the Great on a papal primacy based upon the permanence of Rome--*Roma aeterna, caput mundi--Ep.* 115, 1.

[48]Implicit perhaps in the *Chron.* continuation is the concept, inherited from the exegesis of Origen and Eusebius concerning 2 Thess. 2:7, that Rome is that which restrains the Antichrist. See R. A. Markus, "Chronicle and Theology: Prosper of Aquitaine," in C. Holdsworth and T. P. Wiseman, eds., *The Inheritance of Historiography 350-900*, Exeter Studies in History 12 (Exeter: University of Exeter, 1986), 37, for the explicit understanding of this idea in Jerome's first continuator. For Jerome's exegesis and the same concept, see the following: W. Bousset, *Der Antichrist in der Überlieferung des Judentums des Neuens Testaments und der alten Kirche* (Gottingen: Van den Hoek und Ruprecht, 1895, esp. 149; R. Lerner, "Refreshment of the Saints: The Time after Antichrist as a Station for Earthly Progress in Medieval Thought," *Traditio* 32 (1976): 97-144; Paschoud, *Roma Aeterna*, 214-18; J. Pelikan, *The Excellent Empire. The Fall of Rome and the Triumph of the Church* (New York: Harper and Row, 1987), 43-52; B. Toepfer, *Das kommende Reich des Friedens* (Berlin: Akademie Verlag, 1964), esp. 88; Trieber, "Die Idee der vier Weltreiche," 321-44; and R. Wilken, "The Restoration of Israel in Biblical Prophecy. Christian and Jewish Responses in the Early Byzantine Period," in J. Neusner and E. Frerichs, ed., *"To See Ourselves as Others See Us." Christians, Jews, "Others" in Late Antiquity.* (Chico: Scholars Press, 1985), 443-71. During the devastation of Gaul by barbarians in 406-409 Jerome wrote the widow Geruchia *(Ep.* 123) that remarriage was unthinkable due to the rapid approach of Antichrist and the end, and that if Rome can perish, nothing else is safe. Both *Ep.* 60, 17 and the *Comm. on Isaiah* 7, 22, have it that contemporary sinfulness has led to the barbarian depredations.

## Sources

Jerome fails to mention his sources for the continuation of Eusebius' *Chronicle*. However a number of *verbatim* parallels with earlier fourth-century works still extant show that he depended upon previous written works for many of his notices. It cannot be proven in each case whether Jerome depended upon the extant sources or upon their respective sources, now lost. Similarly, the *verbatim* parallels with Jerome found in later works might have been copied from his own sources.

The only way credible source-critical hypotheses can be developed is by careful investigations in each case. I do not intend to prove any of the several hypotheses developed by modern scholars. Instead I will briefly examine each of the most likely sources, provide examples of the parallels which may help clarify the direction of dependence, and note the hypotheses that attempt to explain the parallels. Appendix C lists the likely source or sources for each of Jerome's notices in the continuation; this list is based upon careful comparisons of the parallels in Jerome and the other works.

The following is a list of Jerome's most likely sources with principal data--full title, the period covered, date of composition, and basic biographical facts of the author, if these are known.

### The Latin Historical Tradition

1. Eutropius' *Breviarium ab Urbe Condita* (dedicated to the Emperor Valens).

    Period covered: foundation of Rome to 364 (death of Emperor Jovian)
    Date of composition: 364-370[49]

---

[49]See C. Santini's edition, *Eutropii Breviarium ab Urbe Condita* (Leipzig: Teubner, 1979), XV, concerning the appearance in some mss. of the title *Gothicus* with Valens' name. If this is original, it dates the work to ca. 370.

Author: Born ca. 321;[50] died after 390.[51] Eutropius held successive
  secretarial posts under late fourth-century emperors,[52] served as
  prefect of Illyricum, and reached the summit of his career as consul
  at Constantinople.[53]

2. Festus' *Breviarium Rerum Gestarum Populi Romani* (dedicated to the Emperor
Valens).

  Period covered: foundation of Rome to 363 (Emperor Jovian's surrender of
    Nisibis to the Persians).
  Date of composition: ca. 369.[54]
  Author: Of Rufius Festus little is known,[55] but he may have been a
    secretary under Emperor Valens and afterwards proconsul of Asia.

3. Aurelius Victor's *De Caesaribus*.[56]

  Period covered: Reign of Augustus to 357 (Julian's victory over the
    Alamanni).

---

[50]H. W. Bird. *Sextus Aurelius Victor. A Historical Study*, ARCA Classical and
Medieval Texts, Papers and Monographs 14 (Liverpool: Francis Cairns, 1984), 5.

[51]H. W. Bird, "Eutropius: His Life and Career," *Echos* 32, 1 (1988): 59.

[52]*Magister epistularum* under Constantius and *magister memoriae* under Valens; for
these positions see A. H. M. Jones, *The Later Roman Empire 284-602* (Baltimore:
The Johns Hopkins University Press, 1986), 1, 50-51, 367-68, 504-5. For Eutropius'
career see Bird, "Eutropius," 51-60.

[53]Bird, "Eutropius," 58-59.

[54]J. W. Eadie, *The Breviarium of Festus*. London: The Athlone Press, 1967, 2-3.
The date is based upon the supposed reference to a treaty between Valens and the
Goths in 369, found in the work's closing sentence. The treaty is discussed by
Ammianus, 27, 5, 7-9.

[55]For discussions of his identity see the following: B. Baldwin, "Festus the
Historian," *Studies on Late Roman and Byzantine History, Literature and Language*
(Amsterdam: J. C. Gieben, 1984), 79-86; W. Den Boer, *Some Minor Roman
Historians* (Leiden: Brill, 1972); Eadie, *The Breviarium*, 1-9; A. Garroni,
"L'iscrizione di Rufio Festo Avieno e l'autor del''Breviarium Historiae Romanae',"
*Bull. Comm.* 43 (1915): 123; T. D. Barnes, review of Eadie in *JRS* 58 (1968): 263;
A. D. E. Cameron, review of Eadie *CR* 19 (1969): 305; J. F. Matthews, "Continuity
in a Roman Family: the Rufii Festi of Volsinii," *Historia* 16 (1967): 484; R. Syme,
*Emperors and Biography* (Oxford: Oxford University Press, 1971).

[56]See the edition of J. Bidez (Paris: Societe d' Edition, Les belles lettres, 1986).

Date of composition: ca. 360.[57]
Author: Born after 320;[58] died ca. 389.[59] Sextus Aurelius Victor held
  secretarial posts under Julian and other late fourth-century
  emperors,[60] and served as governor of Pannonia Secunda under
  Julian and Prefect of Rome under Theodosius.[61]

1.*Epitome de Caesaribus.*

Period covered: Reign of Augustus through 395 (death of Theodosius I).
Date of composition: ca. 400.[62]
Author: unknown pagan[63] probably writing at Rome.[64]

5. The Lost Latin *Kaisergeschichte (KG).*

Period covered: reign of Augustus to 337 (death of Constantine).[65]
Date of composition: ca. 340.
Author: unknown.

---

[57]See Bird, *Sextus Aurelius Victor. A Historical Study*, ARCA Classical and
Medieval Texts, Papers and Monographs 14 (Liverpool: Francis Cairns, 1984), 10
and n. 41.

[58]Bird, *Sextus Aurelius Victor*, 5.

[59]Bird, *ibid.*, 14.

[60]He was either a *notarius* in the corps of imperial notaries or a member of the
*scrinium epistolarum*, which drafted letters to judges and provincial delegates; Bird,
*ibid.*, 8.

[61]Bird, *ibid.*, 11 and 14.

[62]F. Pichlmayr, *Sexti Aurelii Victoris Liber de Caesaribus* (Berlin: Teubner, 1970),
XII.

[63]Ibid., citing *De Caesaribus* 21, 3 on the Furies.

[64]Ibid., citing *De Caesaribus* 3, 9 and other passages on locations.

[65]For the dates of the work I have followed T. D. Barnes, "The Lost
Kaisergeschichte and the Latin Historical Tradition," *BHAC* 1968/69 (1970), 20,
and 39. See below for discussion of the date 337 as the work's *terminus*. Others
have insisted on either a continuation of the *KG* or a later date of composition and
a *terminus* of 357; for the former see A. Enmann, "Eine verlorene Geschichte der
romischen Kaiser," *Philologus* suppl. iv (1884): 432ff.; for the latter, H. W. Bird,
"Further Observations on the Dating of Enmann's Kaisergeschichte," *CQ* 67
(1973): 373-77, and R. Syme, "The Son of the Emperor Macrinus," *Phoenix* 26
(1972): 279. For further bibliography and discussion of the development of the
theory of the *Kaisergeschichte*, see Barnes, "The Lost Kaisergeschichte," 13-17.

## The Greek Christian Historical Tradition

The Lost Greek continuation of Eusebius' *Chron.* referred to as the "Anonymous Arian."

> Period covered: 327 to 378[66] (death of Emperor Valens at Adrianople).
> Date of composition: ca. 379.[67]
> Author: an unknown Arian notably favorable to the Emperor Constantius.

### Discussion of Sources

Eutropius

Numerous verbal parallels between Eutropius and Jerome down to Julian's victory

at the battle of Strasbourg in 357 demonstrate that the two works are related.

These parallels show that Jerome used Eutropius directly.[68] Since the *KG* (above)

ended with 337 A.D. he could not have used it for parallel passages after that date.

---

[66]J. Bidez, in *Philostorgius. Kirchengeschichte, GCS* 21 (2nd. ed.; Berlin: Akademie-Verlag, 1972, CLI-CLII. corrects P. Batiffol, "Un historiographe anonyme arien du IVe siecle," *RQ* 9 (1895): 57-97, who had suggested the accession of the Emperor Julian in 361 as the latest event recorded in this work. See below for references to the fragments listed by Bidez.

[67]The date of composition is of course hypothetical. However certain observations enable us to approximate it. Parallel passages in Jerome, fifth-century ecclesiastical historians, and Byzantine and Syriac chroniclers continue to the death of Valens in 378; Jerome 249c, Theophanes 65, 18, Michael Syrus 294, 31, and the Syriac *Chron. civile et ecclesiasticum anonymi auctoris* (ed. Scharfeh, 97, 25), all describe Valens' refuge in a country house and his subsequent death when the Goths burned the house (see below for texts). Since these parallels are believed to derive from the Arian (see Bidez, *Philostorgius*, 240-41), the lost history must have ended with the same events as Jerome.

[68]For support of this view, see Schoene, *Die Weltchronik des Eusebius*, 217, and Schoene's edition of the *Chron., Eusebii Chronicorum Canonum Quae Supersunt* (Berlin: Wiedmann, 1866), which gives the references to parallels in Eutropius in the right margins; T. Mommsen, "Über die Quellen der Chronik des Hieronymus," *GS* 7 (1909): 606-609; M. Schanz, *Geschichte des römische Litteratur bis zum Gesetzgebungswerk des Kaisers Justinian*, 4, *Litteratur von Constantinus bis zum Gesetzgebungswerke Justinians* (Munich: Iwan von Muller's Handbuch, 1914-1935), 1, 446; and A. Momigliano, ed., *The Conflict between Paganism and Christianity in the Fourth Century A.D* (Oxford: Clarendon Press, 1963), 86.

The following is only one example of the close parallels which are cited as evidence for his use of Eutropius. The verbal parallels are italicized.[69]

> Eutropius 10, 9-11:
> *Constan*tis imperium strenuum aliquamdiu et iustum fuit. . . . militi iniucundus esset, factione *Magnenti*i occisus est. Obiit *haud longe ab Hispani*is *in castro cui Helenae nomen est, anno* imperii septimo decimo, *aetatis tricesimo*, rebus tamen plurimis strenue in militia gestis, exercituique

---

[69]For further examples, see below under *Aurelius Victor* for Jerome's notice (239d) compared to *Brev.* 10, 13 on the usurper Silvanus, as well as the following:

Eutropius 10, 10:

Diversa Constantii fortuna fuit, a Persis enim multa et *gravi*a perpessus, saepe *capt*is oppidis, *obsessi*s urbibus, caesis exercitibus, nullumque ei contra Saporem prosperum *proeli*um fuit, nisi quod *apud Singaram haud dubiam victoriam* ferocia *militum* amisit, qui pugnam seditiose et *stolid*e contra rationem belli die iam praecipiti poposcerunt.

Jerome 236l:

Bellum Persicum nocturnum *aput Singaram*, in quo *haut dubiam victoriam militum stolid*itate perdidimus. Neque vero ullum *Constanti*o ex VIIII gravissimis *proeli*is contra *Pers*as bellum *fuit gravi*us, nam ut alia omittam, Nisibis *obsess*a, Bizabde et Amida *capt*ae sunt.

Eutropius 10, 14:

Iulianum *Caesare*m ad *Gallia*s misit . . . a quo modicis copiis *apud Argentoratum*, *Gallia*e urbem, ingentes *Alamannorum copi*ae extinctae sunt, . . .

Jerome 240g:

Magnae *Alamannorum copi*ae *apud Argentoratum* oppidum *Galliar*um a *Caesare Iulian*o oppressae.

Eutropius 10, 16:

*Iovianus* . . .exercitu quoque inopia laborante uno a *Pers*is atque altero proelio victus pacem cum *Sapore*, *necess*ariam quidem, sed ignobilem, fecit multatus finibus ac nonnulla imperii Romani *parte tradit*a.

Jerome 243e:

*Iovianus* rerum *necess*itate compulsus Nisibin et magnam *part*em *Sapor*i *Pers*arum regi *trad*idit.

per omne vitae tempus sine gravi crudelitate terribilis. . . . Illyricum res
novas habuit, *Vetranio*ne ad imperium consensu militum electo. . . . *Romae*
quoque tumultus fuit, *Nepotia*no, Constantini sororis filio, per gladiatoriam
manum *imperi*um vindicante, . . .

Jerome 237c:
*Magnenti*o aput Augustodunum arripiente imperium *Constan*s *haut longe ab
Hispania in castro, cui Helenae nomen est,* interficitur *anno aetatis tricesimo,*
quam ob rem turbata re publica *Vetranio* Mursae, *Nepotian*us *Romae*
imperatores facti.

In addition to the verbal parallels, Jerome's account also shares Magnentius'

coup and the disturbances at Rome which saw the elevation of Vetranio.

Eutropius' account is fuller, yet Jerome adds the sites of both Magnentius and

Vetranio's seizures of power. Below we shall consider this kind of addition of

place-names as possible evidence for Jerome's use of additional sources. For the

present, however, the parallels serve to illustrate the close relationship between

the texts of Jerome and Eutropius. Such parallels have provided scholars with

evidence for Jerome's direct use of the *Breviarium*. The different character of

Jerome's accounts has been interpreted as evidence for a common source instead

of his use of Eutropius. However, it has also been seen as indicative of his free

adaptation of Eutropius' material and his admixture of material from other works

such as thr *Breviarium* of Festus (below).

Since the putative beginning of the *KG* was the reign of Augustus, verbal

parallels between Jerome and Eutropius prior to Augustus would be evidence for

direct use of Eutropius. If the degree of similarity in such parallels was similar to

that after Augustus, they would presumably be even stronger evidence. In fact,

Jerome did use Eutropius for events prior to Augustus and the degree of similarity

in the verbal parallels is quite like that in the passages after Augustus. The

following are examples of the pre-Augustan parallels. Parallels are italicized.

Eutropius 5, 1, 4 and 2, 1-2:
Cum *Cimbris* itaque conflixit et duobus proeliis *CC milia* hostium cecidit, *LXXX milia* cepit et *ducem* eorum *Teutobodum*, propter quod meritum absens *quinto consul* est factus. . . iterum a *C. Mario* et Q. *Catulo* contra eos dimicata est, . . . *trium*phus decretus est.

Jerome 148gh:
*CC milia Cimbrorum* caesa et *LXXX milia capta* per *Marium* cum *duce Teutobodo*. Gaius *Marius quinquies consul* Eridanum Cimbros superat et de his cum *Catulo triumfat*.

Eutropius 7, 6:
*Antonius*, qui Asiam et Orientem tenebat, *repudiata sorore Caesaris Augusti* Octaviani, *Cleopatram* reginam Aegypti *duxit uxorem*.

Jerome 162f:
*Augusti* et *Antonii* tertiae dissensionis exordium, quod *repudiata sorore Caesaris Cleopatram duxisset uxorem*.

The question of whether Jerome used Eutropius directly rather than the *KG* may be impossible to determine conclusively. However, the fact that Jerome appears to have used Eutropius for events before Augustus is important evidence in favor of the direct use of Eutropius. Parallels prior to Augustus and after 337 like those above show that the *KG* is unnecessary to explain parallels in the continuation. If Jerome did not use Eutropius for republican and imperial history, we have the unlikely scenario that he interrupted his use of Eutropius only to resume again after 337.

Festus

There are two leading hypotheses as to how Festus and Jerome's histories are related. One suggests that Jerome supplemented material from Eutropius with details from Festus.[70] The other holds that both Jerome and Festus used the lost

---

[70]R. Helm, "Hieronymus und Eutrop," *RhM* (1927): 138-70, esp. 160 on Jerome's parallel at *Chron*. 106c with Festus 2, 2--"reges VII . . . annos . . . CCXLIII." See also W. Hartke, *De Saeculi Quarti Exeuntis Historiarum Scriptoribus Quaestiones* (diss. Leipzig, 1932), 37-9, on the parallel between Jerome 194b, Eutropius 8, 8, 2 and 3, 1 and Festus 8, 2 and 20, 2 respectively, regarding the list of peoples conquered by Trajan. Here Jerome appears to take the names of the *Hiberi* and

*KG* also used by Eutropius.[71] The following is an example of the parallels between Jerome and Festus where there are also parallels in Eutropius. Parallels are italicized.

> Festus 27, 1-3:
> *Constantius* in *Persas* vario ac magis difficili pugnavit eventu. Praeter leves excubantium in limite congressiones acriori Marte noviens decertatum est, per duces suos septiens, ipse praesens bis adfuit. Verum pugnis Sisarvena, *Singar*ena et iterum *Singar*ena, praesente *Constantio*, ac *Singar*ena, Constantiensi quoque, et cum Amida *capta* est, grave sub eo principe res publica vulnus accepit. Ter autem a *Pers*is est *obsessa Nisibis*, sed maiore detrimento dum obsidet hostis adfectus est.

> Eutropius 10, 10:
> Diversa *Constantio* fortuna fuit, a *Pers*is enim multa et gravia perpessus, saepe *capt*is oppidis, obsessis urbibus, caesis exercitibus, nullumque ei contra Saporem prosperum *proeli*um fuit nisi quod apud *Singar*am haud dubiam victoriam ferocia militum amisit, qui pugnam seditiose et stolide ... poposcerunt.

> Jerome 2361:
> Bellum Persicum nocturnum aput *Singar*am, in quo *haut dubiam victoriam militum stolid*itate perdidimus. Neque vero ullum *Constantio* ex VIIII gravissimis *proeli*is contra *Persas* bellum fuit gravius, nam ut alia omittam, *Nisibis obsessa*, Bizabde et *Amida capta*e sunt.

Jerome appears to have copied the place-names from Festus, with the addition of Bizabde, while he likewise appears to have used Eutropius. As we have seen, the other explanation would be Jerome's use of the *KG* which would have been the

---

the *Sauromatae* from Eutropius, and those of the *Osroeni Arabae* and the *Bosporani Colchi* from Festus. His phrases also seem to indicate a blending of Eutropius and Festus: "in fidem accepit" is parallel to Eutropius, and "Seleuciam tenuit," to Festus. Both Helm's example above and this example from Hartke pertain to the translation portion of the *Chron.*; nevertheless they are instructive for the relationship of the sources. See Eadie, *The Breviarium of Festus*, 83-84, and 93, for further discussion..

[71]Barnes, *The Lost Kaisergeschichte*, 21.

common source of the other two authors. This could theoretically account for Jerome's additional place-name as well.

The next example, concerning the death of the Emperor Julian, shows a close verbal parallel between Jerome and Festus as well as a briefer one between Jerome and Eutropius. Again we see what appears to be a combination of material from Eutropius and Festus. The parallels between Jerome and Festus are bracketed; those between Eutropius and Jerome are in parentheses.

> Festus 28, 7:
> *cum incautius* per *agm*en *erraret*, excito pulvere erepto suorum conspectu *ab obvio hostium equite conto* per *ilia* ictus inguinum tenus vulneratus est.[72]

> Eutropius 10, 16:
> *hostili* manu interfectus est VI Kal. Iul., imperii *anno* septimo, *aetatis altero et tricesimo*, atque inter Divos relatus est, vir egregius . . .[73]

> Jerome 243b:
> *cum* fame et siti apostatam perdidisset exercitum et inconsult*ius a* suorum *erraret agmin*ibus, *ab obvio* forte *hostium equite conto ilia* perfossus interiit *anno aetatis XXXII*.

Jerome's parallels with Festus in the continuation portion of the *Chron.* are not as numerous or as close as those with Eutropius. They include those shown above and a questionable one between Festus 27, 2 and Jerome 236h.[74] Since they continue after the putative termination of the *KG* in 337, they point to Jerome's use of Festus together with other sources including Eutropius.

---

[72]"when he wandered unguarded through the battle line, summoned from the view of his men by the dust that was stirred up, he encountered an enemy cavalryman who pierced his side with a lance and wounded him down to the groin."

[73]"he was killed by an enemy hand on the sixth of the kalends of July, in the seventh year of his reign, when he was thirty-two years old, and was carried back among the gods, a distinguished man, . . ."

[74]Cf. Festus' "a Persis est obsessa Nisibis" to Jerome--"Sapor ... *obsid*et *Nisibi*n.

Aurelius Victor

Evidence for Jerome's knowledge of Victor's *De Caesaribus* is found in Jerome's request for a copy of the work in exchange for a copy of his own Life of Paul, in an epistle to Paul of Concordia (*Ep.* 10, 3), written in 374:[75]

> Nor must you suppose my demand to be a small one. You are asked to give me the pearl of the Gospel, "the words of the Lord," "pure words, even as the silver which from the earth is tried, and purified seven times in the fire," I mean the *Commentaries* of Fortunatian and--for its account of the persecutors--the *History* of Aurelius Victor, and with these the *Letters* of Novatian . . .[76]

In spite of this reference, the paucity of close verbal parallels between Jerome and Victor leaves Jerome's direct use of the *De Caesaribus* in doubt. However, the following passage may be singled out for the precise detail it shares with Jerome. Although the material immediately preceding this information in both authors is similar, a close examination shows the customary precise verbal similarity between Jerome and Eutropius, but only the more general resemblance between Jerome and Victor.[77] It reveals a precise detail common to Victor and Jerome but lacking in Eutropius. The parallels are italicized.

---

[75]W. Fremantle, trans., *The Principal Works of St. Jerome* (Grand Rapids: Wm. B. Eerdmans, 1954), 12.

[76]Et ne putes modica esse, quae deprecor, margaritam de Evangelio postularis. Eloquia Domini, eloquia casta, argentum igne exanimatum, probatum terrae purgatum septuplum (Ps. 11, 7): scilicet *Commentarios* Fortunatiani, et propter notitiam persecutorum Aurelii Victoris *Historiam*, simulque *Epistolas* Novatiani . . . See F. Pichlmayr, *Sextus Aurelius Victor De Caesaribus* (Leipzig: Teubner, 1970), viii.

[77]Note the following parallels:

Victor 42, 9: *Magnentius fratri Decentio Gallias*, Constantius Gallo, . . . Orientem *Caesaribus commiserant*.

Eutropius 10, 12, 2:

Orienti mox a Constantio *Caesar* est datus patrui filius Gallus, *Magnentiusque*

Victor 42, 15-16:
Is namque *Silvanus in Gallia* . . . tumultu *octavum* circa *ac vicesimum diem*
trucidatus est.[78]

Eutropius 10, 13:
*Silvanus* quoque *in Gallia res novas molitus* ante *diem* tricesimum *extinctus
est* solusque imperio Romano eo tempore Constantius princeps et Augustus
fuit.[79]

Jerome 239d:
*Silvanus in Gallia res novas molitus XXVIII die extinctus est.*

In spite of the temptation here to see Jerome's "on the twenty-eighth day" as
indebted to Victor's "on *about* the twenty-eighth day," the customary lack of verbal
parallels between the two authors allows for an explanation other than Jerome's
use of Victor: Jerome obtained the twenty-eight days, so similar to Victor's "on
*about* the twenty-eighth day," from a common tradition otherwise unknown to us.[80]

---

diversis proeliis victus vim vitae suae apud Lugdunum attulit imperii anno tertio,
mense septimo, *Frater* quoque *eius* Senonis, *quem ad tuendas Gallias Caesarem
miserat,* . . .

Jerome 238h: *Magnentius* Lugduni in Palatio propria se manu interficit et
*Decentius frater eius quem ad tuendas Gallias Caesarem miserat,* . . .

[78]For that Silvanus in Gaul . . .was brutally killed in an insurrection on about the
twenty-eighth day.

[79]Silvanus also stirred up a revolution in Gaul and was put down before the
thirtieth day; from that time Constantius was the only *princeps* and *Augustus* in the
Roman empire.

[80]Another parallel in Jerome and Victor has been adduced as evidence that
Jerome used the *KG*. Both Jerome and Victor note the foundation of Philippopolis
by Philip the Arab. Victor correctly places this foundation in Arabia (28, 1), but
Jerome erroneously identifies it with the city founded by Philip of Macedon in
Thrace (*Chron.* 217g). Barnes argues that Jerome's error preserves that in the *KG*;
"The Lost Kaisergeschichte," 21 and n. 50. However, this does not explain the error
in the *KG*.

In short, though Jerome and Victor cover much of the same period, there is
little evidence to demonstrate Jerome's direct use--particularly in the absence of
*verbatim* parallels like those found for Eutropius and Festus.

Epitome de Caesaribus

Since the *Epitome de Caesaribus* was written later than the *Chron.* it was not a
source for Jerome. On the other hand, substantial verbal parallels like those below
show that the *Epitome* may have used Jerome.[81] Its parallels with Jerome and the
other authors above have been seen as evidence for the *KG*.[82] Yet its verbal
parallels with Jerome continue not only for the period 337-357--including the latest
hypothetical *terminus* for the *KG*[83]--but even afterwards. There are four passages
on events in the period 365-379 with notable verbal similarities to the *Chron.*; the
first two have relatively slight verbal parallels by comparison,[84] while the others,
shown here, are substantially closer:

---

[81]On the sources of the *Epitome*, see esp. Barnes, "The Sources of the De
Caesaribus," 22-23.

[82]Barnes, "The Lost Kaisergeschichte," 22-23.

[83]Bird, "Further Observations on the Dating," 376-77; cf. below on the possibility of
337 as the work's *terminus*.

[84]These both relate events in the reign of Valentinian. The parallels below are
italicized:

Jerome 244a: *Valentinianus* egregius alias imperator et Aureliano moribus similis,
nisi quod *sever*itatem eius nimiam et *parc*itatem quidam crudelitatem et *avaritia*m
interpretabantur.

*Epitome* 45, 5: Hic *Valentinianus* fuit vultu decens, sollers ingenio, animo gravis
sermone cultissimus, quamquam esset ad loquendam *parc*us, *sever*us, vehemens,
infectus vitiis maximeque *avaritiae*; . . .

Jerome 247h: *Valentinianus* subita *sanguinis* eruptione, quod Graece apoplexis
*voc*atur, *Brigitione* moritur.

*Epitome* 45, 8, 10: *Valentinianus* apud *Bergentione*m legationi Quadorum
respondens anno aevi quinto et quinquagesimo impetu *sanguinis voc*e amissa,
sensu integer, exspiravit.

Jerome 248f:
*Alamannorum XXX* circiter *milia aput Argentariam oppidum Gallia*rum ab exercitu Gratiani strata.

*Epitome* 47, 2:
Hic *apud Argentariam oppidum Galliae triginta Alamannorum milia* in bello exstinxit.

Jerome 249c:
*Lacrimabile bell*um in Thracia. . . .Ipse imperator *Valens, cum sagitta saucius* fugeret et ob dolorem nimium saepe equo laberetur, ad cuiusdam *vil*lulae *casa*m *deportat*us est.

*Epitome* 46, 2:
Hic *Valens cum* Gothis *lacrimabili bell*o commisso *sagitt*is *saucius* in *casa deportat*ur *vil*issima; . . .

Such parallels suggest that the *Epitome* used Jerome. Thus the *KG* is not necessary to explain all of the preceding parallels between the two authors.

The Kaisergeschichte

As we have seen, parallels in Eutropius and Jerome continue through Julian's victory at Strasbourg in 357. One explanation already noted is that the *KG* is the common source used by Jerome, Eutropius, Festus and Victor.[85] However, a number of scholars have recently argued for 337 as the *terminus* for the *KG*. Their arguments are based on the fact that the parallels between Victor and Eutropius after the death of Constantine in 337 are neither frequent nor as close verbally as

---

[85]For further discussion in favor of Jerome's use of the *KG* see Barnes, "The Lost Kaisergeschichte," 20ff., emphasizing details on the emperors; Syme, *Emperors and Biography*, 57, 96-97; Bird, "Further Observations on the Dating of Enmann's Kaisergeschichte," *CQ* 67 (1973): 377; and Bird, *Sextus Aurelius Victor*, 18.

those to that point.[86] If this is correct, Jerome could have used the *KG* for his continuation only for the ten-year period 327 to 337. Some of the parallels above, as well as other common material in Jerome and Eutropius, would have to be explained otherwise than by Jerome's use of the *KG*.

Against Jerome's simply using the earlier sources is the fact that there are often details in the *Chron.* which are lacking in the other authors. For example, in his notice of Constantine's death (239c), a passage with close verbal parallels with Eutropius, Jerome adds the specific name of *Acyro*. The fact that such details are often lacking in the earlier Latin authors suggests that they were not found in the *KG*. Further, several such details come after the putative date for the end of the *KG*. Thus Jerome's use of the *KG* does not provide an adequate explanation for such specifics in the *Chron.*

The evidence for Jerome's use of the *KG* is not conclusive. Some additional details in Jerome, such as specific place-names, may be accounted for by his access to oral traditions concerning more recent history or even by literary sources other than those known to us.[87] A different emphasis in Jerome's accounts from that in

---

[86]For the early *terminus* see Barnes, "The Lost Kaisergeschichte," 13-43, esp. 20: "after 337 they [Victor and Eutropius] exhibit no example of either close verbal similarity or common error or shared idiosyncracy. The KG, therefore, finished with the death of Constantine . . ." See also Barnes, *The Sources of the Historia Augusta.* Collections Latomus 155. Brussels: Latomus, 1978, 92; R. Syme, *Emperors and Biography.* Oxford: Oxford University Press, 1971, 222; Bird, "The Sources of the De Caesaribus," 457 n. 5; and Bird, *Sextus Aurelius Victor,* 17 n. 5 and 18 notes 14-15.

[87]See C.V.E. Nixon, *An Historical Study of the Caesares of Sextus Aurelius Victor* (diss., University of Michigan, 1971), 344 and 364; but cf. Bird's caution, "Some Further Observations on the Dating," 377.

earlier sources may only reflect his particular interests.[88] Since our only access to the *KG* is through the analysis of the extant authors, it is difficult to determine Jerome's reliance upon it with any certainty. It is better to assume that he used Eutropius as a major source and supplemented this with material from Festus and others, especially since he clearly used Eutropius for the period before Augustus.

## Jerome and the Christian Chronographical Tradition

The following passages reveal close parallels between Jerome and later Christian chronicles in both the Greek and Syriac traditions. The passages are grouped under subject headings and translations follow in the notes.

1. The rededication of Drepana by Constantine:

> Jerome 231h:
> *Drepanam Bithyniae civitatem in honorem martyris Luciani ibi conditi Constantinus instaurans ex vocabulo matris suae Helenopolim nuncupavit.*

> Chron. Pasch. 527, 9:
> Δρέπανον ἐπικτίσας ὁ βασιλεὺς Κωνσταντῖνος ἐν Βιθυνίᾳ εἰς τιμὴν τοῦ ἁγίου μάρτυρος Λουκιανοῦ ὁμώνυμον τῇ μητρὶ αὐτοῦ Ἑλενούπολιν κέκληκεν, δωρησάμενος ἄχρι τοῦ νῦν ἕως φανερᾶς περιοχῆς πρὸ τῆς πόλεως εἰς τιμὴν τοῦ ἁγίου μάρτυρος Λουκιανοῦ ἀτέλειαν.[89]

> Chron. misc. 129, 20-22:
> wldrpn' ḥdt l'yqrh dlwqynws shd' dtmn sym hw' w'l šm' d'mh hln' hln'pwlys qrh.[90]

---

[88]Cf. Barnes, "The Lost Kaisergeschichte," 17: "even where he is closely following a written source, a writer will often draw on personal recollection of events within living memory in order to produce corrections or additions of his own." Barnes goes on to cite obvious examples from Victor and Eutropius.

[89]The Emperor Constantine, after refounding Drepanum in Bithynia in honor of the holy martyr Lucian, named it Helenopolis, with the same name as his mother, and in honor of the holy martyr Lucian he granted it to the present day immunity from taxation to the extent of the environs visible outside the city. (Whitby and Whitby trans.)

[90]And he [Constantine] refounded Drepana in honor of the martyr Lucian who had been buried there, and he called it Helenopolis from the name of his mother Helena. (I have used Brook's Latin translation [101, 9]. David Levenson checked the Syriac text for me.)

34

Theophanes 28, 3:
Δρέπαναν ἐπικτίσας εἰς τιμὴν Λουκιανοῦ τοῦ ἐκεῖσε μάρτυρος
Λουκιανοῦ ὁμώνυμον τῇ μητρὶ αὐτοῦ ʿ Ἐλενούπολιν κέκληκεν.[91]

Philostorgius 2, 12:
ἡ τοῦ βασιλέως Κωνσταντίνου μήτηρ ʿ Ἐλένη ἐπὶ τῷ στόματι τοῦ τῆς
Νικομηδείας κόλπου πόλιν ἐδείματο. ʿ Ἐλενόπολιν αὐτὴν ἐπονομάσασα·
ἀσπάσασθαῖ δὲ τὸ χωρίον κατ᾽ ἄλλο μὲν οὐδέν, ὅτι δὲ Λουκιανὸς ὁ
μάρτυς ἐκεῖσε τύχοι μετὰ τὸν μαρτύρικον θάνατον ὑπὸ δελφῖνος
ἐκκομισθείς.[92]

2. The burning of Aemilianus:

Jerome 243a:
*Aemilianus* ob ararum subversionem *Dorostori a vicario incenditur.*

*Chron. Pasch.* 548, 17:
ἐμαρτύρησεν δὲ καὶ ἐν Δωποστόλῳ τῆς κατὰ τὴν Θρᾴκην Σκυθίας
Αἰμιλιανὸς ἀπὸ στρατιωτῶν, πυρὶ παραδοθεὶς ὑπὸ Καπετολίνου
οὐικαρίου· πολλοὶ τε ἄλλοι κατὰ διαφόρους τόπους καὶ πόλεις καὶ χώρας
διέπρεψαν τῇ εἰς Χριστὸν ὁμολογίᾳ. ὧν οὐκ ἔστιν ῥᾴδιον τὸν ἀριθμὸν
ἐξειπεῖν καὶ τὰ ὀνόματα.[93]

Theophanes 51, 16:
ἐμαρτύρησεν δὲ καὶ ἐν Δωποστόλῳ τῆς Θρᾴκης Αἰμιλιανὸς ἀπὸ
στρατιωτῶν, πυρὶ παραδοθεὶς ὑπὸ Καπετολίνου· καὶ πολλοὶ ἄλλοι κατὰ
διαφόρους τόπους καὶ τρόπους διέπρεψαν ἐν τῇ εἰς Χριστὸν ὁμολογίᾳ.[94]

Theodoret 3, 7, 5:

---

[91]In the same year he [Constantine] refounded Drepana in honor of Lucian the martyr there and named it Helenopolis with the same name as his mother.

[92]He says that Helen, the mother of the emperor, built the city which was called Helenopolis, at the entrance of the Gulf of Nicomedia: and that the reason of her great predilection for the spot, was because the body of the martyr Lucian was carried thither by a dolphin after his death by martyrdom. (Walford trans.)

[93]And in Dorostolon of Thracian Scythia Aemilianus was also martyred, being consigned to fire by soldiers under the *vicarius* Capitolinus, and many others in various places, cities, and lands distinguished themselves in confession of Christ, whose number and names it is not easy to declare. (Whitby and Whitby trans.)

[94]And at Dorostolon of Thrace Aemilianus was martyred by the *vicarius*, being consigned to fire by Capitolinus; and many others in various places and cities and regions distinguished themselves in confession of Christ.

ἐν Δοροστόλῳ δὲ (πόλις δὲ αὕτη τῆς Θράκης ἐπίσημος) Αἰμιλιανὸς ὁ
νικηφόρος ἀγωνιστὴς ὑπὸ Καπετωλίνου τοῦ τῆς Θράκης ἁπάσης
ἄρχοντος παρεδόθη πυρί.[95]

Such parallels as these have caused many scholars to conclude that the later
works shared one of Jerome's sources for the fourth century. Other parallel
passages seem to provide evidence for Jerome's reinterpretation of material from
the same source.[96] That the lost source was Greek is ascertained from Greek
parallels found in a number of fifth-century ecclesiastical historians and later
Byzantine chronicles. It was unmistakably pro-Arian in character.[97] This is
especially true with regard to the Arianizing emperor Constantius, who ruled from
337 to 361.[98] The unidentified author of the work is usually referred to as the

[95]At Dorostolis, a celebrated city of Thrace, Emilius, an undaunted champion of
the faith, was thrown into the flames by Capitolinus, governor of the province.

[96]An example may be found in the passages on the death of Valens; see esp.
Jerome 249c, Theophanes 65, 17-18, Philostorgius 9, 17, Sozomen 6, 40 and
Theodoret 4, 3, 6.

[97]L. Dindorf and H. Gwatkin were convinced by the undisguised pro-Arian
perspective preserved in the Chron. Pasch. that its source for the fourth century
was Arian; Chronicon Paschale, CSHB 2 vols. (Bonn: Weber, 1832), 1, 379, and
Studies in Arianism: Chiefly Referring to the Character and Chronology of the
Reaction Which Followed the Council of Nicaea (New York: AMS Press, 1978 [repr.
of 1882 ed.], 216-18, respectively. O. Seeck came to the conclusion that almost all
the common material in Jerome and the seventh-century Chronicon Paschale was
derived from a lost Arian source; "Studien zur Geschichte Diocletians und
Constantins," Fleckeisens Neuen Jahrbuch für Philologie 139 (1889): 611. For a
discussion of the scholarship on the lost source down to 1906, see G. Mercati, "A
Study of the Paschal Chronicle," JThS 7 (1906): 397-412. For the more recent
discussion see J. Bidez, Philostorgius Kirchengeschichte mit dem Leben des Lucian
von Antiochen und den Fragmenten eines arianischen Historiographen (Berlin:
Akademie-Verlag, 1972), CLI-CLXIII.

[98]In passages believed by scholars to depend upon the lost work, Constantius is
credited with unusual clemency towards the usurper Vetranio; a benevolent
generosity towards the clergy, the poor, and the people in general; and lavish
endowments at the dedication of Hagia Sophia; Chron. Pasch., 544, 17--545, 5. See
also P. Batiffol, "Un historiographe anonyme arien du IVe siècle," RQ 9 (1895): 94,
and Whitby and Whitby, Chronicon Paschale, 29-30. By contrast, the related
passages in Jerome merely cite Vetranio's demotion (Chron. 238c) and leave the
dedication of Hagia Sophia anonymous (Chron. 241k). In another such passage the

"Anonymous Arian." Some scholars have found the parallels adequate to (1) partially reconstruct the work itself,[99] and (2) to determine that several of the later works dependent upon it had independent access to it.[100]

The lost Arian work appears to have been conceived as a continuation of Eusebius' *Chron.*[101] Therefore it may have been the initial heir of the Eusebian historical tradition in Greek. The significance of the work for this study is two-fold: (1) Such a work, which predated Jerome's, would have suggested the idea of an orthodox continuation of Eusebius. (2) Jerome appears to have relied upon it as a major source of his own Latin work.[102]

---

*Chron. Pasch.* (538) depicts Constantius as the recipient of divine assistance which enables him to save the city of Nisibis from the Persians. See Batiffol, "Un historiographe anonyme," 57-67 and Whitby and Whitby, *Chronicon Paschale*, 28, n. 89. Again by contrast the related passage in Jerome *(Chron.* 234f) credits the security of the same city to the prayers of Iacobus, an orthodox saint. In other passages the story of the emperor's vision of a cross before a key victory makes him comparable to his father Constantine (Philostorgius, 3, 26 and *Chron. Pasch.*, 540) but in the related material in Jerome *(Chron.* 238d and h) the vision is omitted. Finally, parallel passages concerning Constantius' baptism as an Arian by an Arian bishop will be considered below.

[99]See Batiffol's reconstruction in "Un historiographe anonyme arien," 68-90, and the discussion and list of fragments in J. Bidez, ed., *Philostorgius. Kirchengeschichte*, 2nd ed., *GCS* 21 (Berlin: Akademie-Verlag, 1972), 201-413. Cf. the list of Jerome's notices and their probable sources in the present Appendix C.

[100]See Bidez, ed., *Sozomenus. Kirchengeschichte*, *GCS* 50 (Berlin: Akademie-Verlag, 1960), LIII-LIV, and *Philostorgius*, CLV (both on Theophanes); also Whitby and Whitby, *Chronicon Paschale*, xvi and n. 26 (on *Chron. Pasch.* and Theophanes). For example, though related, the account of the vision of the cross seen by Constantius is much fuller in Philostorgius (3, 26), who was himself an Arian of the Eunomian sect, than that in the *Chron. Pasch.* (540).

[101]Batiffol suggested that in its purpose--the praise of the Emperor Constantius--it was also akin to Eusebius' *In Praise of Constantine*; "Un historiographe anonyme arien," 91-2.

[102]It may have supplied information for as much as one-fifth of Jerome's *Chron.*, if Bidez's list of "fragments" is correct.

Further, like the Greek works which relied upon the same source, Jerome's *Chron.* is more valuable due to its access to earlier and non-orthodox ecclesiastical tradition.[103]

The comparison of Jerome and the Greek chroniclers for passages dependent upon the Arian is revealing. One may make the following observations. (1) As one might expect from an orthodox author who experienced the Arian persecutions, Jerome recasts the Arian's materials to his advantage. (2) Philostorgius, an Arian himself, is quite comfortable with his source. (3) The author of the *Chron. Pasch.*, unlike other orthodox authors, freely utilizes the Arian material without any apparent concerns for the heretical implications of his source.[104] (4) Fifth-century historians including Sozomen and Theodoret still exercise caution with their source. (5) Theophanes, though writing later, is quite uncomfortable with some of the material, and attempts to correct it.[105]

The parallels between Jerome and the Syriac chronicles are often close.[106] They provide valuable early evidence for the Arian author in several ways. First, some of the Syriac works including the *Chron. misc. ad a.d. 724* and the continuation of Eusebius to the year 775 attributed to Dionysius of Tellmahre[107]

---

[103]See Dindorf's ed. of the *Chron. Pasch.*, 132, and F. Dvornik, *The Idea of Apostolicity in Byzantium and the Legend of the Apostle Andrew* (Cambridge: Harvard University Press, 1958), 142 for the accuracy of the Arian.

[104]See Whitby and Whitby, *Chronicon Paschale*, xvi.

[105]Whitby and Whitby, *Chronicon Paschale*, 21, citing Theophanes 33, 21-2, which makes Constantine's baptism by Eusebius of Nicomedia an Arian fabrication.

[106]See Bidez, *Philostorgius*, 204f. for additional passages believed to depend upon the Arian; see especially *Chron. misc.* 3 and Jerome 235c and g on an earthquake and the dedication of the "Golden Church" at Antioch.

[107]Mosshammer, *The Chronicle of Eusebius*, 322 n. 23.

predate many of the Byzantine chronicles. Second, they often are closer to Jerome than the Greek sources and they provide more direct access to the Arian.[108] Finally, like the *Chron. Pasch.*, they are dependent upon the Arian to the extent that they sometimes preserve the kind of pro-Arian and pro-Constantius perspective of this source left uncorrected in the *Chron. Pasch.* For example, the *Chron. misc.*, in describing the death of Constantius, states (103, 19) that Constantius "did a beautiful thing in the sight of the Lord and walked in the paths of his father Constantine;" strongly suggesting the emperor's Arianism.[109]

What makes it most likely that the later chroniclers used the lost Arian rather than Jerome? It is the notable pro-Arian perspective of much of the common material in parallel passages like those cited above. It is this perspective in part which enables scholars to identify passages as dependent upon the Arian historian. Most of the works preserving the material in question were composed by orthodox authors long after the suppression of Arianism by the emperors beginning with Theodosius. The dismissal of a common Arian source for these authors and Jerome leaves the pro-Arian perspective inexplicable.

---

[108]Bidez, *Philostorgius*, 226.

[109]See Bidez, *Philostorgius*, 226.

# CHAPTER 2

## *HIERONYMI CHRONICON.* A TRANSLATION OF JEROME'S CONTINUATION OF EUSEBIUS' *CHRONICLE* FROM AD 327 TO 379[1]

(231f) Eusebius, the companion of the martyr Pamphilus, wrote his history to this point. I have appended to it the following.

AD 327

    (231g) Arnobius was considered a distinguished rhetorician in Africa. When he was in Sicca [in Africa] instructing young men in declamation, he was converted to true belief by his dreams; a pagan up to then, he did not receive the faith, that which he had always fought against, from the bishop. He spent his nights composing the most authoritative books against his former religion. Finally he obtained the covenant through certain pledges of faith, as it were.

    (231h) Constantine restored the city of Drepana in Bithynia, and paid honor to the martyr Lucian who was buried there. He renamed it Helenopolis after his mother.

    (231i) In Antioch construction was begun on the Palace, which is called "golden" [or "Golden House"].

---

[1]Helm's Latin text is reproduced in Appendix A. I have omitted from the translation the references to the Olympiads and the regnal years of each emperor, items which are found in the left margin of the Latin text. For ease of reference it seemed best to include in the translation both the year (*anno domini*) and the page and section of Helm's text (e.g. 231f = Helm, page 231, section f).

AD 328

(232a) Constantine killed his wife Fausta.

(232b) Donatus, whose followers throughout Africa were called Donatists, won renown.

(232c) At Antioch Vitalis was ordained as the city's twentieth bishop; he was the successor of Tyrannus. After Vitalis came Filogonius as the twenty-first. Paulinus followed his as the twenty-second. After Paulinus came Eustathius as the twenty-third. From the time he was driven into exile for his faith down to the present day, Arians have continued to control the church in Antioch. The succession of their bishops was as follows: Eulalius, Eusebius, Eufronius, Placillus, Stefanus, Leontius, Eudoxius, Meletius, Euzoius, Dorotheus and Meletius again.

AD 329

I have not provided their dates for this reason: I judge them to have been Christ's adversaries rather than his bishops.

(232d) The priest Iuvencus, a native of Spain, expounded the Gospels in epic poetry [i.e., Vergilian hexameter].

(232e) Porphyrius was recalled from his exile after he sent his distinguished book to Constantine.

AD 330

(232f) At Alexandria Athanasius was ordained as the nineteenth bishop.

(232g) After almost every other city had been plundered, Constantinople was dedicated.

(232h) Metrodorus the philosopher asserted himself.

<u>AD 331</u>

(233a) At Rome Marcus governed the church as the thirty-second bishop for eight months, after which Iulius was ordained the city's thirty-third; he governed the church for sixteen years and four months.

(233b) In accordance with the edict of Constantine, the temples of the pagans were torn down.

<u>AD 332</u>

(233c) The Romans defeated the Goths in the territory of the Sarmatians.

(233d) Constans, the son of Constantine, was promoted to the throne.

(233e) A countless multitude died from the pestilence and famine in Syria and Cilicia.

<u>AD 334</u>

(233f) The Sarmatians assembled a force and drove their masters, the Limigantes, who are now known as the Argaragantes, into Roman territory.

(233g) Calocaerus was suppressed after he stirred up a revolution on Cyprus.

<u>AD 335</u>

(233h) Constantine together with his children sent a letter to honor Antony.

(233i) During the thirtieth anniversary of Constantine's reign ( the *tricennalia*) Dalmatius was named to the office of Caesar.

<u>AD 336</u>

(233k) Pater the rhetorican taught at Rome with great success.

(233l) The daughter of the rhetorican Nazarius equalled her father in eloquence.

(233m) Tiberianus, an eloquent man, governed Gaul as praetorian prefect.

(233n) Eustathius, a priest of Constantinople, won renown. By his industry a martyr's shrine was built at Jerusalem.

## AD 337

(234a) Constantine, baptized in his last days by Eusebius, the bishop of Nicomedia, deviated into the doctrine of the Arians. From then until the present time the plundering of the churches and the discord of the whole world has proceeded apace.

(234b) While Constantine was preparing for war against the Persians he died at a public villa in Ancyra [Ankara] near Nicomedia in the sixty-sixth year of his life. After him his three sons were hailed as *Augusti* rather than *Caesares*. Constantine was the thirty-fifth ruler of the Romans.

Constantius and Constans ruled for twenty-four years, five months and thirteen days.

## AD 338

(234c) The praetorian prefect Ablabius was killed, together with many of noble rank.

(234d) Sapor the king of Persia besieged Nisibis for almost two months after he had laid waste to Mesopotamia.

(234e) Dalmatius Caesar, to whom his uncle Constantine had allotted an equal share of the empire with his sons, was assassinated by a faction of his cousin Constantius in a sudden outbreak of civil war.

(234f) Jacob the bishop of Nisibis won renown. Due to his prayers his city was often freed from crises.

## AD 339

(234g) From this point the Arian impiety, supported by the Emperor Constantius, persecuted Athanasius first of all, then all the bishops who were not Arian, with exile, imprisonment and various kinds of afflictions.

## AD 340

(235a) Constantine (II) was killed near Aquileia at Alsa while making war on his brother.

## AD 341

(235b) Constans carried out a campaign against the Franks with inconclusive results.

(235c) Many of the cities of the East rested together from a frightful earthquake.

(235d) Audeus was a famous man in Coelo-Syria. The Audian heresy was named after him.

## AD 342

(235e) Constans thoroughly defeated the Franks and established peace with them.

(235f) Hermogenes, the Master of the Soldiers, banished the bishop Paulus following the order of the emperor and the Arian party. Accordingly Hermogenes was abused by the populace at Constantinople.

(235g) The Golden Palace [see above] was dedicated at Antioch.

(235h) Macedonius, skilled in the art of embroidery, was appointed bishop in place of Paulus by the Arians. The Macedonian heresy of the present derives from him.

(235i) Due to Arian stratagems and the cruelty of the prefect Phillippus (who was a partisan of the Macedonian sect) Paulus was strangled.

### AD 343

(236a) Maximinus, the bishop of Treves, was a famous man. He honorably received Athanasius, bishop of Alexandria, when Constantius sought to punish him.

### AD 344

(236b) Sapor the king of Persia persecuted the Christians.

(236c) Neocaesaria in Pontus was destroyed except for the church and the bishop and the others who had taken refuge there.

### AD 345

(236d) Titianus, an eloquent man, administered the praetorian prefecture in the Gallic provinces.

### AD 346

(236e) Athanasius returned to Alexandria due to a letter from Constans.

(236f) Dyrrachium was ruined by an earthquake. For three days and nights Rome trembled and a great many of the cities of Campania were shaken.

(236g) At great expense the state constructed a port at Seleucia in Syria.

(236h) Sapor again besieged Nisibis for three months.

### AD 347

(236i) Eusebius Emisenus, a standard bearer of the Arian sect, wrote many things on a variety of subjects.

(236k) There was an eclipse of the sun.

### AD 348

(2361) There was a night battle with the Persians at Singara. In this we squandered a certain victory because of our soldiers' sluggishness. In fact there was not any more serious battle for Constantius out of nine very serious battles against the Persians. For as I shall omit others, Nisibis was besieged, Bizabde [on the Tigris] and Amida [again, on the Tigris; northwest of Nisibis] were taken.

(237a) Maximus, the fortieth bishop of Jerusalem and successor to Macarius, died. After him the Arians seized the church; that is, these Arians were its bishops: Cyril, Eutychius, Cyril again, Irenaeus, Cyril for a third time, Hilarius, and Cyril for the fourth time. Of these men Cyrillus served as a deacon in the Church. Although he had been ordained a priest by Maximus, after the latter's death the see was offered to him by Acacius and other Arians if he would reject Maximus' ordination For this impiety concerning the priesthood he was compensated with a bribe. The dying Maximus had substituted Heraclius in his own place. Worrying this man with a variety of deceits, Cyril demoted him from bishop to priest.

AD 349

(237b) Liberius was ordained the thirty-fourth bishop of the Roman church. When he was driven into exile for his faith, all the clergy swore that they would support no one else. But when the Arians had substituted Felix in the priesthood, most of them violated their oaths. A year later they were cast out with Felix, because Liberius, overcome by the weariness of exile and subscribing to a heretical depravity, had entered Rome like a conqueror.

AD 350

(237c) While Magnentius was usurping the imperial throne at Augustodunum [in Gaul; modern Autun] Constans was not far from Spain in a camp which is called Helena. Constans was killed in his thirtieth year and as a result the state was thrown into disorder. Vetranio was declared emperor at Mursa [in Pannonia], and Nepotianus, at Rome.

(238a) At Rome, when the people rebelled against the party of Magnentius, they were betrayed by a senator named Heraclides.

(238b) Nepotianus' head was carried around through the city on a javelin, and many nobles were proscribed and put to death.

## AD 351

(238c) At Naissus [in Moesia] Constantius removed the imperial insignia from Vetranio.

(238d) Magnentius was defeated at Mursa. In this battle the might of Rome perished.

(238e) Gallus, the cousin of Constantius, was made *Caesar*.

## AD 352

(238f) The Jews seized weapons for a rebellion when they had killed the soldiers at night. Gallus caught them by surprise and slaughtered many thousands of men, even those of an innocent age, and he burned Diocaesaria, Tiberias, Diospolis and many towns.

(238g) Gallus had some of the nobles of Antioch killed.

## AD 353 (A jubilee year according to the Hebrews)

(238h) Magnentius killed himself with his own hand in the palace at Lugdunum [Lyons]. His brother Decentius, whom he had sent as *Caesar* to protect the Gallic provinces, ended his life among the Senones by hanging himself.

(239a) Gennadius was considered a distinguished forensic orator at Rome.

(239b) Minervius the rhetorician from Burgdigala [Bordeaux] taught at Rome in a most distinguished manner.

## AD 354

(239c) Gallus Caesar was vexed by his cousin Constantius; Gallus had come under the latter's suspicion for his extraordinary talent. He was killed at Histria [in Moesia by the Black Sea].

(239d) Silvanus stirred up a revolution in Gaul but was put down within twenty-eight days.

(239e) The rhetorician Victorinus and the grammarian Donatus, my teacher, were considered outstanding men at Rome. One of them, Victorinus, was even honored with a statue in the Forum of Trajan.

(239f) Paulinus and Rodanius, bishops of the Gallic provinces, were driven into exile for their faith.

## AD 355

(239g) The rhetoricians Alcimus and Delfidius taught in Aquitania most eloquently.

(239h) Donatus was driven out of Carthage. The Donatists in Africa were named after him, as I have recounted above. They also call certain followers of his "Montensians," because initially they began to hold their assembly on a hill at Rome.

(239i) The following were condemned to exiles far apart from one another by Constantius and the Arians: Eusebius, the bishop of Vercellae, Lucifer, Dionysius of Caralitana, the bishops of the church of Milan, and also Pancratius, a Roman priest, and Hilarius, a deacon.

(240a) Julian, the brother of Gallus, was named *Caesar* at Milan.

AD 356

(240b) The monk Antony died in the desert in his one hundred and fifth year of age. He used to tell the story of Paulus, a certain Theban who was wonderfully blessed, to many of those who came to him. I have given an account of Paulus' death in a brief book.

(240c) Hilary, the bishop of Pictavi [Poitiers] was driven into exile in Phrygia for three years by a faction of Saturnius, the bishop of Arles, and those of the Arians who were associated with him.

There he composed books about our religion.

(240d) The relics of the Apostle Timothy were carried into Constantinople.

(240e) Sarmata, Amatas and Macarius, disciples of Antony, were esteemed as remarkable men.

(240f) Liberius the Roman Bishop was sent into exile.

(240g) A great hoard of the Alemmani was crushed by the *Caesar* Julian at the Gallic town of Argentoratum [Strasbourg].

AD 357

(240h) The Saracens rushed into the monastery of the blessed Antony and killed Sarmata.

(240i) Upon Constantius' entry into Rome the bones of the Apostle Andrew and the Evangelist Luke were received from the people of Constantinople with extraordinary good will.

<u>AD 358</u>

(241a) Nicomedia was entirely devastated by an earthquake while the neigh-boring cities were shaken in part.

(241b) Paulinus, the bishop of Treves, who was living in Phrygia as an exile, died.

(241c) Evanthius, the most learned of grammarians died at Constantinople; Chrestus was brought from Africa to replace him.

<u>AD 359</u>

(241d) Synods were held at Ariminum [Rimini] and Seleucia of Isauria, in which the ancient faith of the fathers was condemned first by the treason of ten legates and then by that of an who were present.

(241e) Honoratus was made the first urban prefect of Constantinople after serving as praetorian prefect of the Gallic provinces.

(241f) Gratian who is now the emperor was born.

(241g) Hilary returned to Gaul after he had offered his book on his own behalf to Constantius at Constantinople.

(241h) Macedonius was driven from Constantinople.

(241i) Almost all the churches in the whole world were polluted under the pretense of peace and the partnership of the king of the Arians.

<u>AD 360</u>

(241k) The greatest of the churches was dedicated at Constantinople.

(241l) Meletius of Sebastia, the bishop of the Armenians, was transferred to Antioch by the Arian bishops Acacius and George. After a brief interval in which he restored the priests deposed by his predecessor Eudoxius, Meletius mocked the most just cause of exile by an improvised change of faith.

(242a) Gaul--through the agency of Hilary--condemned the treacheries of the falsehood of Ariminum.

## AD 361

(242b) Constantius died at Mopsucrene between Cilicia and Cappadocia in his forty-fifth year. Julian was the thirty-sixth ruler of the Romans. He reigned for one year and eight months.

## AD 362

(242c) Julian converted to idol-worship; then a mild persecution was alluring rather than compelling Christians to sacrifice. In this persecution many of our people fell into ruin willingly.

(242d) When George, the man who had been ordained by the Arians to replace Athanasius, was burned during an insurrection, Athanasius returned to Alexandria.

(242e) Eusebius and Lucifer returned from exile. Lucifer, after he had taken in two other confessors, made Paulinus the bishop of the Catholic party of Antioch. Paulinus was a priest of the bishop Eustathius and he had never polluted himself with the communion of the heretics.

## AD363

(242f) Prohaeresius the Athenian sophist abandoned his school of his own accord after the enactment of the law which forbade Christians to teach the liberal arts. This was in spite of the fact that Julian made an exception for him so he could teach as a Christian.

(243a) Aemilianus was burned to death by the *vicar* for overthrowing the altars of Dorostorus [in Moesia].

(243b) The church of Antioch was closed shut, and God by His will quieted the severest storm of an impending persecution. For when Julian set out against the Persians he had sworn that he would offer our blood to the gods after his victory. He was conducted to the desert by a certain man playing the part of a deserter, when the same apostate had ruined his army with hunger and thirst. Then when he very ill-advisedly strayed from the ranks of his own soldiers, he by chance encountered an enemy cavalryman who pierced his side with a spear. He died in his thirty-second year of age. On the very next day Jovian was raised from commander of the household troops to be Julian's successor. Jovian was the thirty-seventh ruler of the Romans; he reigned for eight months.

AD 364

(243c) Jovian was compelled by the necessity of the situation to surrender Nisibis and a large part of Mesopotamia to Sapor, the Persian king.

(243d) A synod at Antioch was held by Meletius and his supporters; after they had rejected the *homoousios* and the *anomoeos*, they espoused a middle position between these dogmas--the *homoeousion* of the Macedonians.

(243e) Jovian died at Dadastana [on the border of Bithynia and Galatia] in his thirty-fourth year. His death was due to either indigestion or the fumes of live coals, of which he had ordered too many burned. After him Valentinian, a tribune of the targeteers in the household troops from Pannonia Cibalensis [i.e., the area of Cibalae] was named *Augustus* at Nicaea. He took his brother Valens who was at Constantinople as his colleague in power. The reign of Valentinian and Valens was the thirty-eighth of the Romans; they ruled for fourteen years and five months.

AD 365

(244a) Valentinian was a distinguished emperor in some regards, similar to Aurelian in character, except that certain persons interpreted Valentinian's excessive severity and stinginess as cruelty and greediness.

(244b) Apollinaris, the bishop of Laodicea [in Asia] composed a great number of works on our religion.

(244c) An earthquake shook the whole world and the sea advanced onto the shore; the tremors shook the cities of Sicily and many of the islands, and thereby crushed countless people.

(244d) Procopius, who had seized power at Constantinople, was killed in advantageously situated Phrygia and a great many of the Procopian party were put to death and their property was proscribed.

(244e) Damasus was ordained as the thirty-fifth bishop of the Roman church. After a brief interval of time, certain individuals established Ursinus as bishop. He and his followers invaded the basilica of Sicininus, where the people of Damasus' party were assembling, and carried out the cruelest executions of both sexes.

(245a) After Valens was baptized by Eudoxius, the bishop of the Arians, he persecuted our people.

AD 367

(245b) Gratian, the son of Valentinian, was made emperor at Ambiani [in Gaul].

(245c) Such a great storm arose at Constantinople that several persons were killed by hail of an astonishing size.

(245d) At Atrabatae [in northern Gaul] wool mixed with rain floated down from the sky.

(245e) Hilary, the bishop of Pictavi (or Limonum; modern Poitiers) died.

AD 368

(245f) Nicaea, which had often suffered damage in the past, was completely overthrown by an earthquake.

(245g) Libanius of Antioch was esteemed as a distinguished rhetorician.

AD 369

(245h) Valens returned the public games to Constantinople.

(245i) Athanaric, the king of the Goths, killed a great number of Christians when he had incited a persecution. He also drove many from their own settlements into Roman territory.

(245j) Eusebius, the bishop of Vercellae, died.

AD 370

(245l) The martyrs' shrine for the Apostles was dedicated at Constantinople.

(245m) There was a great famine in Phrygia.

(246a) Lucifer, the bishop of Carales [Cagliari in Sardinia], died; like Gregory, a bishop in Spain, and Philo of Libya, he never joined himself to the Arian depravity.

AD 371

(246b) Maximinus, prefect of the grain supply, obeyed the emperor's order to investigate criminals, and put to death a great many of the nobles at Rome.

(246c) Valentinian was suppressed in Britain before he could seize power.

(246d) A priest of Sirmium [in Pannonia] was unjustly beheaded because he had refused to hand over Octavian (whom he had sheltered in his home) in accordance with the proconsul's order.

## AD 372

(246e) Didymus of Alexandria, utilizing secretaries, wrote numerous commentaries on many things concerning our doctrine. He was deprived of his eyesight in the fifth year after his birth and therefore he was wholly illiterate.

(246f) Probus the prefect of Illyricum exacted the most unjust tribute from the provinces he was governing before they were laid waste by the barbarians.

## AD 373

(246g) Eunomius, a disciple of Aetius of Constantinople, won notoriety; the Eunomian heresy derives from him.

(246h) The Saxons were cut to pieces at Deuso in the territory of the Franks.

(247a) Almost eighty-thousand Burgundians descended to the Rhine--something which never happened before.

(247b) Clearchus, the prefect of the city at Constantinople was a famous man. He brought the necessary long-prayed-for water into the city with his aqueduct.

(247c) Peter was ordained the twentieth bishop of Alexandria. He was so easy about accepting heretics after the death of Valens that he aroused in some the suspicion that money was involved.

AD 374

(247d) Melania, noblest of Roman women and the daughter of Marcellinus who was once consul, abandoned her only son, the urban *praetor,* and sailed to Jerusalem. She lived there in such miraculous virtue, especially humility, that she received the name of Thecla.

(247e) After the belated death of Auxentius of Milan, Ambrose was appointed bishop and all Italy was restored to the right faith.

(247f) The clergy of Aquileia were regarded as if they were a choir of the blessed.

AD 375

(247g) Because the Sarmatians had laid waste the Pannonian provinces in the previous year, the same consuls remained in office.

(247h) Valentinian died suddenly at Brigitio [or Brigetio, in Pannonia] due to a sudden eruption of blood, which is called *apoplexis* in Greek. After him Gratian ruled, together with his uncle Valens. Gratian took his brother Valentinian as his colleague in power.

(248a) Many of the monks of Nitria [a monastic center west of the Nile delta] were killed by the tribunes and their soldiers.

(248b) After he had passed a law that the monks should serve in the army, Valens ordered those who refused to be clubbed to death.

AD 376

(248c) Theodosius, the father of the Theodosius who was afterwards emperor, and very many nobles were put to death.

(248d) Photinus died in Gaul. The Jewish doctrine called Photinian is named after him.

(248e) Basil of Caesarea, the bishop of Cappadocia, was a famous man. By the one fault of pride he ruined his many good qualities of chastity and talent.

AD 377

(248f) About thirty thousand Alamanni were laid low by Gratian's army at the Gallic town

of Argentoratum [modern Strasbourg].

(248g) Florentinus, Bonosus and Rufinus were regarded as distinguished monks. Of these Florentinus was so merciful to the destitute that he was named "father of the poor" by the common people.

(248h) The race of the Huns devasted the land of the Goths. The Goths were received by the Romans without having to lay down their arms. They were driven to rebel due to famine brought on by the greed of the general Maximus.

(249a) After they overcame the Romans in combat the Goths poured into Thrace.

AD 378

(249b) Valens, compelled to leave Antioch, recalled our people from their exile in his belated repentance.

AD 379

(249c) There was a lamentable war in Thrace. In this the protection of the calvary was lacking. The Roman legions were surrounded by the Goths and slaughtered to the last man. The Emperor Valens himself fled when he was wounded by an arrow and often nearly fell from his horse due to the very severe pain. He was carried off to the house of a certain modest villa.

The barbarians followed him there and they set fire to the house; he failed to even acquire a proper burial place.

(249d) From the founding of Rome to the last year of this work there were 1,131 years, which may be considered in the following manner:

Under the kings, 260 years. Under the consuls, 464 years. Under the *Augusti* and *Caesares*, 427 years.

(250) All the years down to the sixth consulship of Valens and the second of the Emperor Valentinian the younger are reckoned here:

From the fifteenth year of Tiberius and the preaching of our Lord Jesus Christ, 351 years. From the second year of Darius, king of Persia, at which time the temple of Jerusalem was restored, 899 years. From the first Olympiad, in which age Isaiah was prophesying among the Hebrews, 1,155 years. From Solomon and the first construction of the temple, 1,411 years. From the downfall of Troy, at which time Samson was among the Hebrews, 1,561 years. From Moses and Cecrops, the first king of Attica, 1,890 years. From Abraham and the reign of Ninus and Semiramis, 2,395 years.

All the list from Abraham down to the time written above which contains 2,395 years.

From the Flood, moreover, to Abraham, the years are estimated to be 942 years. From Adam to the Flood, 2,242 years. From Adam down to the fourteenth year of Valens, that is, to his sixth consulship and the second of Valentinian, all the years that elapsed were 5,579 years.

# CHAPTER 3

## COMMENTARY

The present commentary has notes listed under the corresponding numbers of the notices in Helm's edition. For additional material the reader should refer to the Appendices. The notes which follow identify the most important historical events and personalities, list the chief parallel ancient sources and provide very selective references to modern secondary literature.

231f. See Eusebius' *Chron.* (Helm's ed.) 1, 34, 2.

231g. This notice is an example of Jerome's own compositions for the continuation. It is more detailed than many of those essentially copied from Eutropius and others. The work of Arnobius cited here is the *Adversus Nationes*. At 1, 13, 1, 39 and 3, 24 in this work Arnobius cites his conversion, but with no mention of dreams. Lactantius was a pupil of Arnobius; see Jerome *Ep.58*, 10 and *Ep. 75.*

On Arnobius' reputation as an anti-Christian polemicist and his conversion, see W. H. C. Frend, *The Rise of Christianity*, (Philadelphia: Fortress Press, 1984), 450; his conversion by dreams compared to other similar conversions, R. MacMullen, *Christianizing the Roman Empire (A.D. 100-400)* (New Haven: Yale University Press, 1984), 134 n. 15; his writings on various subjects, J. Burckhardt, *The Age of Constantine the Great*, trans. by M. Hadas (Berkeley: University of California Press, 1983), 131, 165, 208, 213 and 222.

231h. Lucian of Antioch: Jerome, *De vir. il* 77. On the Arians tracing their heritage back to Dionysius of Alexandria through Lucian, see G. Bardy, *Recherches sur Saint Lucien d'Antioch et son école* (Paris: Gabriel Beauchesne et ses fils, 1936); on Arius naming Eusebius of Nicomedia as his "co-Lucianist," see R. C. Gregg and D. E. Groh, *Early Arianism. A View of Salvation* (Philadelphia: Fortress Press, 1981), 164; see also E. Boularand, "Les débuts d'Arius," *Bulletin de littérature ecclésiastiques* 65 (1964): 178-9 on Arius' supposed study with Lucian.

The *Chron. Misc.* (4b; Bidez, *Philostorgius*, 205), *Chron. Pasch.* (527, 9), and Theophanes (28, 3) used Jerome's source; Philostorgius (201, 4), Socrates (1, 17) and the *Life of Lucian* are closely related to one another for the same events; Bidez,

*Philostorgius*, 205. Nicephorus 8 later copied Philostorgius *verbatim*. Cedrenus (295d) shows his usual dependence upon Theophanes.

231i. Antioch: for the many references to the city in the *Chron.*, see the index of names in Helm's edition. The church cited was known by several names: the "Golden House" (*Domus aurea*), the "Great Church," the "Palace" (*Dominicum* or *Kyriakon*), "Harmony," (*Harmonoia*), "Church of the Golden Dome," the "Octagonal Church." See Frend, *The Rise of Christianity*, 530; R. MacMullen, *Constantine* (New York: Harper and Row, 1971); A. H. M. Jones, *The Later Roman Empire, 284-602* (Baltimore: Johns Hopkins Press, 1986), 1, 90. Begun in 327 and finished in 341, it is described both in Eusebius' *Life of Constantine* 3, 50 and in the *De laud. Constantini*; see G. Downey, *Antioch in the Age of Theodosius* (Norman: University of Oklahoma Press, 1961), 343 notes 107-8 and for Downey's description, see ibid., 342-9. On the use of the term "Newer Church," see ibid., 336 n. 82 and 345 n. 125. For the church's location in Antioch, see the map in Downey, *Antioch*, 343 n. 105. For the use of the term *Dominicum* for churches in the period, see Frend, *The Rise of Christianity*, 475 for an inscription at Altava in Mauretania. On imperial building projects at Antioch, see also J. H. W. Liebeschuetz, *Antioch: City and Imperial Administration in the Later Roman Empire* (Oxford: Oxford University Press, 1972), 135.

Eusebius' detailed account of ther structure in the *De laud. Constantini* is unparalleled in the other sources. The octagonal shape is cited by Theophanes (and Michael, ultimately depending upon him). Theophanes has preserved Jerome's source; Jerome's account reads like a translation of the Greek except that he calls the church golden instead of octagonal. Cedrenus preserves Theophanes, citing, for example, the "octagonal church [*kyriakon*] in Antioch." The ninth century chronicle attributed to Julius Pollux (see I. Hardt, *Julii Pollucis Historia Physica seu Chronicon ab Origine Mundi usque ad Valentis Tempora* [Munich and Leipzig: Joseph Lindauer, 1792], 274) and the *Chron Misc.* (5a; Bidez, *Philostorgius*, 205) are similar in describing "the great church in Antioch." Again the Arian may be the key to the parallels. Pollux (318, 320) appears at first to have used Photius for the dedication of the church as Constantius' opportunity for calling a synod; however, Pollux is more specific, citing ninety-nine bishops in attendance.

232a. Fausta: cf. *Chron.* 229d. Her death not directly linked to her son Crispus', Frend, *The Rise of Christianity*, 501; her execution followed by those of former associates of Constantine, *ibid.*, 496 n. 116, citing Eutropius 10, 6, 3; uncertainty regarding Constantine's motive, R. Browning, *The Emperor Julian* (Berkeley: University of California Press, 1971), 16 and 32; jealousy between Fausta and Helena, *ibid.*, 516 n. 146 and A. H. M. Jones, *Constantine and the Conversion of Europe* (New York: Collier Books, 1962), 198; on the removal of her name (with that of Crispus) from monuments, MacMullen, *Constantine*, 187; site of execution at the baths of Trier, *ibid.*, 50; the charge of adultery, Jones, *Constantine*, 199, citing an imperial constitution of 326 A.D.

Cf. Eutropius 10, 6, 3 and Zosimus 2, 29.

232b. Donatus: cf. *Chron.* 239h; *De vir il.* 93; *Ep.* 133, 4 (esp. for the phrase "throughout Africa"--*per Africam*).

On Donatus and the rise of Donatism, see Frend, *The Donatist Church: A Movement of Protest in North Africa* (Oxford: Clarendon Press, 1952; also MacMullen, *Constantine*, 107; *Christianizing the Roman Empire*, 93-4, 160-1; Burckhardt, *The Age of Constantine*, 306; A. di Berardino, *Patrology*. vol. 4. *The Golden Age of Patristic Literature From the Council of Nicea to the Council of Chalcedon*. trans. by P. Solari (Westminster, Md.: Christian Classics, Inc., 1986), 4, 115-16; A. Piganiol, *L'empire chrétienne, 325-395* (Paris: Presses Universitaires de France, 1947), 80; E. Stein, *Histoire du Bas-Empire: De l'état romain a l'état byzantin, 284-476*, French ed. by J.-R. Palanque (Amsterdam: Adolf M. Hakkert, 1968), 100, 136, 173; T. Barnes, *The New Empire of Diocletian and Constantine* (Cambridge: Harvard University Press, 1982), 238 (Ch. 15, "Constantine and the Donatists"); P.-A. Fevrier, "Toujours le Donatisme: a quand l'Afrique?" *Riv. storia e lett. religiosa* 2 (1966): 228-40; S. Lancel, "Aux origines du Donatisme et du movement des circoncellions," *Cahiers tunisiennes* 15 (1967): 183-88.

Cf. Optatus of Milevis 1, 24ff. (*CSEL* 26).

232c. Antioch and its bishops: see P. Monceaux, "Saint Jerome au desert de Syrie," (*Revue des Deux Mondes* 58 (1930), 154; Downey, *A Study of the Comites Orientis and the Consulares Syriae*, diss. (Princeton University, 1939), and *Antioch*; A.-J. Festugiere, *Les moines d' Orient, IV, 1: Enquête sur les moines d' Egypte* (Paris: 1964); and Liebeschuetz, *Antioch*. On the schism at Antioch, see F. Cavallera, *Le Schisme d'Antioche (ive-ve siècle)* 1905 and Frend, *The Rise of Christianity*, 645 n. 3. On individual bishops, see under names as follows:

Vitalis, bishop, 314-319 A.D. Cf. Jerome, *Ep.* 15, 2 and *Ep.* 16, 2. On beginning the "Apostolic Church" or "Old Church" in Antioch, see Downey, *Antioch*, 336.

Philogonius, bishop, 319-324: on the completion of the church begun by Vitalis, Downey, *Antioch*, 336. See also W. Ensslin, "Philogonios," *RE* 19 (1938): 2483; as supporter of Alexander during the Arian controversy, Frend, *The Rise of Christianity*, 497 and 514 n. 108.

Paulinus: cf. Jerome *Ad Pammach. adv. Ioan.* 41; *Ep.* 15, 2; *Ep.* 16, 2; *Ep. ad Rufin.* 22. From Tyre, bishop of Antioch for only six months, Downey, 1961, 352. Jerome cites Paulinus as bishop between Philogonius and Eustathius; he is the only source for this bishop. The importance of Athanasius' decision to back him, Frend, *The Rise of Christianity*, 616 and 632; see also Downey, *Antioch*, 351 n. 151 citing F. Loofs, *Paulinus von Samosata: eine Untersuchung zur altkirchlichen Literatur und Dogmengeschichte* (Leipzig: 1924) and G. Bardy in A. Fliche and V. Martin, *Histoire de l'église, depuis les origines jusque à nos jours, sous la direction de A. Fliche et V. Martin* (Paris: 1946), 387-90. See also C. C. Mierow, *The Letters of St. Jerome* (New York: Newman Press, 1963), 208 n. 54; 210 n. 1; 213 n. 1; 223 n. 1; Piganiol, *L'empire chrétienne*, 135, 163, 216, 227, 228; and Stein, *Histoire*, 176, 198.

Eustathius, bishop, 325-326: cf. Jerome, *De vir. il.* 85, *Ep. adv. Rufin.* 42. Elected by a synod which condemned Arianism, Downey, *Antioch*, 145; his dethronement due to a remark vs. Helena, H. Chadwick, "The Fall of Eustathius of Antioich," *JThS* 49 (1948): 27-35 and Downey, *Antioch*, 145-6. See R. V. Sellers, *Eustathius of Antioch and His Place in the Early History of Christian Doctrine* (Cambridge: Harvard University Press, 1928), for Eustathius' place in the development of Christian doctrine. Influence on Ancyra, Frend, *The Rise of Christianity*, 497; as opponent of Origenism, *ibid.*, 503; fall from power, 526; views similar to Paul of Samosata, *ibid.*, 759; "Word-man" christology, J. N. D. Kelly, *Early Christian Doctrines* (New York: Harper and Row, 1960), 302; see also Berardino, *Patrology*, 210.

Eulalius, successor to Paulinus and followed by Euphronius: see Downey, *Antioch*, 352 and n. 157, citing Chadwick, "Fall of Eustathius," (as providing the only plausible chronology of the Antiochene bishops' succession).

Euphronius: see Piganiol, *L'empire chrétienne*, 53.

Leontius: protected the Arian apologist Aetius against the Caesar Gallus, Downey, *Antioch*, 152.

Eudoxius, d. in 370: cf. Jerome, *Dial. c. Lucif.* 20. On the creed ascribed to him, Kelly, *Early Christian Doctrines*, 282; baptizer of Constantius, Frend, *The Rise of Christianity*, 629. See Piganiol, *L'empire chrétienne*, 103, 105-6, 136, 161-2; Stein, *Histoire*, 175.

Meletius: cf. *Ep.* 15, 2; *Ep.* 16, 2. Bishop of Beroea, chosen bishop of Antioch after Eudoxius, Downey, *Antioch*, 370; witness of martyrdom of Christian soldiers under Julian, Downey, *ibid.*, 173; council at Alexandria's attempt to reunite Meletians and those loyal to Paulinus, Downey, *ibid.*, 177; on the division of the Antiochenes among followers of Meletius, Paulinus and Euzoius (below), *ibid.*, 182; as a "New Nicene," Frend, *The Rise of Christianity*, 609; presiding at the synod of Antioch in 363 which accepted the *homoousios* and the creed from Nicaea, *ibid.*, 616; years in exile, Frend, *ibid.*, 629; acknowledged by Basil, *ibid.*, 632; Jerome and Damasus' disapproval, *ibid.*, 633 n. 82 citing *Ep.* 15, 2.

Euzoius, bishop, 361-378: see Downey, *Antioch*, 176. Elected in the confusion after the transfer of Eudoxius to the see of Constantinople, *ibid.*, 157; on the extreme Arianism of the creed issued under his aspices at the synod of 361, Downey, *ibid.*, 370.

Jerome's account, primarily a list of the bishops, makes it difficult to determine its relationship to other sources. The bishops named in the accounts of Socrates and Sozomen vary, but those in Theodoret agree with Jerome and point to a common source. Both of the ancient biographies of Athanasius include accounts of Meletius (*Vita Ath.* 22 and *Vita Ath. aceph.* 5), but they lack substantial parallels with Jerome. Gelasius *HE* 3, 16, 20 discusses only Eustathius. *Chron. misc.* (24b; Bidez, *Philostorgius*, 215) names the Arian Leontius (above) as the twenty-ninth bishop of Antioch; cf. Jerome, who refuses to give dates (i.e., the order of succession) for Arian bishops.

232d. Iuvencus: cf. *De vir. il.* 84. See Berardino, *Patrology*, 5, 15-16, 265-69, 312, 324; Piganiol, *L'empire chrétienne*, 387.

232e. Porfirius Optatianus, not to be confused with the pagan polemicist Porphyry: see Porfirius 2, 31 and 9, 35.

232f. Athanasius: see the references in Berardino and in Stein. For Jerome's references to Athanasius cf. *Chron.* 234g, 236a, 236e, 242d; *Apol. c. Rufin.* 2, 17; 2, 20; 2, 21; *De vir. il.* 87, 88, 95, 98, 125; *Ep. adv Rufin.* 42; *Vita Pauli* 12.

*Chron. Pasch.* preserves the close connection between the consecration of Athanasius and the foundation of Constantinople also found in Jerome (see 232g below for Constantinople). Philostorgius is more precise on the exact location and the indecisive nature of the voting for Athanasius' election. Sozomen (2, 17) cites Athanasius' own resistance to the election and Alexander's participation in the choice of Athanasius. A source very different from Philostorgius' is evident here; Sozomen relates a secret ordination of Athanasius by seven bishops rather than a forced election. The source is other than Socrates, upon whom Sozomen sometimes depends. The former (1, 15) has a quite different account, referring to a "sacred game" played by Athanasius and his friends. This is dependent upon Rufinus. Theodoret (1, 26) has no mention of Alexander's part in the election; however, like Sozomen he cites Athanasius' assistance of Alexander in favor of the "Nicene belief." Gelasius (3, 15, 8ff.) describes Athanasius as coming to the priesthood on favorable terms. Rufinus' account (10, 15) emphasizes that Athanasius was destined for both the priesthood and controversy. The *Vita Ath.* (5) relates the immediate succession of Athanasius after Alexander's death and the subsequent resistance of other forces. The *Vita Ath. aceph.* (2) cites the desire of the Alexandrians for Athanasius' consecration. Due to the terse character of Jerome's notice it is difficult to determine its relationship to the other sources.

232g. Constantinople: cf. *Chron.* 223c, 235f, 240di, 241ceghk, 243e, 245chl, 246g, and 247b; *Apol. c. Rufin.* 2, 27; *De vir. il.* 7; 127; *Ep.* 90, *passim.* See Berardino, *Patrology,* 35, 383; Mierow, *The Letters of St. Jerome,* 201 n. 1 (on *Ep.* 10); 210 n. 1 (*Ep.* 15); 212 n. 21 (*Ep.* 16); 214 n. 1 (*Ep.* 18A); 223 n. 1 (*Ep.* 19).

On pagan and Christian authors' attitudes towards the new capital, see H. W. Bird, "Three Fourth Century Issues. A Roman Bureaucrat's Personal Views," *Échos* 20, 30 (Oct. 1976); also K. Sugano, *Das Rombilds des Hieronymus,* Europäischen Hochschulschriften, Reihe 15. Klassischen Sprachen und Literaturen, Band 25 (Frankfurt-am-Main: Peter Lang, 1983), 11-12 and O. Zwierlein, "Der Fall Roms im Spiegel der Kirchenvater," *ZPE* 32 (1978): 50-1 and 55; Stein, *Histoire,* 127, 131, 135, etc. On the plundering of other cities, Burckhardt thought the reference was to population (*Age of Constantine,* 350), but Kelly has it relate to art (*Jerome,* 71).

In favor of Kelly's interpretation above, Theophanes (23, 26) cites the beautification of the "New Rome" by the transfer of statues, marble, etc., from other cities. Likewise Socrates (1, 16) refers to statues brought from other cities, while Sozomen (2, 3) mentions the expenses incurred. *Chron. Pasch.,* as we have seen, is similar to Jerome in combining the ordination of Athanasius and the foundation of the new capital. Pollux (272) cites the generosity of the public dole in the new city on the occasion of its foundation, while Theophanes has the distribution of food due to famine. Philostorgius (2, 9) also relates a lavish dole on the occasion of the city's foundation, an event also related by Sozomen and by the *Origo Constantini Imperatoris* (5, 29). It is Philostorgius (*ibid.*) who preserves the story of Constantine being led by a divine entity to mark the city's boundaries. While Socrates cites a single law engraved on a column, Eutropius (10, 3) mentions laws associated with the city's new status. Zosimus (2, 30, 35) gives a full account of the buildings of Constantine in Constantinople; though he says something about the movement of many citizens into it-- the source of Burckhardt's theory above--he says nothing of the exprense incurred by other cities as a result. *Chron. misc.* (8a; Bidez, *Philostorgius*, 206) merely cites the emperor's establishment of Constantinople as that of a "famous city," also known as Byzantium.

232h. Metrodorus: see Piganiol, *L'empire chrétienne*, 56.

Socrates (1, 19) cites Metrodorus' travel to India as an example for the philosopher Meropius. Rufinus used the same source, citing the travels of both men. Gelasius (3, 9, 3) is directly related to Rufinus, with references not only to both philosophers but to Adesius and Frumentius, who are also named by Rufinus.

233a. Marcus, bishop of Rome from Jan. to Oct., 336: perhaps the same Marcus mentioned by Constantine in a letter to Pope Miltiades in 313 requesting a synod to hear the case of Caecilian of Carthage; Kelly, *The Oxford Dictionary of Popes* (Oxford: Oxford University Press, 1986), 28-9; see also V. Monachino, *La cura pastorale a Milano, Cartagine e Roma nel iv secolo* (Rome: 1947), 282 and 300 and A. Ferrua, "La basilica di papa Marco," *Civilta cattolica* 99 (1948): 503-13 (on the basilica credited to Marcus).

Julius, bishop of Rome from Feb., 337 to April, 352: famous for championing Nicene teaching and for defending Athanasius; it was at his request that Constantius II and Constans called the general synod at Serdica in 342 or 343; Kelly, *Dictionary of Popes*, 29-30. See also Berardino, *Patrology*, 34, 580 and Piganiol, *L'empire chrétienne*, 82, 94 and 381 as well as H. Hess, *The Canons of the Council of Serdica a.d. 343* (Oxford: Oxford University Press, 1958).

Jerome gives the reign of Marcus as eight months and that of Julius as sixteen years and four months. Theophanes (28, 21 and 29, 3), preserved by Pollux (342) gives just fifteen years for Julius. Sozomen (2, 20) simply says Marcus held his see for a short time, while Theodoret (2, 15, 10 and 5, 40, 4) omits Marcus altogether.

233b. Constantine: cf. *Chron.* 6, 7, 225g and Rom., 229dk, 230e, 231ade, 232ae, 233dhi, 234ab Rom. and e; *De vir il.* 80, 81, 82, 84, 86, 88, 93; *Vita Pauli* 8.

That Constantine issued an edict for the destruction of pagan temples is "out of the question;" Burckhardt, *Age of Constantine*, 305. See also P. P. Joannou, *La législation impériale et la christianisation de l'empire romain (311-476)* (Rome: Orientalia christiana analecta 192, 1972), on Constantine's laws relevant to Christianity.

*Chron. Pasch.* (525, 19) places the emphasis on the destruction of idols rather than temples: "he threw down all the idols." This account depended upon the same source as Sozomen (2, 5), for example, on the redistribution of the temples' wealth. Close verbal parallels also point to a common source for the *Artemii Passio* (5) and *Chron. Pasch.* The use of the lost Arian again offers the solution to the parallels. Theophanes (24, 1 and 28, 32) and *Chron. misc.* (7b; Bidez, *Philostorgius*, 206) appear to have used Jerome's source for the destruction of temples. Georgius Monachus (4, 178, 1 and 9, 1) later preserved material from both Theophanes and Malalaas (5, 11, 3), as verbal parallels on the destruction of temples and the opening of churches show.

233c. Goths: cf. *Chron.* 220l, 221k, 245i, 248h and 249c; *De vir. il.* 135; *Hebr. quaest. in gen.* 10, 21. See under names of individuals (e.g., Athanaric at 245i).

Again Theophanes (27, 31) may preserve Jerome's source; he has a victory over the Goths and Sarmatians, compared to Jerome's victory over the Goths in Sarmatian territory. Likewise Sozomen (18) cites the defeat of Goths and Sarmatians, with a treaty that followed. Eutropius (10, 7, 1) gives the victory over the Goths but no reference to the Sarmatians. Here as elsewhere (see, for example 234b) the author of the *Origo Constantini Imperatoris* (6, 30) appears to have used Jerome. This work not only recounts the defeat of Goths; it also has the Sarmatians asking for Roman help. Jerome's account appears to be related to that of the *Consularia Constantinopolitana* (hereafter cited as *Cons. Const.*), which in its early form predated the *Chron.* Both have notices of the Roman defeat of the Goths in Sarmatian territory.

233d. Constans: cf. *Chron.* 234 Rom., 235b, Rom., 236c, 237c; *De vir. il.* 87. On his birth, death, engagement to the daughter of the Consul Ablabius, Barnes, *The New Empire*, 45; residences and journeys, Barnes, *ibid.*, 86-87; for an examination of his life and career, G. E. Garrido, "Observaciones sobre un emperador cristiano Fl. Jul. Constante," *Lucentum* 3 (1984): 261-78; the crisis of the years 345 to 346, H. R. Baldus, "Constantius et Constans Augusti. Darstellungen des kaiserlichen Bruderpaares auf Pragungen der Jahre 340-350 n. Chr.," *JNG* 34 (1984): 77-106; also Piganiol, *L'empire chrétienne*, 75, 78, Stein, *Histoire*, 131-39.

Like Jerome, both the *Cons. Const.* (ca. 367) and Victor (41, 13) cite the elevation of Constans just after the defeat of the Goths. Eusebius' *Vita const.* (4, 40) names the three sons of Constantine made Caesars but makes no reference to the Goths. Libanius (*Or. 59, 39*) merely refers to the Emperor's children being given power. Again Theophanes (17, 21) may have used Jerome's source, citing Constans as Constantine's son and his promotion to Caesar, in that order. Zosimus (2, 35) places the emphasis on Constantine II and the promotion of his brothers as Caesars only later.

233e. See Appendix B on natural phenomena as one of Jerome's subjects.

Theophanes (29, 14) is close to Jerome, citing the same famine in Syria and particularly in Antioch.

233f. Sarmatians, etc.: see Jones, *Constantine*, 169; MacMullen, *Constantine*, 146-47.

Eusebius' *Vita const.* (4, 6) has a fuller account of the Sarmatians and other barbarians but omits the Limigantes. The *Origo Const. Imp.* (6, 32) again may have used Jerome, mentioning the rebellion of the Sarmatians' subjects and the Sarmatians' entry into Roman territory, but it also cites three hundred thousand barbarians settled in Thrace, Scythia, etc. Jerome again appears to be related to *Cons. Const.*, as shown by the verbal parallel "Sarmatae . . . dominos suos . . .in Roman . . . expulerunt." Ammianus (17, 12, 18 and 19, 21) does not name the Limigantes but supplies many details including personal names.

233g. Calocaerus: Jerome's notice is one of only several bits of evidence for Calocaerus; the others are Victor 41, 11-12; Theoph. 29, 28-31; and *Origo Const. Imp.* 534, 29.

Theophanes used Jerome's source for *Kalokairos* on Cyprus and his subsequent defeat by the Romans. The *Origo Const. Imp.* (534, 29) appears to depend upon Jerome for Calocaerus' revolution and its suppression. See I. Koenig, *Origo Constantini. Anonymus Valesianus*, Teil 1, Text und Kommentar (Trier: Trierer Historische Forschungen 11, 1987), 19-28 for the use of Jerome by the *Origo*; against this see Barnes, "Jerome and the Origo Constantini Imperatoris," *Phoenix* (Summer 1989): 159-61.

233h. Antony: cf. *Chron.* 218e, 240beh; *De vir. il.* 87, 88, 99, 102; *Ep.* 22, 36; 57, 6 (citing Evagrius' prologue to the *Vita Antonii*); 68, 2; *Vita Pauli* 7-16; *Vita Hilar.* 3, 29, 31, 32.

See H. Gwatkin, *Studies of Arianism: Chiefly Referring to the Character and Chronology of the Reaction Which Followed the Council of Nicaea* (New York: AMS Press, 1978 repr. of 1882 ed.) 103; Mierow, *The Letters of St. Jerome*, 190, 201 n. 1, 206 n. 15, 245 n. 32; Piganiol, *L'empire chrétienne*, 60, 233, 377; Stein, *Histoire*, 147-50; Pelikan, *The Christian Tradition*, 135-37. The *Life of Antony* by Athanasius was translated into Latin ca. 365, probably at Rome. In about 370 Jerome's friend Evagrius provided a new translation, based on classical principles (Migne, *PL* 73). The prologue to this translation is especially important to Jerome, who adopts its principles and cites Evagrius in *Ep.* 57 (above) adressed to Pammachius.

The Emperor's letter to Antony is also mentioned in Athanasius' *Vita Antonii* (81) together with Antony's delayed response. Rufinus (10, 8) also records the Emperor's letter.

233i. Dalmatius Caesar: on his birth, death, and education, see Barnes, *The New Empire*, 45. A letter from Dalmatius to his father (consul in 333) is preserved in the *Codex Iust.* 5, 17, 7; see Barnes, *ibid.*, 16, 87, 105. On his role in events in the aftermath of Constantine's death, see Browning, *Julian*, 34-35; cf. Burckhardt, *The Age of Constantine*, 284. On the date of his promotion and that of Constans, see Jones, *Later Roman Empire*, 1, 85 n. 108, citing *Chron. Min.* 1, 232, 234-5. On the allotment of provinces to *Caesars*, Jones, *ibid.*, 1, 85; see also *ibid.*, 101-2. On the role of the *Caesars* in the period, Browning, *Julian*, 16.

*Chron. Pasch.* (531, 14) used Jerome's source, citing Constantine's *Tricennalia* celebration together with the promotion of Dalmatius. Theophanes (29, 28, 37) seems to rely upon the same source. Victor (41, 15) has a military emphasis and points out Dalmatius' name as identical to his father's. The *Epitome* (41, 15) is clearly based upon Victor; both give Constantine's age after mention of Dalmatius. The *Origo Const. Imp.* (6, 35) includes details omitted by Jerome, while the latter is again related to the *Cons. Const.* (a. 335) for the *Tricennalia* and Constans' promotion.

233k. Jerome's source for the rhetorician Pater is unknown.

233l. Nazarius: see Berardino, *Patrology*, 150. Cf. *Anthologia Latina* 767/8.

233m. Tiberianus: see Piganiol, *L'empire chrétienne*, 74 n. 5, 323.

Tiberianus is attested as "Vicar of Spain" at *CTh* 3, 5, 6 and as "Count of Africa" at *CTh* 12, 5, 1. He is also named in *Codex Iustin.* 6, 1, 6.

233n. See 232c on Eustathius.

Eusebius refers to the martyr's shrine at Jerusalem in *Vita const.* (3, 25f. and 40; and 4, 47) but fails to mention Eustathius. The *Laud. Const.* (9) describes the building projects in Palestine but also omits Eustathius. Theophanes (33, 11) used Jerome's source, and cites Eustathius as a presbyter of Constantinople responsible for the shrine in Jerusalem.

234a. Eusebius of Nicomedia: Browning, *Julian*, 35-37, 39; MacMullen, *Constantine*, 173; Jones, *Constantine*, 129-32. "Public villa" seems to indicate one of the imperial *mansiones* maintained by the state; MacMullen, *Constantine*, 224.

Eusebius' *Vita const.* (4, 61f.) is an early source for Constantine's death outside Nicomedia, but parallels suggest that Theophanes (17, 28 and 33, 19) and the *Chron. Pasch.* (532, 10) used Jerome's source for Constantine's baptism (see below). Socrates (1, 39, followed by Sozomen 2, 34), Philostorgius (2, 16) and Rufinus (10, 12) depended upon the same source tradition for an Arian presbyter's role in handling the will of Constantine; cf. Theophanes 34, 1. Theodoret (1, 32) and Theophanes' source alike (for 17, 28) related Constantine's preference for a baptism in the Jordan River. Among later authors, Cedrenus (271c) preserved Theophanes, while Photius (88) and Georgius Monachus (4, 187) derive their cautions against heretical claims to the baptism from Theophanes as well; as usual, verbal parallels reveal that Julius Pollux (314) preserved material directly from the earlier authors, here including Socrates (on the suburb of Nicomedia), Sozomen (on Constantine's sister Constantia and the Arian presbyter), and Theodoret (on the preference for the Jordan).

234b. Constantine's postponement of baptism was representative of the custom followed in the period; the emphasis was that of cleansing from sins rather than initiation into the community; Jones, *Constantine*, 196. In this instance, as we have seen, Constantine had hoped for baptism in the Jordan; see MacMullen, *Constantine*, 223-4.

Jerome appears to have used Eutropius (10, 8, 2). However, Theophanes (33, 15) seems to have used Jerome's source for the length of Constantine's reign and the reference to his sons. Again the *Origo Const. Imp.* (6, 35) appears to have used

Jerome (note the parallel "cum bellum pararet in Persas . . . villa publica iuxta Nicomediam"). Both Libanius (*Or.* 59, 72) and Eusebius (*Vita const.* 4, 56) refer to the *defeat* of the Persians as that of barbarians.

234Rom. *Chron. Pasch.* (533, 21) and Theophanes (34, 8) preserve Jerome's source, citing Constantine's thirty-five years, his three sons, and the numeral 34; cf. also Jerome 234d and *Chron. Pasch.* 533, 18-19. Both Theophanes and *Chron. Pasch.* mention Constantius' reign in connection with Sapor of Persia. *Chron. misc.* (14a; Bidez, *Philostorgius*, 211) gives twenty-five years for the reign of Constantine II; cf. Jerome's "twenty-four years, five months and thirteen days" for the reigns of Constantius and Constans.

234c. Ablabius: see Piganiol, *L'empire chrétienne*, 51, 58, 74, 75; Jones, *Constantine*, 178-79; MacMullen, *Constantine*, 209, 213, 209, 224; Stein, *Histoire*, 131, 473.

Ablabius is discussed in Eunapius' *Lives of the Sophists* at *Aed.* 41, where he is credited with murder as well as "all these evils," and is named as Praetorian prefect. The murder of nobles is emphasized by the fact that Ablabius "did not even attain to the humble middle class" (Loeb trans., 384-5). Zosimus (2, 40) used Eunapius (above), citing Ablabius' murder of the philosopher Sopater. Palladius' *Hist. Laus.* (56) cites Olympias, the granddaughter of Ablabius.

234d. Sapor, or Shapur II: cf. *Chron.* 236bh, 243c.

Theophanes (34, 32) and *Chron. Pasch.* (533, 18) used Jerome's source on the Persian king in Mesopotamia. The *Chron. misc.* (13g; Bidez, *Philostorgius*, 210) also preserved Jerome's source, citing Sapor in Mesopotamia and then his siege of Nisibis; similarly to Jerome, who has "almost two months," it has "sixty-six days." In his *Panegyric* for Constantius (1, 27 and 2, 62-63), Julian describes the massive siege operations at Nisibis, including the Persians' diversion of the Mygdonius River against the city's walls.

234e. See 233i on Dalmatius.

Jerome used Eutropius (10, 9, 1). Theophanes (35, 7) and Socrates (2, 25) used a common source on Dalmatius.

234f. Iacobus: cf. Gennadius *De vir. il.* 1. See Piganiol, *L'empire chrétienne*, 75; Stein, *Histoire*, 137.

*Chron. Pasch.* (536, 18 and 537, 6) may point to Jerome's source, but it is much less precise than Jerome. It mentions Nisibis as saved by its citizens' prayers, but fails to name Iacobus. Verbal parallels show that Theophanes (39, 19) used the same source, but Iacobus is credited with saving the city. Philostorgius (3, 23) mentions Iacobus but as one who "fought wonderfully . . . on behalf of the city's safety. *Chron. misc.* (13g; Bidez, *Philostorgius*, 210) not only mentions Iacobus' prayers driving the enemy away, but gives the figure of sixty-six days, close to Jerome's "almost two months;" see 234d above. "Theodoret (2, 30, 11), followed by Pollux (352), has a miraculous arrival of flies to torment the Persian elephants. Gennadius (*De vir. il.*, 1) provides a brief biography of Iacobus.

234g. Athanasius: on the nature of his stance against Arianism, Kelly, *Early Christian Doctrines*, 233, 240-47; E. P. Meijering, *Orthodoxy and Platonism in Athanasius: Synthesis or Antithesis?* (Leiden: E. J. Brill, 1968, *passim*; R. W. Thomson's ed. of Athanasius' works (New York: Oxford University Press, 1971); Frend, *The Rise of Christianity*, 524-5. Suspected of treason by Constantius, Frend, *ibid.*, 534 and 536. For an overview of the problems of the relationship of emperors and their Christian subjects in the period, see K. M. Setton, *The Christian Attitude Towards the Emperor in the Fourth Century* (New York: Columbia University, 1941), *passim*.

Theophanes (34, 1) and others, as noted above (234a), records the role of an Arian presbyter in the transmission of Constantine's will. Philostorgius (2, 11) and Theodoret alike (2, 3) relate calumnies spread concerning Athanasius at the end of Constantine's reign; Philostorgius recorded the charge that Athanasius had relations with a prostitute, while Theodoret names several "accomplices" of the unnamed Arian presbyter who assisted him in undermining Athanasius' reputation before Constantius. Theodoret (2, 3) records Constantine's "lapse" and has the story of the Arian and the will in some detail (cf. above on 234a). Rufinus (10, 12f.) and Theodoret are closely related on details concerning Constantia, the Emperor's sister and widow of Emperor Licinius.

235a. Constantine II: see 234 Rom. For recent works, especially relating to his coinage, see W. Weber, "Constantinische Deckengemalde aus dem römische Palast unter dem Trierer Dom," *Museumsfuhrer Bischofl. Dom-Diozesanmus.* (1984); P. Brun, "Gloria Romanorum," *Studia Kajanto*, Arctos suppl. II (Helsinki: Classical Association of Finland, 1985), 23-31 (coins struck at Trier depicting him with Constantius); G. Dagron and D. Feissel, "Inscriptiones inedites du musee d'Antioche (Antakya)," *Travaux et Memoires*, Centre de recherche d'histoire et de civilisation byzantine 9 (1985): 421-61 (on an inscription at Antioch, 336 A.D.). As Caesar with the title *Alemannicus*, gained by 331, and his Danube command, Jones, *Later Roman Empire*, 2, 1082 n. 15 citing *ILS* 6091 and *Anonymous Valesianus* 31; see also Browning, *Julian*, 16.

*Chron. Pasch.* (518, 2) and Theophanes (35, 30) seem to have used Jerome's source. The former has the army of Constans responsible for Constantine II's death and Theophanes says Constantine (II) was defeated "by the soldiers" of Constans. However, the verbal parallel with Eutropius (10, 9, 2; note especially "bellum fratri inferens . . . Aquileiam") suggests Jerome's use of the *Breviarium*. Rufinus (10, 16) is related to Jerome in citing Constantine's death at Alsa near Aquileia.

235b. Franks: cf. 235e, 246h. See Piganiol, *L'empire chrétienne*, 121, 124, 223, 254.

Socrates (2, 10) used a source other than Jerome's for the Franks' attack on Gaul, and he omits Constans' name. Sozomen (3, 6) characteristically depends upon Socrates, here for the earthquake at Antioch.

235c. On earthquakes, cf. 174d, 236f, 241a, 244c, 245f. See D. Soren, "The Day the World Ended at Kourion. Reconstructing an Ancient Earthquake," *National Geographic* 174 no. 1 (July 1988): 30-53; on contemporary interpretations of earthquakes, M. Henry, "Le témoignage de Libanius et les phenomenes seismiques du ive siècle de notre ère. Essai d'interprétation," *Phoenix* 39 (1985): 36-61; Libanius' grouping of earthquakes, etc., around the death of Emperor Julian, *ibid*.

Sozomen (3, 6) follows Socrates (2, 10), omitting only the detail of a year's duration.

235d. Audeus (also *Audaeus*): see Helm, *Chron.*, 235, n. 12. On Audianism as an ascetic cult, Frend, *The Rise of Christianity*, 578.

Epiphanius (*Panar. haer.* 70, 3, 1) records the establishment of the Audian heresy in Syria. Theodoret (*Haer. fab.* 4) gives Audaeus' origin as Syria across the Euphrates, and describes Audian tenets. Augustine (*De haer.* 50) refers to the *Audiani* while Jerome here names the *haeresis Audiana*.

235e. Theophanes (37, 13) used Jerome's source. He places Constans' defeat of the Franks immediately before the earthquake in Cyprus. While Jerome cites the ruin of many cities, Theophanes names Salamine in particular. On the Franks, Libanius (*Or.* 59, 131f.) relates that the Emperor "turned their insatiable lust for war to a desire for peace;" however, the Emperor in Libanius is Constantius, not Constans.

235f. Paulus: cf. *Chron.* 235hi. See Stein, *Histoire*, 134, 151. Paulus' remains were later brought to Constantinople by Emperor Theodosius I; see J. Matthews, *Western Aristocracies and Imperial Court, A.D. 364-425* (Oxford: Clarendon Press, 1975), 123; on Hermogenes, ordered by Constantius to restore order at Constantinople, Jones, *Later Roman Empire*, 1, 124.

Again Theophanes (42, 25) used Jerome's source, citing Hermogenes as general (*stratelates*), the exile of Paulus, and Hermogenes' death at the hands of the people.

235g. Dedication of the "Golden Church" at Antioch: see 231i. Jerome errs in placing the dedication in 342, since the date of the "Council of the Dedication" in 341 is certain; Downey, *Antioch*, 343 and n. 106, citing W. Eltester, "Die Kirchen Antiochias im IV Jahrhundert," *ZNT* 36 (1937): 254-5.

Sozomen (3, 5) preserved Socrates (2, 8) on the construction under Constantine and completion under Constantius. Eusebius (*Laud. Const.* 15), like Jerome, emphasizes the Church's great size and beauty. Among later authors, Malalas (5, 2, 7) should be noted for providing the text of the dedicatory inscription.

235h. Macedonius: cf. 235i, 241h. Constantius ordered the exile of Macedonius both because of doctrinal issues and the dispute that was brought on by the bishop's decision to move the body of Constantine to the Church of St. Acacius; see M. Whitby and M. Whitby, *Chronicon Paschale 284-628 A.D.* (Liverpool: Liverpool University Press, 1989), 34 and G. Dagron, *Naissance d'une capitale: Constantinople et ses institutions de 330 à 451* (Paris: Bibliotheque Byzantine, études VII, 1974), 436-42.

Macedonian heresy: cf. 243d, *De vir il.* 89. See also Theodoret, *Haer. fab.* 4, 5. The Macedonians were also called "Pneumatomachians" ("Spirit-fighters"); on Gregory of Nyssa's famous sermon vs. Macedonius as the Pneumatomachian leader, J. Quasten, *Patrology*, vol. III, *The Golden Age of Greek Patristic Literature from the Council of Nicea to the Council of Chalcedon* (Westminster, Md.: The Newman Press, 1963), 3, 259. See also Kelly, *Early Christian Doctrines*, 259 and 1986, 33; Berardino, *Patrology*, 322, 324; Piganiol, *L'empire chrétienne*, 83, 105, 106, 219, 371. Helm cites Joseph Scaliger, *Thesaurus Temporum*, 2nd ed. (Osnabruck: Zeller, 1968 repr. of 1658 ed.) as giving the Greek term *poikilotechnes*, literally, "many-colored skill," for Macedonius' trade; 235 n. 21.

Theophanes (42, 24) used Jerome's source; he has Paulus' banishment by Constantius, Paulus' death, and the ascendancy of the Macedonians together with Philippus' support of Macedonius. Sozomen (2, 16) has again relied upon Socrates (3, 9). The latter used the same tradition as Theophanes and thus has references to the bath of Zeuxippus and to Paulus' being taken to Thessaloniki. Like Jerome, Athanasius (*Apol. de fug.* 3) has the strangulation of Paulus and the role of the prefect Philippus. The *Vita Athan. Aceph.* (2-3) also relates Hermogenes' persecution of Paulus as well as Paulus' strangulation. Theodoret (*Haer. fab.* 4, 5) describes Macedonius' repudiation of the *homoousios* creed and his adoption of the *homoeusios* instead. Rufinus (10, 26), like Theodoret (ibid.), describes the Macedonians' error concerning the Holy Spirit.

235i. Paulus: see 235f and 235h.

236a. Maximinus of Treves: see Berardino, *Patrology*, 96-101, 392. Constantius: see 234d.

Theophanes (32, 12) may have used Jerome's source for Athanasius' exile at Treves. He includes an account of two letters of Athanasius, one authentic and the other spurious. Sozomen (2, 28) appears to depend upon Socrates (1, 35) for the role of Emperor Constantius. Theodoret (1, 31, 5) is related to Socrates; like him he records the exile but does not mention Maximinus. Athanasius (*Apol. ad Constant.* 3) describes his own tribulations at Treves; the *Vita Athan.* (5, in Photius, 258) emphasizes the anger of Constantius towards Athanasius.

236b. Theophanes again appears to preserve Jerome's source, here for Sapor's persecution of the Christians.

236c. Neocaesarea: cf. *vir il.* 65. *Reperti sunt*: Jerome uses the perfect where we would expect the pluperfect in classical Latin.

Again Theophanes (37, 18) had access to the same source as Jerome, and records the earthquake and the survival of those in the church.

236d. Titianus: the following inscriptions attest to Titianus as prefect: *C.I.L.* 6 1166/7; 1653/4; 1717, 10, 476.

236e. Athanasius: see 232f. On Constans' support of Athanasius, Frend, *The Rise of Christianity*, 529 and Kelly, *Early Christian Doctrines*, 238.

Theophanes (43, 13) may reflect Jerome's source; he has Constans' concern over the exile of Athanasius, the exchange of correspondence, the threat of war pending Athanasius' restoration, and the return of Athanasius to his see. Philostorgius (3, 12) appears to have used the same source as Theophanes for many details. Socrates (2, 22-3) likewise followed the same source: "he [Constans] encouraged him [Constantius] to restore Paulus and Athanasius to their sees." Likewise Sozomen (3, 20) has "but Constans wrote his brother to restore Athanasius and Paul to their churches," and Sozomen is verbally closer to Theophanes than Socrates is. Verbal parallels also reveal that Theodoret (2, 10, 3-12) used the common source, and like Socrates, he quotes the letter of Constantius to Athanasius. In the *Vita Athan.* (17-18), Julius, the bishop of Rome, plays a key role in Athanasius' release from exile.

236f. Dyrrachium: cf. *Chron.* 97; Campania: cf. 152g, 171d, 177b.

Theophanes (37, 32) used Jerome's source for the earthquake at Dyrrachium, Rome in darkness for three days, and the damage to the cities in Campania.

236g. Seleucia: cf. *Chron.* 127c, 194b. See Berardino, *Patrology*, 37.

Theophanes (38, 6) may provide evidence for Jerome's simplification of data from the Arian: in the former, the Arian Emperor Constantius receives credit for the construction, while in Jerome, the builder is unnamed. Like Theophanes, *Chron. misc.* (21a; Bidez, *Philostorgius*, 214) ascribes the building to Constantius. Cf. Julian, *Or.* 1, 40.

236h. Sapor: see 234d.

Julian (*Or.* 1, 27a and 2, 62d) has a four-month siege. *Chron. Pasch.* (536, 18) has one hundred days like Theophanes (38, 9). Theodoret (2, 30, 4) gives seventy days.

236i. Eusebius of Emesa: cf. *vir il.* 91, 119, 129. See Berardino, *Patrology*, 209, 232, 233.

Jerome is unique in referring to this Eusebius as an Arian author. Socrates (2, 9) provides a capsule biography, the details of which he credits to George, the bishop of Laodicea.

236k. Eclipse: Theophanes (38, 12) preserves Jerome's source: "An eclipse of the sun occurred."

236l. Singara: see Piganiol, *L'empire chrétienne*, 18, 76, 107, 146. A comparison with the source, Eutropius 10, 10, 1, reveals an interesting reinterpretation of the events. While Eutropius blames the loss on the soldiers' arrogance and their demands for an engagement, Jerome cites their "stupidity"--*stoliditate*--instead. Eutropius' account allows for the soldiers' rash courage, not mere foolishness. His hint at the threat of sedition also removes the burden of the responsibility from Constantius. By contrast, Jerome's remark may suggest a lack of military prowess on the Emperor's part: in spite of the fact that there were nine serious engagements, the Emperor played no significant role. For more on Constantius, see the following: birth, marriage to the daughter of Julius Constantius, and death, Barnes, *The New Empire*, 45; title of *Persicus*, taken for a victory in 366, Barnes, "Two Victory Titles of Constantius," *ZPE* 52 (1983): 229-35 and cf. J. Arce, "The Inscription of Troesmis *ILS* 724 and the First Victories of Constantius II as Caesar," *ZPE* 48 (1982): 245-9; as *Caesar* in Gaul, Jones, *Later Roman Empire*, 2, 1082 n. 15, citing Julian, *Or.* 1, 11d, 12a; and his departure for the East, *ibid.*, 136.

Ms. S, lines 25-6, reads *Constans III* while OMA shows *novem*. The omission of *gravius* from some mss. is significant for Jerome's precise meaning, since this would clearly mean Constantius had no part in war whatsoever. *Persas* may be a gloss, as it is written above line 26 in ms. S. For the difficulties of the text, lines 23-26, see Helm's apparatus, 236, in Appendix A of the present work.

Amida: see Piganiol, *L'empire chrétienne*, 18, 57, 101, 251; Stein, *Histoire*, 154, 171.

Jerome used Eutropius (10, 10, 1) and Festus (27, 1-3), as verbal parallels demonstrate. However, like Theophanes (46, 9), he has the capture of Bizabde, so the Arian may provide a detail here. Ammianus (18, 5, 7) is independent here, especially in his explicit acknowledgement of a bloody Roman defeat at night. Libanius (*Or.* 59, 120), similarly to Jerome, emphasizes the fact that the Romans should have won: "If we took up arms, clearly the victory would be ours."

237a. "had been ordained a priest" (*presbyter*): I have translated *presbyter* as "priest;" cf. W. Berschin, *Griechisch-lateinisches Mittelalter. Von Hieronymus zu Nikolaus von Kues* (Bern: Francke, 1980), 66, translating Evagrius of Antioch's prologue to the *Vita Antonii: Presbyter Evagrius*--"Der Priester Evagrius." The ecclesiastical orders were well-defined by this period. *Ep.* 51, 2 mentions bishop (*episcopus*), priest (*presbyter*), deacon (*diaconus*), subdeacon (*subdiaconus*). *Ep.* 108, 14 terms priests and deacons those of "Levitical rank." In the *Adv. Iovin.* 34 Jerome enumerates bishop, priest and deacon, arguing that these are names of duties rather than merits: "Episcopus et presbyter et diaconus non sunt meritorum nomina, sed officiorum." For other ecclesiastical terms of the period borrowed from Greek, see E. A. Bechtel's list in *Sanctae Silviae Peregrinatio: The Text and Study of the Latinity* (Chicago: University of Chicago diss., 1902), 130-32 (esp. 131 for *martyrium*, found at *Chron.* 233n).

Theophanes (27, 5; 30, 18; 36, 14; 41, 27) may have used Jerome's source, but Jerome's account is much fuller. Like Jerome, *Chron. misc.* (8a; Bidez, *Philostorgius*, 206) has Maximus as the fortieth bishop of Jerusalem. Socrates (2, 45) appears to have access to the same tradition as Jerome, listing Cyril, Herennius, Heraclius, Hilary and Cyril. The only discrepancy with Jerome is the omission of Cyril after Herennius--Jerome's Irenaeus. Sozomen (2, 20) discusses problems with the ordination of Maximus as successor to Macarius; he relies in part (4, 30) upon Socrates, especially for the succession of bishops. Epiphanius has a different succession, placing one Cyril after Herennius. Theodoret (2, 26, 6) gives a less detailed account but bears similarity to Jerome: Maximus succeeds Macarius at Jerusalem; Cyril is involved in struggles for the same see; and Acacius deposes Cyril. Rufinus (10, 24) records Cyril as bishop after Maximus, and then relates the rise of Georgius at Alexandria.

237b. Liberius: cf. 240; *De vir. il.*, 95, 97, 98. See Berardino, *Patrology*, 65, 71, 144, 572, 580; Piganiol, *L'empire chrétienne*, 94, 97, 103, 162, 192; Stein, *Histoire*, 151, 174. In the *De vir. il.* 97, Jerome condemns the author Fortunatianus for his role in pressuring Liberius; see Kelly, *Jerome*, 60. Felix: cf. *De vir. il.* 98. See Piganiol, *ibid.*, 95, 96, 104 n. 77, 192; Stein, *ibid.*, 152, 174. Singled out by Athanasius for his loyalty: Quasten, *Patrology*, 3, 35, citing *Apol. c. Arian.* 89-90. See also *ODCC*, both "Liberius" and "Santa Maria Maggiore."

Athanasius not only mentions the exile of Liberius in the *Apol. c. Arian.* (as a fellow minister who chose to be banished); in the *Ad Const.* (27) it is Liberius' refusal to subscribe to the condemnation of Athanasius which brings about Liberius' exile (cf. *Avell. Coll.* 1) and in the *Ad monach.* (33-41), the emphasis is upon Liberius' courage in confronting Constantius. Both *Lives* of Athanasius name Liberius as the distinguished successor of Julius, relate Liberius' exile, name Felix as his replacement, and cite divine punishment for Liberius' persecutors through blindness and sickness. Socrates (2, 37) is similar to Jerome in mentioning Felix's removal by force. Sozomen (4, 11-15) and Philostorgius (4, 3) used a common source for the Romans' pressure on Constantius for the restoration of Liberius. Philostorgius seems to have used Jerome's source for Felix's promotion, Liberius' submission, and Liberius' recall.

237c. On the circumstances of Magnentius' elevation, as well as his "barbarian" origin, see Burckhardt, *The Age of Constantine*, 289; F. Lot, *The End of the Ancient World and the Beginning of the Middle Ages*, trans. by P. and M. Leon and ed. by G. Downey (New York: Harper and Row, 1961), 198-9. On the barbarians and the lack of defense for the frontier due to Magnentius and Constantius' actions, see *ibid.*, 188. On Magnentius' coinage, see P. Bastien, "Le monnayage de l'atelier de Lyon: De la reouverture de l'atelier en 318 a la mort de Constantin (318-337)," *Numis. romaine* XIII Wetteren Soc. d'ed. Num. rom. (1982). On the war between Magnentius and Constantius, see J. Sasel, "The Struggle Between Magnentius and Constantius II for Illyricum," *Ziva Antika* 21 (1971) 205-16. Magnentius' religion: Bidez, *Philostorgius*, 52; and MacMullen, *Christianizing the Roman Empire*, 48 n. 23. On Vetranio, cf. *Chron.* 238c, and see Piganiol, *L'empire chrétienne*, 85, 87; Stein, *Histoire*, 140, 150; and Jones, *Later Roman Empire*, 1, 113. On the part played by Constantius' sister Constantina in Vetranio's election, see Browning, *Julian*, 50 and cf. Burckhardt, *The Age of Constantine*, 289 on the army. See also A. H. M. Jones, J. R. Martindale, and J. Morris, *The Prosopography of the Later Roman Empire* (hereafter abbreviated *PLRE*) (Cambridge: Harvard University Press, 1971), 1, "Vetranio" and D. Bowder, *The Age of Constantine and Julian* (London: 1978) 46-47, 92.

Jerome used Eutropius, as verbal parallels on Constans' death at the camp of Helena show. *Chron. Pasch.* (518, 3) relates the seizure of power by Magnentius and his subsequent role in Constans' death. Theophanes (43, 32) preserves the same source, and these two works also show parallels concerning Vetranio and Nepotian. Philostorgius (3, 22) is closely related, citing Constans' death at the hands of Magnentius, and the rise of *Vetranis*. Socrates (3, 25) bears a general resemblance to the account of *Chron. Pasch.* and Theophanes: "Magnentius the tyrant [i.e., usurper] arose in the

West; through treachery he killed Constans, who was ruling that part of the empire while staying in the Gauls." Theodoret (2, 15, 1) simply states that after Constans' death Magnentius began to rule the West. Zosimus' account (2, 42-43) provides more precise locations: Constans is assassinated at Helena; Vetranio arises at Mursa; and Nepotianus, at Rome. Both the *Artemii Passio* (10) and Zosimus cite Magnentius' generals, while Zosimus names the *magister officiorum* Marcellinus. *Chron. misc.* (24c; Bidez, *Philostorgius*, 215) merely cites the deaths of Constantine II and Constans without distinguishing between the respective dates of each.

238a. See 237c.

*Chron. Pasch.* here (535, 11) and above appears to copy the *Cons. Const.*, in this instance citing in a similar fashion the battle at Rome between the other citizens and the "Magnentians." Jerome is the only source which gives the betrayal of the senator Heraclas by the Magnentians.

238b. Again, see 237c.

*Verbatim* parallels show that Jerome used Eutropius (10, 11, 2). Zosimus (2, 43) provides additional details including the roles of the praetorian prefect Anicetus and the *magister officiorum* Marcellinus.

238c. Vetranio: *magister peditum*, persuaded by Constantina to seek the throne; his coins with the inscription *Hoc signo victor eris* provide the earliest independent testimony for Constantine's famous vision. See Jones, *PLRE* 1, "Vetranio 1," and Bowder, *The Age of Constantine*, 46-7, 92.

Jerome used Eutropius. Ammianus (16, 1, 2) includes the story of Apodemius, who flattered Constantius by reference to his demotion of Vetranio. Victor (42, 1), like *Chron. Pasch.* (539, 5) and Theophanes 44, 28), names Naissus as the place where Vetranio was dethroned. Philostorgius (3, 22) used the same source as Theophanes, recording Vetranio's dining with Constantius. Socrates (2, 28), followed closely by Sozomen (4, 4), relates the career of Georgius at Alexandria, the desertion of Vetranio's soldiers, and Vetranio's subsequent plight: "he immediately threw himself at the emperor's feet." Zosimus (2, 44) has much in common with Theophanes; cf. 238d below, for which they share the idea of Constantius and Vetranio joining forces against Magnentius. Zosimus also shares details with Philostorgius, including the removal of Vetranio's robe, his banishment to Bithynia, and his idleness there.

238d. Mursa: on the accuracy of Eutropius and Jerome concerning the massive losses at this battle, see R. C. Blockley, "Constantius, Gallus and Julian as Caesars of Constantine II," *Latomus* 31 (1972): 467 and n. 2: "Constantius' forces cannot have recovered."

Jerome used Eutropius (10, 12, 2; see Introduction under "Aurelius Victor"). Socrates (2, 32) records Magnentius' executions of senators at Rome, for which he is followed by Sozomen (4, 7). Both describe the flight to Lugdunum (Socrates has "the remotest parts of Gaul") and subsequent suicide. Zosimus (2, 50-53) gives a detailed asccount of the battle at Mursa, including the entrapment of Magnentius' Gallic troops in the stadium.

238e. Gallus: cf. 238fg, 239c, 240a. See Piganiol, *L'empire chrétienne*, 75, 87, 91, 111, 112. On the circumstances of his promotion and his marriage to Constantina, eldest of Constantine's sisters, see Browning, *Julian*, 51-52.

*Chron. Pasch.* (540, 8) and Theophanes (40, 15) used Jerome's source; the former is more specific, naming Gallus as "the son of Constantius, brother of Dalmatius." Philostorgius (3, 25) used the common source as well, and like both *Chron. Pasch.* and Theophanes, he mentions the Persians and the East in conjunction with Gallus' promotion to Caesar. However, he approaches Gallus' relationships differently, and emphasizes that Gallus' father Constantius was the brother of Constantine. Socrates (2, 28), followed by Sozomen (4, 4), has Gallus sent to Syria after his promotion to defend the East. Zosimus (2, 45) is more precise, and names Lucillianus as Gallus' subordinate assigned to the Persian campaign. Both Zosimus and the *Epitome* (42, 1) mention the marriage of Gallus to Constantina. Of the sources, Socrates, Sozomen, the *Cons. Const.* (a. 351), and Philostorgius all relate the story of a miraculous cross apparition in the East on behalf of Constantius. *Chron. misc.* (25b; Bidez, *Philostorgius*, 220) states only that Constantius decided to have Gallus Caesar rule with him.

238f. On the Jewish revolt see B. G. Nathanson, "Jews, Christians and the Gallus Revolt in Fourth Century Palestine," *BA* 49 no. 1 March (1986): 26-36.

Theophanes (40, 20) records the same events as Jerome--the revolt in Palestine, the loss of life, and the destruction of Diocaesaria. Socrates (2, 33) is followed by Sozomen (4, 7) for an account of the revolt and the ruin of Diocaesaria. Victor's account (42, 11), independent of Jerome's, names Patricius as the general who crushed the revolt.

238g. Gallus at Antioch: see Nathanson, "Jews, Christians and the Gallus Revolt," above. For the rescue of senators from Gallus' decree by Honoratus, Count of the East, see Downey, "Study of the Comites Orientis," 12. See also Jones, *PLRE* 1, "Constantius 4."

*Chron. Pasch.* (541, 15) used Jerome's source. Included among its details are the following: the executions of the praetorian prefect and the quaestor, followed by Constantius' summons of Gallus to Antioch. Philostorgius (3, 28) used the same source and refers to the executions, naming the prefect Domitian, and to the summons. Socrates (2, 34) reports the same events and includes Domitian. Both he and Sozomen (4, 7) name the quaestor Magnus; however, Sozomen gives the seventh regnal year of Constantius, compared to the emperor's seventh consulship in Socrates. While Sozomen places the death of Gallus at *Havonius*, Socrates names Flanona (located on the Istrian peninsula) instead; see 239c below. Ammianus (14, 1, 4f.) names the prefect Thalassius instead of Domitian.

238h. See 237c. On the danger of rebellion due to Magnentius' survival of his defeat, see Browning, *Julian*, 61-62.

Jerome used Eutropius (10, 12, 23) on Magnentius at Lugdunum, etc. Although the *Epitome* (42, 2f.) shows a dependence upon Victor for its reference to Magnentius' brother Decentius and his promotion to Caesar, it has a fuller account of Magnentius' suicide than any other source. *Chron. Pasch.* (541, 10) and Theophanes (44, 15) shared a common source for their description of Magnentius' defeat at Mount Seleucus. Socrates (2, 32) relates the death of Magnentius' mother and agrees with Theophanes in citing another brother of Magnentius without giving his name. Zosimus (2, 53-54) has an independent account which includes Magnentius' suicide and like the *Epitome* gives hanging as the method for Decentius' suicide.

238i. The jubilee: the number is omitted, but this would refer to the eighty-seventh; see Helm 223h.

239a. Jerome's source for Gennadius as a forensic orator is unknown.

239b. Again, Jerome's source for the rhetorician Minervius is unknown. Ausonius' *Commemorato Professorum Burdigalensium* 2, 4 praises Minervius, but it was written after the *Chron.*, no earlier than 385; see H. G. White's ed., *Ausonius* (Cambridge: Harvard University Press, 1968), xxi.

239c. See 238e and g. On Gallus' fall, see Browning, *Julian*, 62-63, 73, 101 and esp. 62 on Constantius' vacillation on Gallus' fate.

*Chron. Pasch.* (541, 15) , like Jerome and Ammianus, gives the place of execution as Histria. Philostorgius (4, 1) records the execution in greater detail, but the place is simply referred to as "an island in Dalmatia." The palace eunuchs were involved in Gallus' downfall; Zosimus (2, 55) names Dynamius and Picentius, while both Philostorgius and Julian (*Letter to the Senate and People of Athens*) name Eusebius. *Chron. misc.* (28b; Bidez, *Philostorgius*, 223) says only that it was a brief time after the Caesar's promotion that Constantius killed him. Eutropius (10, 13) depicts Gallus as a tyrant, but Jerome here describes him as distinguished enough to attract suspicion. Other orthodox authors are generally well-disposed towards Gallus (e.g., Theodoret, 3, 3), while Ammianus is as hostile towards him as Eutropius (e.g., at 14, 1, 2, where both Gallus and his wife are "insatiable for human blood"--"humani cruoris avida." By contrast, the pagan Victor is neutral (42, 9 and 12), and Festus omits Gallus entirely.

239d. Silvanus: see Piganiol, *L'empire chrétienne*, 88, 93. On his "barbarian" background, see Jones, *Later Roman Empire*, 116, 135 and Lot, *The End of the Ancient World*, 199; as a usurper of higher rank, Jones, *ibid.*, 328; on the circumstances of his fall, Jones, *ibid.*, 334-35; also *PLRE* 1, "Silvanus 2."

Jerome used Eutropius (10, 13) but he has twenty-eight days like Victor; see Introduction under "Aurelius Victor." Sozomen (4, 7) relied upon Socrates (2, 32) for the *tyrannos* (i.e., usurper) *Silouanos*. Ammianus (15, 5, 31) supplis details such as Silvanus' father being a Frank named Bonitus; like Julian (*Or.*1, 48), he depicts Silvanus' brief rule as marred by abuses.

239e. Victorinus: see Gennadius, *De vir. il.* 61. Donatus: cf. Jerome, *Comm. in Eccl.* 1, 9-10. See Piganiol, *L'empire chrétienne*, 98, 239, 385; G. Good, *Harvard Studies in Classical Philology* 74 (1970), *passim*; Kelly, *Jerome*, 10-14.

Jerome here relies upon personal knowledge, at least in part.

239f. Paulinus of Treves: see Piganiol, *L'empire chrétienne*, 94; Stein, *Histoire*, 151. On Rodanius' exile in Asia, see Frend, *The Rise of Christianity*, 535.

The *Vita Athan.* (21) cites the exiles of Paulinus and Rodanius together with those of Eusebius, Dionysius, and Lucifer. The *Vita Athan.* in Photius (258) concurs with this list as with other details (e.g., a reference to Milan preceding the reference to the exiles). The *Avell. Coll.* (2, 21) names Paulinus as an exile after referring to the synod at Ariminum, and distinguishes him as Paulinus of Treves. Socrates (2, 36) is followed by Sozomen (4, 9) in part, but the latter includes Rodanius and Lucifer in addition to Paulinus, Dionysius, and Eusebius as listed by Socrates.

239g. Rhetoricians in Aquitania: see Ausonius, *Prof. Burd.* 3, 6 and Ammianus 18, 1, 4, where Delphidius is remembered as a most eloquent orator--*orator acerrimus*.

239h. See 232b. On the Montensians, see Gennadius, *De vir. il.*5.

Optatus (2, 4) gives the same explanation as Jerome for the Montensians' name but in more detail. Augustine discusses the Montensians in his *De haer.* (69). Socrates (3, 5) and Sozomen (4, 9) are of little assistance on the subject of the Montensians.

239i. Eusebius of Vercellae: cf. 242e, 245k, *De vir. il.* 96. See Berardino, *Patrology*, 4, 62-64, 65, 93-94. Lucifer of Cagliari: cf. 242e, 246a, *De vir. il.* 95. See Berardino, *ibid.*, 4, 13, 44, 63, 64-69, 91 and Piganiol, *L'empire chrétienne*, 95, 135-36, 192, 226. On Lucifer as fomenting discord as a bishop, Frend, *Christianizing the Roman Empire*, 616. Pancratius: cf. *De vir. il.* 95. Pancratius is not named among the exiles listed by Hilary in his *C. Const.*

The various sources refer to different bishops among the exiled. For example, Sozomen (4, 9) names Dionysius of Alba, while Jerome has Dionysius of Caralitana. The *Vita Athan.* in Photius (258) relates the exiles of Dionysius, Lucifer, and Eusebius, but omits those of the deacon Hilary and the priest Pancratius, included by Jerome. Rufinus (10, 21) lists Dionysius, Eusebius, Paulinus, Rodanius and Hilary. In his *C. Const.* Hilary lists himself, Paulinus, Eusebius, and Lucifer. Like Jerome (240c), Hilary refers to the key role played by Saturninus among the Arian leadership.

240a. Julian: cf. 240g, 242Rom., 243b; *De vir. il.* 95, 96, 102, 117; *Vita Hilar.* 34, 40. See Berardino, *Patrology*, 15, 38, 115; Piganiol, *L'empire chrétienne*, 75, 94, 107, 110f., 127f. Julian made Caesar: J. Bidez, *La vie de l'empereur Julien* (Paris: Societe d'edition, 1930), 123; persecution of Christians, *ibid.*, 291-99; MacMullen, *Christianizing the Roman Empire*, 45-47, 53; see also 242c below. Julian's defeat and death: Bidez, *ibid.*, 315-31; Browning, *Julian,* 187-218; and E. Demougeot, *La formation de l'Europe et les invasions barbares: Des origines germaniques à l'avénement de Dioclétien* (Paris: 1979), 86-105. For chronology in this period, see Barnes, "Imperial Chronology, A.D. 337-350," *Phoenix* 34 (1980): 160-66.

*Chron. Pasch.* (541, 19) and Theophanes (45, 7) appear to have used Jerome's source for their accounts of Julian's promotion. In Jerome, however, Milan is named, while in the others the Gallic provinces are mentioned instead. Philostorgius (4, 2) used the same source as Theophanes, not only for Julian's promotion, but for his marriage to Helena, Constantius' sister. Likewise, Socrates (2, 34) used the common source of Philostorgius (e.g., for a phrase on the barbarians) and *Chron. Pasch.* (e.g., note the use of the same verb, *apesteilen*). Sozomen (4, 21) nearly copies Socrates (omitting the phrase on the barbarians). The *Vita Athan.* in Photius (258) and the *Artemii Passio* (15) are related to Philostorgius. Zosimus (3, 1) used other sources. For example, unlike the others, he refers to Julian's summons from Athens. He also adds that Constantius sent Marcellus and Salustius to Gaul in order to secure Julian's loyalty. *Chron. misc.* (28b; Bidez, *Philostorgius*, 223) has Constantius' execution of Gallus followed by the Caesar's replacement by his brother Julian. The particulars in the Latin tradition include the following: the *Epitome* (42, 12) refers to Julian's promotion with regard to his age, twenty-three; Eutropius (10, 14, 1) calls Julian Constantius' cousin (*patruelis*); and Ammianus (25, 8, 11) cites the imperial robe as the "ancestral purple," and emphasizes the delight of the soldiers at the promotion.

240b. See 233h. Paul of Thebes: cf. *De vir. il.*, 135; *Vita Pauli, passim*; and Athanasius, *Vita Ant.*, 89. See also D. J. Chitty, *The Desert a City*. Oxford: Mowbray 1977 repr. of 1966 ed., *passim*.

Theodoret (4, 27) relates Antony's career, including his departure from the desert to warn the citizens against Arianism.

240c. Hilary of Poitiers: cf. 245e; *Comm. in Isaian*, pref., 60, 13; *Comm. in Matt.*, pref., 96; *C. Pelag.* 3, 19; *De vir. il.* 86, 100; *Ep.* 5, 2; 57, 6; 61, 12; 70, 5; *Hebr. quaest. in Gen.* 1, 1; Origen, *In Luc.*, pref. See Berardino, *Patrology*, 3-5, 14, 16-19, 33-59, 93-94, 186, 195, 235, 539; J. Doignon, "Tradition classique et tradition chretienne dans l'historiographie d'Hilaire de Poitiers au carrefour des IVe-Ve siecles," *Caesarodunum* 15 (1980): 216; Piganiol, *L'empire chrétienne*, 95, 102, 103, 106, 117, 191, 371. Stein, *Histoire*, 152, 197. For his teaching on the *homoousios*, Kelly, *Early Christian Doctrines*, 254-55. For his exile, see Doignon, *ibid., passim*, and Frend, *The Rise of Christianity*, 535. See also *OCD*, "Hilary." On his diatribes against Emperor Constantius, the author of his exile, see his *C. Const.* (*PL* 10). For the impact of Hilary's *De syn.* on Jerome's historical consciousness, see F. X. Murphy, *A Monument to St. Jerome. Essays on Some Aspects of His Life, Works and Influence* (New York: Sheed and Ward, 1952), 133. Saturninus: cf. *De vir. il.* 100. See Berardino, *Patrology*, 35, 118.

Jerome has much of the same material found here in his *Vita Hilar.* Venantius Fortunatus (*Vita Hilar.*, 5, 17) relates Hilary's exile to Phrygia and cites three books addressed to the emperor: "he poured forth his prayers to the emperor in three little books he offered him." Cf. Rufinus (10, 32), who also refers to Hilary's books. Sozomen (5, 13) has the return of the bishop Eusebius to Antioch, the schism between the followers of Paulinus and Meletius, etc., but fails to mention Hilary. Theodoret (3, 4, 2) relates Meletius' return to Antioch and Athanasius' to Alexandria; then he lists Hilary with Eusebius and Lucifer as spending their time of exile in Thebes.

240d. Relics: Constantius' role in the translation of the relics as a precedent for later such translations, J. M. Peterson, *The Dialogues of Gregory the Great in Their Late Antique Background*, Studies and Texts 69 (Liverpool: Liverpool University Press, 1984), 146 and n. 98. See Jerome, *C. Vigilant.*, 1, 5 (*PL* 23) and Paulinus of Nola, *Carm.* 19, 349-51, 1.

*Chron. Pasch.* (542, 7) and Theophanes (227, 12) used Jerome's source for the movement of the relics. *Chron. Pasch.* describes the placement of those of Timothy under the altar in the Church of the Holy Apostles, as does Philostorgius (3, 2). Theophanes preserves the Latin name of the month (June), while *Chron. Pasch.* has the Greek; he also cites the relics of all three saints--Timothy, Luke and Andrew--enumerated in Jerome. The *Cons. Const.* (a. 356) has the arrival of Timothy's relics only.

240e. Sarmata and Amatas as disciples of Antony: information unique to Jerome.

Socrates (4, 23 and 24) names Macarius twice in a description of monks. Sozomen (3, 14) cites two different Macariuses. Both he and Socrates refer to Macarius of Alexandria, but there are differences. While Socrates reports miraculous cures and Macarius' austerities, Sozomen has him raise a man from the dead and relates his early study of philosophy. Jerome had another source other than that of Socrates and Sozomen, for he names Macarius as a disciple of Antony, which they fail to do. Further, he cites Sarmata and Amatas as Macarius' fellow disciples, and these are absent from Socrates and Sozomen. Theodoret (4, 21, 5-7) discusses an episode in Macarius' life lacking in the other sources, namely, his exile to an island. One thing it has in common with Socrates' account is an exorcism, but Socrates cites numerous ones and Theodoret reports only one. Rufinus (11, 4) includes both Macariuses like Sozomen. His account shared a source of Socrates, since both authors have Pambo (or Pambonius) and Isidorus as disciples of Antony in their discussions of the Nitria community.

240f. See 237b.

Both Socrates (4, 11) and Sozomen (2, 37) inform that Felix was not an Arian by choice, and both relate the people's pressure for Constantius to return Liberius to them as their bishop. Theodoret (2, 16, 27) records Liberius' hearing before Constantius and the subsequent exile to Berea. Ammianus (15, 7, 10) has an early indication of the growing importance of the Roman see; he emphasizes Constantius' desire to have Athanasius' condemnation confirmed by Liberius, "bishop of the eternal city."

240g. Alemanni: cf. 248f. Julian's defeat of the Alemanni at Strasbourg in 357: Browning, *Julian*, 85-88; Jones, *Later Roman Empire*, 1, 684.

Verbal parallels show that Jerome used Eutropius (10, 14, 1). Sozomen (5, 1) has Julian's conversion after his success against the barbarians. Zosimus (3, 3) gives special attention to Julian's resourcefulness in preparing for the campaign, and he calls the battle at Strasbourg "a victory which defies exaggeration" (Ridley trans., 50).

Both Zosimus and the *Epitome* (42, 13) emphasize the barbarians' numerical supe-
riority, but the *Epitome* stresses the carnage: "blood flowed like rivers." Ammianus
(16, 12) gives a detailed account which includes the previous defeat of the Caesar
Decentius by the barbarian King Chonodomarius, Julian's speech to the soldiers, and
much attention to Julian's personal courage and leadership.

240i. Cf. 240d.

Ammianus (16, 10, 13) describes Constantius' entry into Rome without any mention
of Christian relics; instead he addresses the emperor's own awe at the sights of the
ancient capital.

241a. See 234b.

*Chron. Pasch.* (543, 5) and Theophanes (45, 25) have the death of Cecropius, bishop
of Nicomedia, due to this earthquake. Sozomen (4, 16) follows Socrates (2, 39) in
describing the earthquake at Nicomedia that prevents the convening of a synod there;
the bishops' failed attempt to meet at Nicaea; and finally the selection of Seleucia as
the meeting place. Sozomen also cites the death of Cecropius, like *Chron. Pasch.* and
Theophanes, but he includes the death of only one other bishop, while they report
more. He also provides the story of the Persian monk Arsacius, who predicted the
catastrophe but died in it nevertheless. Philostorgius (4, 10) has the earthquake *inter-
rupt* the synod already in progress at Nicomedia--one that would have favored the
orthodox--and the synod at Ariminum afterwards, in favor of the Arians. Like those
mentioned, he has the death of Cecropius, but with precisely fifteen others. Victor
(16, 12) records the earthquake at Nicomedia but likewise a destructive fire at
Carthage. Ammianus (17, 7, 1) reports earthquakes throughout Asia, Macedonia, and
Pontus but especially at Nicomedia. Details include fires that burned for days afterwards.

241b. See 239f.

Theodoret (2, 15, 4), Athanasius (*Apol. de fug.*, 4), and the *Avell. Coll.* (2, 77)
record Paulinus' exile together with others.

241c. See *Gramm. Lat.* 6, 554, 4; 565, 5.

241d. Ariminum: cf. 241d, 242a. On the Anomoeans or strict Arians prevailing upon
Constantius to summon this council, and the subsequent victory of the Homoian
Arians, see Quasten, *Patrology*, 3, 201-2. See also Jones, *Later Roman Empire*, 1,
118; Frend, *The Rise of Christianity*, 540-43; Kelly, *Early Christian Doctrines*. On
Ariminum and Seleucia's synods as held under the supervision of Constantius' favor-
ites, see Jones, *Later Roman Empire*, 1, 118.

Socrates (2, 37 and 39) ostensibly preserves various speeches and correspondence, as
well as the creed, of the Ariminum synod. Sozomen (3, 19) relates a pro-Arian vision
of the cross on the part of Constantia and credits Aetius with being the first to deny
the Son's consubstantiality with the Father. He also describes (4, 17-19) Valens and

Ursacius as the synod's leaders, and their insistence upon the creed of Sirmium in the face of resistance from the "pro-Nicene" bishops. Finally, he credits Constantius with persuading the bishops to subscribe to the pro-Arian formula of faith.

241e. Honoratus, first prefect of Constantinople: see Jones, *PLRE* 1, "Honoratus 2." For the office, see Dagron, *Naissance d'une capitale*, 215-17, 241-42.

*Chron. Pasch.* (543, 10) gives the precise date of Honoratus' promotion (Sept. 11). Socrates (2, 41) has Honoratus' appointment associated with the abolishment of the proconsulship. Sozomen (4, 23) instead cites Honoratus' immediate assignment--the investigation of Aetius and his heresy. Refer also to Hydatius' *Chron.* under the consulship of Eusebius and Hypatius.

241f. Gratian: cf. Helm, *Chron.*, pref., 7; 245b, 247h, 248f; *De vir. il.*, 116; 127. See Berardino, *Patrology*, 138, 146-7, 162, 169, 278; Piganiol, *L'empire chrétienne*, 176, 201, 241, 393; Stein, *Histoire*, 181-5, 189. Refer also to Matthews, *Western Aristocracies*; Jones, *PLRE* 1, 401, "Gratianus 2."

*Chron. Pasch.* (543, 9) may have used Jerome's source for Gratian's birth.

241g. See 240c.

Sozomen (5, 13) echoes Socrates (3, 10) on Hilary's role in refuting Arianism in Italy through the medium of his books (see 240c above for Venantius Fortunatus' reference to three books).

241h. See 235h. Constantius ordered Macedonius' exile both because of doctrinal issues and the dispute brought about by the bishop's decision to move Constantine's remains to the Church of St. Acacius; see Whitby and Whitby, *Chronicon Paschale*, 34 and Dagron, *Naissance d'une capitale, 436-42*.

*Chron. Pasch.* (543, 18) credits Macedonius' exile to his "many personal faults" (Whitby and Whitby trans., 34). Theophanes (46, 7) points to Constantius' own anger at Macedonius. Philostorgius (5, 1) has Acacius behind Constantius' decisions to remove Macedonius and promote Eudoxius. Both Socrates (2, 42) and Sozomen (4, 24) have Acacius' supporters responsible for the exile. Socrates is specific concerning the charges brought against Macedonius, including his admission to communion of a deacon accused of fornication.

241i. See 232c. On Constantius and the Church, see R. Klein, *Constantius II und die christliche Kirche* (Darmstadt: Wissenschaftliche Buchgesellschaft, 1977); J. Moreau, "Constantius II," *JAC* 2 (1959): 178; K. M. Girardet, "Constance II, Athanase et l'edit d'Arles (363)," *Politique et theologie* (1977): 63-92. See also Bowder, *The Age of Constantine*, 42-53.

241k. Cf. 232g on the favor shown Constantinople. On Hagia Sophia, referred to here, see MacMullen, *Constantine*, 154 for its beginnings under Constantine. See D.

J. Geanakoplos, "Church Building and 'Caesaropapism,' A.D. 312-565," *GRBS* 7 (1966): 167-86, on the importance of imperial sponsorship of the new churches; also T. Klauser, "Die Hagia Sophia," *Jahrbuch für Antike und Christentum* 13 (1970): 107-18.

*Chron. Pasch.* (543, 16) records the dedication, on Feb. 15, of the "Great Church." Philostorgius (3, 2) takes the opportunity to credit Constantius as the builder. Socrates (2, 43) has the consecration of the church on Feb. 15 after Eudoxius was made bishop of the capital. Sozomen (4, 26) gives part of Eudoxius' dedicatory sermon. The *Vita Athan.* (23) is closely related to Sozomen, citing the consecration in the tenth year of Constantius' reign and the third consulship of Julian, as does Sozomen, and preserving the same sermon excerpt.

241l. Georgius, bishop of Alexandria from 357 to 361: see Piganiol, *L'empire chrétienne*, 95, 112, 116, 128; on his lynching when news of Constantius' death reached Alexandria, see Downey, *Antioch*, 176. Georgius was called the "Cappadocian monster" by Gregory Nazianzen; MacMullen, *Christianizing the Roman Empire*, 159 n. 9. He was hated by orthodox Christians as well as others; MacMullen, *ibid.*, citing G. Ricciotti, *Julian the Apostate*, trans. by M. J. Costelloe (Milwaukee: The Bruce Publishing Co., 1960), 182. For more on Georgius, see 242d below.

*Chron. Pasch.* (547, 23) appears to have used Jerome's source for the return of other exiled clergymen after Meletius' promotion to the see of Antioch. Both Philostorgius (5, 1, 5) and Socrates (2, 44) may also reflect Jerome's source, with Meletius' summons from Sebastia by Acacius as well as his change of faith. Sozomen (4, 25) relates Meletius' replacement at Sebastia by the heretic Eunomius. Theodoret (2, 31, 2) has an independent account including Constantius' command for Meletius to expound upon *Prov.* 8, 22 and details on Meletius' background, his support of the orthodox, and the Arians' belief that he would aid their cause instead.

242a. Hilary: see 240c and 241d. Jerome represents the synod of Ariminum as endorsing Arianism; in fact, it was the "mediating doctrine favored by the emperor [Valens]" that was approved there; Kelly, *Jerome*, 64 notes 31 and 32. For sources, see 241g.

242b. See 234Rom.

*Chron. Pasch.* (545, 8) and Theophanes (46, 13-14) depended upon Jerome's source, but Theophanes replaces the baptism of Constantius by an Arian with the statement that the emperor realized his error, i.e., Arianism. Philostorgius (6, 5), a Eunomian, duly records the baptism. Socrates (2, 47) gives apoplexy as the cause of death. Sozomen (5, 1) follows Socrates in part, but he provides the additional fact that Constantius interrupted his Persian campaign when he learned of Julian's preparations against him. Zosimus (3, 11) has the news of Julian's march reach Constantius by messengers from Constantinople.

242Rom. The *Epitome* (42, 17) gives Constantius' age as forty-four and his regnal year as the thirty-ninth, while Ammianus (21, 15, 2-3)--close to Jerome--gives the age as "forty-four years and a few months" and the year of the reign as the thirty-eighth. *Chron. Pasch.* (545, 15) is close to Jerome for Julian's dates: age thirty-six and a reign of two years (compared to Jerome's year and eight months). Theophanes (46, 23) gives Julian's age as thirty-one and lists other parallel dates, as is customary in his work, including the year of the bishop of Rome. Socrates (3, 21) gives the age of thirty-one like Theophanes, and cites his death during his third regnal year and fourth consulship.

242c. Jerome here refers to the moral ruin of apostasy; Julian himself is involved: "*Iuliano . . . converso.*" On Julian's persecution, see Browning, *Julian*, 181-82, esp. 182 on the burning of the temple of Apollo at Daphne in 362 as causing a turning point in his policy. For an example of his actions, see Quasten, *Patrology*, 3, 359 on *Ep.* 52 to the people of Bostra in 362, ordering them to exile their bishop.

*Chron. Pasch.* (548, 12) is close to Jerome on the apostasy of Christians, but it is specific as to the causes: the constraints or offers of promotion by superiors and the requirements of the military service under pagan auspices. Theophanes (50, 34) refers to the military reason: "the army was deceived into defecting." Socrates (3, 13) cites Julian's idolatry and his sacrifices in particular, and credits three future emperors-- Jovian, Valentinian, and Valens--for their steadfastness during this time of peril. Sozomen (5, 4), independent of the other extant sources, furnishes details of the persecution of the church in Caesarea of Cappadocia. Ammianus (22, 5, 2) has it that Julian restored the sacrifices and reopened the temples as soon as he could be sure that it was safe to do so.

242d. "Insurrection," *seditio*: more than a mere riot--*tumultus, motus, turba.* For more on Athanasius see 232f, 234g, and 236a as well as the following: F. L. Cross, *The Study of Athanasius, an Inaugural Lecture Delivered Before the University of Oxford on 1 Dec., 1944* (Oxford: Clarendon Press, 1946), for what E. R. Hardy called "a masterful survey;" *Christology of the Later Fathers*, LCC, trans. by E. R. Hardy and C. C. Richardson (Philadelphia: The Westminster Press, 1954), 53; K. Hoss, *Studien über das Schriften und die Theologie der Athanasius auf Grund einer Echtheitsuntersuchung von Athanasius contra gentes und de incarnatione* (Freiburg: 1899); J. Lebon, "Pour une edition critique de Saint Athanase," *Revue d'histoire ecclésiastique* 21 (1925): 324-30; G. J. Ryan and R. P. Casey, *The 'De Incarnatione' of Athanasius*, Studies and Documents XIV (Philadelphia: University of Pennsylvania Press, 1945-46); Hardy, *Christology*, 43-49; and *OCD* "Athanasius." More specifically, see Frend, *The Rise of Christianity*, 630-31 on his career; *ibid.*, on his theology; Pelikan, *Christian Tradition*, 193-200 on his relations with the Arians. On Julian's instructions protecting Georgius' library, presumably for his own use, see Frend, *ibid.*, 595. Georgius was killed by pagans for his "repeated acts of pointed outrage, insult and pillage of the most sacred treasures of the city;" MacMullen, *Christianizing the Roman Empire*, 90. On Julian's contacts with Georgius, see Browning, *Julian*, 40.

*Chron. Pasch.* (546, 4) has Georgius' body placed on a camel and carried through the city, and then burned together with the carcasses of various animals. Theophanes (47, 16), on the contrary, has Georgius still alive on the camel. Philostorgius (7, 2) men-

tions the fact that Georgius was presiding over a synod when he was seized; he reports that the Arians blamed Athanasius for the killing. Both Socrates (3, 2) and Sozomen (5, 6-7) have pagan perpetrators of the crime. However, like Theophanes, Socrates has Georgius still alive on the camel, while Sozomen, like *Chron. Pasch.*, has the body instead. Thus it is uncertain whether Georgius was killed by some other means or burned alive. Theodoret (3, 4, 2 and 5, 40, 6) catalogues the evils of Georgius in Alexandria. These include the abuse of the corpses of those already dead. Julian (*Ep.* 10) scolded the Alexandrians for their behavior, but took the opportunity to boast of his own clemency: "It is a fortunate thing for you, men of Alexandria, that this transgression of yours occurred in my reign" (Wright trans., 67).
*Chron. misc.* (14a; Bidez, *Philostorgius*, 211) erroneously cites "*Gregorius*"--not Georgius--as the nineteenth bishop of Alexandria.

242e. See 232c on the Antiochene bishops.

Socrates (3, 5-6), like Jerome, reports the recall of Lucifer and Eusebius, and Lucifer's ordination of Paulinus as bishop of Antioch, but he adds that the two reinstated bishops consulted together in order to strengthen the orthodox teaching. Socrates blames Euzoius (above) for the schism at Antioch. Sozomen (5, 12) follows Socrates partially, but while Socrates says that the two bishops planned a synod, he gives details concerning the synod when it was held at Alexandria, including Athanasius' speech in defense of his earlier flight. Theodoret (3, 4, 2 and 5, 1), like Socrates and Sozomen, relates how Lucifer and Eusebius planned the defense of the orthodox teachings, with special concern in regard to repairing the schism at Antioch.

242f. Prohaeresius: the leading teacher of rhetoric at the time, he was a native of Armenia; see Browning, 1976, 64. On Julian's request that he write a history of that emperor's conflict with Constantius, and on the similarity of Marius Victorinus' abandonment of his position to the action taken by Prohaeresius, see Browning, *Julian*, 172. See also Jones, *PLRE* 1, "Prohaeresius," and Eunapius, *Lives of the Philosophers* (in the Loeb ed. of Philostratus).

Theophanes (48, 18) relates how Julian made it illegal to believe "the teachings of Greek Christians," i.e., the great Christian teachers in the East. Socrates (3, 12) cites Julian's law against Christians teaching the classics. Sozomen (5, 18) has the same prohibition as Socrates but with additional details, including Julian's resentment towards outstanding Christian teachers such as Basil. Theodoret (3, 8) has Julian's prohibition of Christians teaching rhetoric or philosophy, and the expulsion of Christians from the army. Julian himself refers to his measure concerning teaching in terms of a choice: if Christians really wish to interpret the classics, "let them first imitate the ancients' piety towards the gods" (Browning trans. of Julian's rescript, which followed the original edict on teaching, 1976, 171). See also his *Ep.* 14, addressed to Prohaeresius. Ammianus (22, 10, 7 and 25, 4, 20), though a pagan, does not hesitate to call the law against teaching a harsh (*inclemens*) one. See also *CTh* 13, 3, 5 for the law itself.

243a. *vicar*: title of a diocesan governor responsible to the emperor; see Barnes, *The New Empire*. "The vicar seems to have deputised for the praetorian prefects in all their manifold functions," Jones, *Later Roman Empire*, 1, 47.

*Chron. Pasch.* (549, 17), Theophanes (51, 16), and Theodoret (3, 7, 5) may all have used Jerome's source for the execution of Aemilianus at Dorostolon by the *vicar*, but they preserved the vicar's name--Capitolinus.

243b. Julian's closing of the "Golden Church" at Antioch: Browning, *Julian*, 182. See 240a on Julian above. On the background of Julian's Persian campaign, see A. Ferrill, *The Fall of the Roman Empire. The Military Explanation* (London: Thames and Hudson, 1986), 52 and Browning, *ibid.*, 187-89.

A textual problem is left unsolved here in Helm's text: "Cum fame et siti apostatam perdidisset exercitum . . ." Ms. L has "cum fame et siti *idem apostata;*" P likewise has "*apostata.*" If we correct "*apostatam*" to "*apostatum,*" we translate "when he had lost his *apostate army.*" However, an "apostate army" is difficult, since the remainder of the same army nominates the Christian Jovian as the new emperor. L is the most satisfactory reading--"*idem apostata*"--in which case we have "when the same apostate had lost his army." "*Idem apostata*" may be a scribal gloss, yet Jerome's own vitriolic might allow for such a phrase.

Jovian: cf. 243Rom., 243ce; *Vita Hilar.* 34. See Stein, *Histoire*, 170-72, 174, 178, 186-89; Matthews, *Western Aristocracies*, 34-35. Instead of *primicerius*, Ammianus calls Jovian "domesticorum ordinis primus"--"first of the rank of domestic troops." *Primus* here (25, 5, 4) may signify "excellent" or "first-class," as elsewhere in late Latin; Loefstedt, *Late Latin*, 46 and *Syntactica: Studien und Beitrage zur historischen Syntax des Lateins* (Lund: Gleerup, 1956), 2, 385-87.

*Chron. Pasch.* (551, 12) records Julian's death, not in battle, but following his vision of an armed consul stabbing him with a spear. Theophanes (50, 14-16) seems to have relied upon Jerome's source, citing Julian's closing of the great church in Antioch, and specifically, the confiscation of its sacred vessels. Philostorgius (7, 15) also echoes Jerome's source, describing the emperor as led into "a pathless desert" in which a large part of the army perished. Socrates (3, 21-22, 25) supplies the detail that Julian wore no armor at the time he was wounded, while he also cites the hunger and thirst of the army. In addition he has the story, reportedly obtained from the poet Callistus' verses celebrating Julian's deeds, that it was a demon who wounded the emperor. Sozomen (6, 1) cites the lack of provisions, but provides a very different story of how Julian staged chariot races to divert his men's attention after the Persians had gained the strategic advantage. Philostorgius and Sozomen have in common the story that an old Persian, determined to aid his countrymen, deceived Julian into marching into the desert. Theodoret (3, 25 and 4, 1) reports the famine in the army as due to Julian's negligence. Like Socrates, he has the story that a supernatural being wounded the emperor. Libanius (*Or.* 18, 268; see Norman trans., 460) has an account biased in favor of Julian: the Persians are ready to sue for peace when a dust storm causes Julian to be wounded. Zosimus (3, 29), like Libanius, gives details highly favorable to Julian: "At the time of his death, he had almost entirely destroyed the Persian empire" (Ridley trans., 65). The *Epitome* (43, 1-3) has Julian deceived by a deserter (cf. Philostorgius and Sozomen above) and led into ambush. Eutropius (10, 16, 1 and 17, 1), like Zosimus and Libanius, relates the successes of the campaign up to the disaster of Julian's death. citing the surrender of many towns and fortresses. Festus (28, 3) was probably one of Jerome's sources, as the verbal parallel shows. Ammianus (22, 13, 2; 25, 3, 6 and 5, 4) has the burning of the temple of Apollo at Daphne, with Julian's suspicion of the Christians; in regards to the battle in which the emperor lost his life, he has Julian vainly trying to signal to his men that the Persians are in flight when he receives the fatal spear wound.

243Rom. Theophanes (54, 19), Philostorgius (8, 8), and Socrates (3, 26) all cite Jovian's son, Varronianus, as honored with a consulship. Ammianus (25, 10, 11) cites this as well, but as a bad omen. Socrates, like Eutropius (10, 18, 2), gives seven months for Jovian's reign, compared to eight in Jerome. *Chron. Pasch.* (552, 17) and the *Epitome* (44, 1) agree with Jerome on eight months.

243c. Nisibis: see 234d. On the humiliation of Jovian's settlement, see Ferrill, *Fall of the Roman Empire*, 55-56. For Jovian, see also Jones, *PLRE* 1, "Iovianus 3," and *Later Roman Empire*, 1, 138 (also on the treaty). Perhaps because Jovian was a Christian, Jerome omits the disgraceful aspect of his territorial concessions. In the bargain, Rome left its Armenian ally, King Arsaces, at the mercy of the Persians; see Frend, *Rise of Christianity*, 613 n. 80.

*Chron. Pasch.* (553, 19) and Theophanes (53, 31) probably used Jerome's source; both cite the surrender of Nisibis, but *Chron. Pasch.* gives details of the peace negotiations with the Persians, including the names of the envoys (the Persian Surenas and the Roman Arinthaeus). Philostorgius (8, 1) may have used the same source, but he adds the surrender of Roman fortresses as far as Armenia. Socrates (3, 22) is similar to Jerome on the necessity of the Romans' surrendering territory: "the exigencies of the present situation obliged him [Jovian]." He includes the emperor's declaration before the troops that he is a Christian, followed by the soldiers' acclamation. He is followed in this by Sozomen (6, 3); however, Sozomen also describes the Jovian's restoration of the churches, while Socrates only refers to the new hopes of the Christians. Theodoret (4, 2) provides a summary of the new emperor's achievements, including the recall of exiled bishops and a thirty-years' peace treaty with Persia. *Chron. misc.* (39a; Bidez, *Philostorgius*, 237) describes Jovian's concessions in some detail, including the fact that Nisibis was evacuated by the Roman population. Making it clear that the concessions were necessary, it praises Jovian for establishing peace and harmony between the two empires. Jovian is also cited for his personal holiness; cf. Socrates and Sozomen on the emperor's declaration of his Christian faith before the army. Similarly to Sozomen, who has the restoration of the churches themselves, *Chron. misc.* (*ibid.*) credits Jovian with the restoration of the churches' treasures. Zosimus (3, 31) records the thirty-years' peace and names individual cities ceded to Persia. In addition to the individual envoys named by *Chron. Pasch.* (above), he has the praetorian prefect Sallustius. Eutropius (10, 17, 1), like Jerome and Socrates, points to the necessity of Jovian's concessions. Festus (29) is not as kind; he says that Jovian was more interested in royal power than military glory. Ammianus (25, 7, 4f.) names the same envoys as Zosimus. He is harsher still than Festus, and claims that Jovian could have carried out a successful retreat, had he been inclined.

243d. Antioch: see 231c. Meletius: see 243d. *Homoousios* and *anomoeos*: theological terms of the orthodox and the Homoeousians. The latter were moderates who disliked the term *homoousios* but were "virtually orthodox;" Kelly, *Early Christian Doctrines*, 249-50; see also Pelikan, *Christian Tradition*, 209-10. On the Macedonians, see 235h. Jerome errs in dating the synod at Antioch under Meletius 60 364--it really occurred in 363; Frend, *Rise of Christianity*, 616. He also errs in having the council endorse the Macedonian tenets--it actually subscribed to the Nicene faith, as is related by Socrates, Sozomen, and later, by Julius Pollux (384); Frend, *ibid.*

Sozomen (6, 4) follows Socrates (3, 25) on the Acacians conferring with the Meletians at Antioch and on the drawing up of a credal formula for presentation to the Emperor Jovian. Both have the Nicene faith confirmed at this synod (above) and both list bishops who were in attendance, including Meletius, Eusebius of Samosata, though Socrates lists several more than Sozomen.

243e. For Jovian, see 243bc. Jovian's death: See Stein, *Histoire*, 172. On Valentinian I, cf. *De vir. il.* 95, 96, 100, 107, 110, 111. See Piganiol, *L'empire chrétienne*, 147, 149, 170, 339, 353, 355, 407; Stein, *Histoire*, 146, 172-75, 178-84, 192. On his accession and early career, see Matthews, *Western Aristocracies*, 35-39; V. Neri, "Ammiano Marcellino e l'elezione di Valentiniano," *Rivista storica dell'antichita* 15 (1985): 153-82; Jones, *Later Roman Empire*, 1, 135, 328. On his reign, see Jones, *ibid.*, 139-51. On his defense of the empire, see Ferrill, *Fall of the Roman Empire*, 56-57 and E. A. Thompson, *Romans and Barbarians. The Decline of the Western Empire* (Madison: University of Wisconsin, 1982), 123, 237-38. Valentinian "died of an apoplectic fit, riled by the defiance of Germanic envoys at his headquarters on the Danube;" Frend, *Rise of Christianity*, 619. "Targeteers," or "shield-bearers," a group of *scholae* or household troops established by Diocletian; S. Williams, *Diocletian and the Roman Recovery* (New York: Methuen, Inc., 1985), 59. It is unclear whether they were recruited from barbarians or native elements; Jones, *Later Roman Empire*, 1, 54. For examples of their employment, see Jones, *ibid.*, 120, 613 and Ricciotti, *Julian*, 112, 136, 147; see also R. I. Frank, *Scholae Palatinae. The Palace Guards of the Late Roman Empire* (Rome: The American Academy in Rome, 1969). On Valens, cf. Helm, *Chron.*, pref., 7, 17, 247ch, 248b, 249bc, 250 (line 2). See Stein, *Histoire*, 149, 162, 172-78, 180-83, 183-92, 197, and Jones, *PLRE* 1, "Valens 8." For Valens' Gothic policy, see Matthews, *Western Aristocracies*, 88-90; Valens and the senate, A. Demandt, *Der Fall Roms. Die Auflösung des römischen Reiches im Urteil der Nachwelt* (Munich: C. H. Beck, 1984), 34; Valens and Arianism, *ibid.*, 129-30, and see 245a below; Valens' family, Jones, *PLRE* 1, 1130, stemma 4.

Verbal parallels reveal Jerome's use of Eutropius (10, 18, 2), where both accounts of the emperor's death are also given. *Chron. Pasch.* (555, 8 and 18) records the death, but says nothing of how it occurred, and describes a dream of Julian which had forewarned of Valentinian's rise to the throne. Philostorgius (8, 8) relates Jovian's death as due to the fumes from freshly-plastered walls. Socrates (3, 26) reports an oration in praise of Jovian before his delivered by Themistius, and gives an unspecified disease as the cause of death. He may have used Jerome's source here, for he has the birthplace of Valentinian, his promotion at Nicaea, and his subsequent promotion of Valens. Sozomen (6, 6) has a different emphasis, relating Valentinian's career under Julian. Theodoret (4, 5-6) gives no information on Jovian's death, but only laments the fact. He enumerates the positive aspects of Valentinian's reign, including the loyalty of the army and the emperor's concern for orthodoxy in religious matters. Zosimus (3, 35-36) cites the sudden illness and death of Jovian without specifics, and describes the election of Valentinian as necessary following a failed attempt to promote the prefect Salustius to the throne. Ammianus (25, 10, 12) gives the same two possible causes of Jovian's death as Jerome, but he goes on to compare the death of Scipio Aemilianus, whose suspicious end was likewise not carefully investigated. He also (26, 4, 3) provides details concerning the promotion of Valens.

244Rom. While Jerome gives the reign of the two emperors together as fourteen years and five months, *Chron. Pasch.* (555, 20), like Zosimus (3, 36), has Salustius actually turn down the throne in favor of Valentinian. The *Epitome* (45, 1) gives the reign of Valentinian as almost twelve years, and that of Valens as thirteen years and five months.

244a. Valentinian: refer to 243e above.

Similarly to Jerome, Ammianus (28, 1, 20) relates Valentinian's severity, exemplified in this case by his investigation of the soothsayer Amantius, and, again similarly to Jerome, he relates (30, 8, 8) how some tried to excuse Valentinian's greed by comparing him to the emperor Aurelian.

244b. Apollinaris of Laodicea: cf. *Apol. c. Rufin.* 1, 13; 16; 21; 24; 25; 33; 34; *Ep. adv. Rufin.* 13; 16. See Stein, *Histoire*, 165, 300, 306, 308. Apollinaris was strictly anti-Arian, yet he was ultimately judged heretical for his own teaching that Christ lacked a perfect human soul; see Whitby and Whitby, *Chronicon Paschale*, 38 n. 122 and Kelly, *Early Christian Doctrines*, 289-95.

*Chron. Pasch.* (548, 9) briefly identifies Apollinaris as a heretic. Theophanes (48, 19), on the other hand, says that Apollinaris wrote the Emperor Julian "on behalf of the truth," and cites his proficiency in scriptural studies. Philostorgius (8, 11, 14) likewise praises Apollinaris for his biblical studies. Socrates (2, 46) records the beginning of Apollinaris' heresy and afterwards (3, 16) describes how Apollinaris avoided Julian's ban on Christian teaching by writing on biblical subjects in various Greek literary genres. Sozomen (5, 18) follows Socrates for Apollinaris' writings, but provides more details on the particular works involved; in addition (6, 25), he gives a description of the new heresy. Theodoret (5, 3, 2) gives another summary description of the heresy.

244c. The verb *oppressere*, "crushed" (perfect indicative) lacks a subject, perhaps "earthquakes" or "tremors." Otherwise, the text may be problematic; see Helm's apparatus in Appendix A. Jerome has used the perfect here where we should expect the pluperfect. He mistakenly places this earthquake in 366, while it reaqlly occurred in 365.

*Chron. Pasch.* (556, 15) reports that this earthquake razed Nicaea. Theophanes (56, 10) includes the detail that ships in Alexandria were left stranded on dry land.

Socrates (4, 3) used Jerome's source, since he has the alteration of the coastline; like Theophanes, he has the stranded ships as well. Ammianus (26, 10, 15) also has ships on the dry land, but specifically, resting on the tops of buildings.

244d. Procopius: a "tyrant" or usurper; cf. Claudian, *De bell. Gild.* 1, 147, which describes the usurper Gildo as a *tyrannus*. See Stein, *Histoire*, 169, 171, 175f., 186; Jones, *Later Roman Empire*, 1, 123 on Procopius' role during Julian's Persian campaign; and *ibid.*, 139, on his claims, defeat, and the reprisals taken against his followers. "Procopius, already suspect as a relative of Julian, was stimulated to revolt by the harsh exactions of Valens and his father-in-law Petronius; he was finally betrayed by his allies and handed over to Valens;" Whitby and Whitby, *Chronicon Paschale*, 46 n. 139. See also Jones, *PLRE* 1, "Procopius 4."

*Chron. Pasch.* (556, 20) and Theophanes (55, 28) may have referred to Jerome's source for the death of Procopius in *"Phrygia Salutaris."* Philostorgius (9, 5), Socrates (4, 5), and Sozomen (6, 8) all relate that Procopius was betrayed by his own generals. Zosimus (4, 5-8) furnishes a detailed account which clarifies the treason of the general Gomarius. Ammianus (26, 5, 8) discusses the beginning of this revolt in the East, and (26, 9, 7-10 and 10, 14) gives details concerning Procopius' defeat and execution.

244e. Damasus, bishop of Rome from 366 to 384: cf. *De vir. il.* 103; *Ep.* 15-16; 17, 2; 18; 19 (to Jerome from Damasus); 20-21; 22, 3; 43, 3; 123, 10; *Homil.* 3; Origen, *In Cant. Cant.*, pref.; *Gospels*, pref. See Berardino, *Patrology*, 6, 67, 220, 222-28, 273-78; Piganiol, *L'empire chrétienne*, 163, 191-92, 207, 209-10, 217, 225, 228, 231, 237, 370, 381; Stein, *Histoire*, 174, 197-99. On Ursinus, cf. *Ep.* 15, 3. See also Berardino, *ibid.*, 273; Piganiol, *ibid.*, 192, 227, 366. On Siscininus, Jerome has simply *Siscininum*; see Jones, *Later Roman Empire*, 2, 846, 862.

Theophanes (41, 9) cites Damasus as the thirty-sixth Roman bishop. Socrates (4, 29) clearly places the blame for the violence on Ursinus and his supporters, as does Sozomen (6, 23). Socrates also cites the punishment of citizens for the fighting by Maximin. Theodoret (5, 2, 2 and 40, 4) gives the edict of the Emperor Gratian which commanded the bishops to follow the leadership of Damasus and reports Damasus' high reputation for personal holiness. Ammianus (27, 3, 12) emphasizes the bitterness of the fighting over the Roman see and gives the number of dead in the basilica as one-hundred-thirty-seven.

245a. Valens: see 243e. For Eudoxius, see 232c. On his transfer to the see of Constantinople, see Downey, *Antioch*, 157.

*Chron. Pasch.* (556, 9) cites Valens' Arianism. Socrates (4, 1, 9, 11), followed by Sozomen (6, 6), gives the baptism of Valens by Euzoius. Theodoret (4, 12) credits Valens' wife with leading him into Arianism, but also points to the influence of Eudoxius.

245b. Gratian: see also 241f above. Marina, Gratian's mother, prevailed upon his father, Valentinian, to promote him to the throne; see Jones, *PLRE* 1, "Marina Severa 2."

*Chron. Pasch.* (557, 7) and Theophanes (55, 1) relate Gratian's elevation to the throne by his father Valentinian. Philostorgius (8, 8) informs that Valentinian was a responsible father regarding Gratian's training. Socrates (4, 11) merely cites the elevation to the throne as occurring on Aug. 24. Sozomen (6, 10) similarly cites the elevation, and adds in passing that Gratian had been born before his father took the throne. Zosimus (4, 12) has it that Valentinian was recovering from a severe illness, when, following the advice of his court, he secured the throne for Gratian. Ammianus (27, 6, 4 and 30, 7, 7) is similar to Zosimus on this, but furnishes more information, including the ceremony itself, Valentinian's speech to the army, and the soldiers' acclamation which followed.

245c. Constantinople: see 232g.

*Chron. Pasch.* (547, 4) and the *Cons. Const.* (a. 357), like Jerome, have hail compared to stones. Socrates (4, 11) reports the rumor that God was intervening with this deadly hail due to the exiles of the orthodox clergy. In Sozomen (6, 10) the hail is reported as falling in several different places, and the author attributes this and the earthquake at Nicaea (see 245f below) to divine action.

245d. Atrabatae was famous for its wool; see Jones, *Later Roman Empire*, 2, 846, 862.

245e. Hilary: see 240c.

245f. Nicaea earthquake: *Chron. Pasch.* (557, 13) says that Nicaea was razed, as does Socrates (4, 11), and both give Oct. 11 as the date. Thus they appear to preserve data from Jerome's source. For Sozomen (6, 10), see 245c above.

245g. Antioch: see 231i.

Socrates (3, 1) describes how Julian, forbidden to attend Libanius' school at Nicomedia, studied his orations privately. Sozomen (6, 1, 17) cites Julian's funeral oration composed by Libanius.

245h. Constantinople: see 232g. Valens: see 243e.

*Cons. Const.* (a. 369) includes Valens' restoration of the games to Constantinople.

245i. Goths: see 233c. On Athanaric, see Matthews, *Western Aristocracies*, 88 and 92.

Socrates (4, 33) has Athanaric's initial advantage over Fritigern, but this is followed by the final victory of Fritigern's party with help from the Emperor Valens. The aftermath of the victory is then said to have witnessed many conversions to Christianity. Sozomen (6, 37) first has the Goths' flight from the Huns and their request for admission to the empire, then he follows Socrates for the war among the Goths. Ambrose (*In Luc.*, 2, 37) cites the conversion of the Goths together with the presence of martyrs among them.

245j. The death of Eusebius of Vercellae is recorded only in Jerome.

245l. Constantinople: see 232g.

*Chron. Pasch.* (559, 13) used Jerome's source in placing the consecration of the Church of the Holy Apostles, called the "martyrs' shrine"--*martyrium*--of the Apostles by Jerome, in the year 370. Cf. also *Cons. Const.* (a. 370): "the holy church was dedicated where the blessed apostles were placed."

245m. Famine in Phrygia: Socrates (4, 16) relates the story that this famine was a divine punishment for Valens' executions of orthodox clergymen. *Cons. Const.* (a. 370) simply records the fact of the famine.

246a. Lucifer: see 239i. For Gregory *Baeticus* (i.e., the bishop of Eliberum in Spain), see *De vir. il.*, 105.

246b. Prefect of the grain supply: see Jones, *Later Roman Empire*, 2, 106, 375, 404, 486, 600, 690-92, 698.

Socrates (4, 29) cites the role of Maximin in punishing the violence after Damasus' election (see 244e above). Ammianus (28, 1, 5-7) describes the abuses at Rome during Maximin's tenure.

246c. Valentinian: Jerome seems to identify by this name one *Valentinus*, a Pannonian who had been exiled to Britain. If so, the revolt really occurred in Britain in 368; S. Johnson, *Later Roman Britain* (London: Grafton Books, 1982), 122-23. "The plot was nipped in the bud;" *ibid.*

Both Zosimus (4, 12) and Ammianus (28, 3, 3-5) record Valentinus' exile to Britain as the result of unspecified charges. Ammianus relates the rebellion and its suppression in detail.

246d. An unnamed priest of Sirmium: Ammianus (29, 3, 4) records a priest who was a favorite of Octavian, but his text is corrupt; see Rolfe trans., vol. 3, 235.

246e. Didymus of Alexandria: cf. *De vir. il.* 109, 120, 126, 135. See Pelikan, *Christian Tradition*, 218 and 223 on his doctrine of the Trinity, and *ibid.*, on his relations with the Arians.

Socrates (4, 25) gives a detailed biography of Didymus, naming him as a great bulwark against the Arians. Both Socrates (*ibid.*) and Sozomen (3, 15) record Didymus' communication with Antony. Sozomen (6, 20) names Didymus as one of several orthodox Christians who inspired imitation by others. Theodoret (4, 29, 3) emphasizes Didymus' great knowledge in several fields, including scriptural studies.

246f. *Antequam*, "before," with a subjunctive verb, *vastarentur*: this suggests deliberate timing for the action of the main verb, perhaps with a view to prevent other action. See B. L. Gildersleeve, *Latin Grammar* (New York: St. Martin's Press, 1971 repr. of 1895 ed.), 577.

On Probus as prefect, see Jones, *PLRE* 1, "Probus 5," and for more on his career, Jones, *Later Roman Empire*, 1, 141-42 and 160 (for his promotion under Gratian).

Ammianus (30, 5, 4-6) relates the various abuses as well as the increase of taxes under Probus, and the Emperor Valentinian's investigation.

246g. Eunomius "won reknown (i.e., notoriety):" cf. *Homil.* 2; 14; 36; 51; 57; 59. The Eunomians: see Stein, *Histoire*, 136, 153-55, 175, and Kelly, *Early Christian Doctrines*, 249, 256, 427, and 487. For Eunomius, see Pelikan, *Christian Tradition*, 196 and 228, as refuted by Basil and Theodore of Mopsuestia, respectively. See also Gregg and Groh, *Early Arianism*, 75 n. 82. On the psuedo-Aristotelian dialectic employed by Eunomius, see Kelly, *ibid.*, 249.

Theophanes (58, 5) describes Eunomius' break with Eudoxius at that point at which the latter would have nothing to do with Eunomius' teacher, Aetius. Philostorgius (3, 20) tells how Eunomius and Aetius resided together at Antioch, and likewise (8, 2), at Constantinople; he then discusses their subsequent opposition to Eudoxius. Socrates (2, 35) furnishes a biography of Aetius and discusses Eunomius' role as Aetius' secretary; he goes on to supply a biographical sketch of Eunomius himself and his eventual promotion to the see of Cyzicus. Sozomen (6, 26) discusses Eunomius and Aetius together, emphasizing their errors concerning baptism. He also cites Eunomius' replacement of Meletius as bishop of Sebastia (4, 25). Theodoret (2, 24, 6 and 29, 11) gives details concerning Eunomius' ordination by treachery and his flight to avoid censure by Constantius.

246h. Defeat of the Saxons: see Lot, *End of the Ancient World*, 189; Ferrill, *Fall of the Roman Empire*, 58-59; and Jones, *Later Roman Empire*, 1, 140.

Ammianus (28, 5, 1-7 and 30, 7, 8) gives a full description of Valentinian's operations against the Saxons under the direction of the generals Nannenus and Severus, in which an ambush resulted in the slaughter described by Jerome.

247a. The Burgundian threat: see Ferrill, *Fall of the Roman Empire*, 59. For the way this was turned against the Alemanni by Valentinian, see Lot, *End of the Ancient World*, 189. On the Burgundians' settlement afterwards, see Thompson, *Romans and Barbarians*, 23, 26; J. B. Bury, *History of the Later Roman Empire from the Death of Theodosius I to the Death of Justinian (395-565)*, 2 vols. (New York: Dover, 1958 repr. of 1923 ed.), 102; and Lot, *ibid.*, 207.

Ammianus (28, 5, 11) credits the firmness of Valentinian with the Burgundians' decision to withdraw to their own territory.

247b. Clearchus: on his demonstrations of piety through plaques erected in the circus, see MacMullen, *Christianizing the Roman Empire*, 63 n. 8, citing Eunapius, frg. 78 (*FHG* 4, 49); see also A. Chastagnol, *La Préfeture urbaine à Rome sous le Bas-Empire* (Paris: 1960), 81 n. 1.

Theophanes (56, 31-57, 3) cites the baths built in Constantinople under the Emperor Valens and refers to the aqueduct referred to here. Socrates (4, 8) records Clearchus' construction of baths in addition to the aqueduct.

247c. Peter, bishop of Alexandria from 373 to 380, successor to Athanasius: on Basil's efforts to win his approval of Meletius, bishop of Antioch (above), see Frend, *Rise of Christianity*, 632. On his reputation for personal sanctity and the edict of Theodosius, *ibid.*, 636 and refer to *CTh* 16, 1, 2--"*Cunctos Populos.*"

Theophanes (59, 29), instead of his ready acceptance as bishop, has Peter's removal by the Arians through the agency of an official named Magnus. Socrates (4, 20) refers to Peter as "devout and eloquent." Sozomen (6, 19) records Magnus' imprisonment of Peter and Peter's subsequent escape to Rome. Theodoret (4, 20) relates that Peter was Athanasius' own choice for his successor and gives details of Peter's arrest, his secretive flight, and refuge in Rome. He goes on (4, 22) to quote a letter from Peter concerning the atrocious behavior of his Arian replacement, Lucius.

247d. Melania: cf. *Ep.* 3, 2; 4, 2; 39, 4; 43, 4. See Frend, *Rise of Christianity*, 710 on Melania as exemplary of the trend towards asceticism. See D. Groce, *Vie de Sainte Melanie* (Paris: Sources chrétiennes, 1962), for Melania's life.

Paulinus of Nola (*Ep.* 29, 5) refers to Melania as "the holy and illustrious woman among God's saints." Palladius (*Hist. Laus.* 46) gives a biography of Melania, in which he cites her foundation of the monastery in which she lived for twenty-seven years (5) and her assistance in reuniting schismatic monks (6).

247e. Ambrose of Milan, bishop from 373 to 397: cf. *Apol. c. Rufin.* 1, 2 and 3, 14; *Comm. in Eph.*, pref.; *Comm. in Hag.* 2; *Comm. in Luc.* 10, 113; *De spir. sanct.* (*PL* 23, 108A-B); *De vir. il.* 124; *Ep.* 15, 4; 22, 22; 48, 14-16; 49, 14; 54, 17; 69, 2, 9; 84, 7; 112, 20; *Ep. adv. Rufin.* 14; *Homil.* 26. See also Paulinus, *Vita Ambr.*, and Rufinus, *Apol. c. Hier.* 2, 22, 24. See Berardino, *Patrology*, 144-52 (for his career), 152-80 (for works), 195. 197, 209-10; Kelly, *Jerome*, 106 n. 10; Piganiol, *L'empire chrétienne*, 194, 207, 227, etc. M. Simonetti, "Saint Ambroise et saint Jerome, lecteurs de Philon," *Aufstieg und Niedergang der römischen Welt: Geschichte und Kultur Röms im Spiegel der neuern Forschung*, ed. by H. Temporini and W. Haase (Berlin: Walter D. Guyter, 1984), vol. 2, 21, 1, 731-59; Stein, *Histoire*, 148, 174, 197-99, 201-4, etc.; D. S. Wiesen, *St. Jerome As a Satirist. A Study in Christian Latin Thought and Letters* (Ithaca: Cornell University Press, 1964), 240-41, 243; and Matthews, *Western Aristocracies*, Ch. 8.

Auxentius, bishop preceding Ambrose: cf. *Ep.* 1, 15; 15, 3. See Berardino, *Patrology*, 46, 65, 93-94, 96, 105, 131, 147; Piganiol, *L'empire chrétienne*, 95, 191, 194. Concerning the "belated death" of Auxentius, note that Hilary of Poitiers and Eusebius of Vercellae had failed to oust him in 364; Berardino, *ibid.*, 93-94. In *Ep.* 1, 15, Jerome praises Evagrius for figurativel burying Auxentius. His death is probably "belated" as well because he is the biographer of the Arian missionary Ulfilas and one of the chief authors of the Creed of Ariminum; see Frend, *Rise of Christianity*, 618.

Theophanes (60, 23) records how Ambrose was sent by Valentinian I as the provincial governor to restore peace to Milan, where rival factions were struggling to obtain the office of bishop. Socrates (4, 30) gives the same information, but adds Valentinian's approval of Ambrose's own election as bishop. Sozomen (6, 24) emphasizes Valentinian's insistence upon Ambrose's ordination. Theodoret (4, 6, 6-7), like Sozomen, mentions the fact that Ambrose had not been baptized. Again, like Sozomen, he records Valentinian's insistence that Ambrose should remain the new bishop. He also cites Ambrose together with Damasus as champions of orthodoxy in the West. Athanasius (*Ad mon.* 75) refers to Auxentius as more of a lawyer than a bishop.

247f. Aquileia: see 235a. Jerome's description of the clergy of Aquileia was based upon personal knowledge. See Kelly, *Jerome*, 33.

247g. Pannonia: see 243e.

Socrates (4, 31), followed by Sozomen (6, 36), relates Valentinian's campaign against the Sarmatians and his fatal meeting with their ambassadors; see 247h below.

247h. Valentinian: cf. 243e. Gratian: cf. 241f. Valens: cf. 243e. The place was a Roman fortress at Brigetio (now Szoeny) in Pannonia.

*Chron. Pasch.* (560, 15) names the fortress of Vergitinae as the precise location. Philostorgius (9, 16) describes the promotion of Valentinian the Younger, supported by his mother Justina and the soldiers, after his father's death. He claims that Gratian disapproved when he learned of the promotion and that he even punished some individuals, but this probably shows the author's bias against Gratian; see Walford trans., 498 n. 3. For Socrates and Sozomen, see 247g above. Theodoret (5, 1) looks ahead to Gratian as the sole ruler of the empire after Valens' death. Zosimus (4, 17) informs that Valentinian had been in the area for nearly nine months, and records omens that accompanied his death (18). Ammianus (30, 5, 15) reports a series of omens that warned of the emperor's death and describes his fit of anger in the presence of the embassy from the Quadi (30, 6, 3-5). He provides background for the promotion of Valentinian the Younger. This consists (30, 6, 3-5) of the machinations of Merobaudes, the *magister militum*, who saw to it that Sebastianus, a successful general popular with the soldiers, would be inaccessible for a coup.

248a. Nitria, the monastic community: cf. *Ep.* 3, 2; 22, 33; 87, 92; 108, 14; *Ep. adv. Rufin.* 22. On Jerome himself as founder of "domestic monasteries," see Peterson, *The Dialogues*, 68 and 159.

Socrates (4, 22-24) has the Arians' assault against the desert communities, including the slaughter of defenseless monks. He digresses (23) to name some of the outstanding monks. After describing Nitria and other monastic communities in Egypt, Sozomen (6, 31) relates the story of Melas, an abbot who shamed his Arian persecutors.

248b. Valens: see 243e. Monks clubbed to death: this was ordinarily the punishment for cowardice within the army. Eusebius relates the persecution of Christians already in the army at *Chron.* a. 2317; see A. Harnack, *Militia Christi. The Christian Religion and the Military in the First Three Centuries*, trans. by D. M. Gracie (Philadelphia: Fortress Press, 1981), 94. On the problem of military service for Christians in general, see *ibid.*, Ch. 2, and among the primary sources refer to *CTh* 12, 1, 63 and Sozomen 6,40, 1.

248c. Theodosius the Elder: see Claudian, 15, 216 and 22, 422 (Platnauer's ed., Loeb series, 1976).

Theodosius' execution is recorded by Socrates (4, 19). Sozomen (6, 35) includes the story of a tripod on which the pagans tried to divine the name of Valens' successor.

248d. Photinians: a sect that adhered so closely to Jewish law that it was considered Jewish; see S. Kraus, "The Jew in the Works of the Church Fathers. VI: Jerome," *JQR* 6 (1894): 238. They held an "adoptionist" view of Christ; see L. A. Spellar, "A New Light on the Photinians," *JTS* n.s. 34, 1 (1983): 99-113. See also Theodoret, *Haer. fabul.* 2, 11 and Gennadius, *De vir. il.* 14.

Socrates (2, 18) discusses Photinus' background in Asia Minor and as a disciple of the deposed bishop Marcellus. Afterwards, he provides a biographical sketch (2, 29). Sozomen (4, 6) describes the synod called at Sirmium which condemned Photinus' views; he includes a debate between Photinus and Basil of Ancyra. Theodoret (*Haer. fabul.* 11, 11) describes Photinianism as comparable to Sabellianism, and cites the author Diodorus' writings against both groups. Philastrius (*Divers. haeres.* 65), similarly to Theodoret, compares Photinus' errors to those of Sabellius.

248e. Basil of Caesarea, bishop from ca. 330 to 379: cf. *De vir. il.* 116, 120 and 128. He abandoned rhetoric for the ascetic life and became a founder of eastern Christian monasticism. He followed Eusebius of Caesarea, author of the *Chron.*, as bishop. On his efforts to heal the Meletian schism, see Quasten, *Patrology*, 3, 207. On the "classical orthodox doctrine of Christ," see Hardy, *Christology*, 23-24; teaching on the Trinity, Pelikan, *Christian Tradition*, 218-24. See also *OCD*, "Basil." For his life and works, see R. J. Deferrari, *Saint Basil. The Letters*, 4 vols. (Cambridge: Harvard University Press, 1972), 15-38; for his works as historical sources, see Jones, *Later Roman Empire*, 1, 154-55; his popularization of monasticism, *ibid.*, 929; and for complete descriptions of his monasticism, see V. K. L. Clarke, *Saint Basil the Great: A Study in Monasticism* (Cambridge: Harvard University Press, 1912) and E. F. Morrison, *St. Basil and His Rule: A Study in Early Monasticism* (Oxford: Oxford University Press, 1912).

On the "many deficiencies"--*multa bona*--*bona* means "moral goods," i.e., traits.

Socrates (4, 26) says that when Eunomius tried to enter the controversy with Basil of Caesarea, he appeared to be illiterate by comparison. Sozomen (6, 15-16) recounts Basil's dispute with Eusebius of Caesarea, in which Basil's reconciliation thwarted the Emperor Valens' plans to further the cause of Arianism in Caesarea. Philostorgius (8,

12) cites Basil's writings against Eunomius. Theodoret (4, 19, 1-3) describes how Valens tried to coerce Basil into subscribing to Arian views through the agency of the prefect Modestus. He then relates the story of Valens' near repentance when his son was dying.

248f. Alemanni: see 240g. On Gratian's victory, see Lot, *End of the Ancient World*, 194. The site of the battle was Horburg on the Il River, near Colmar. Galliae: see 238h; plural here for the several Gallic provinces. Argentorate (Strasbourg) was the site of Julian's great victory over the Alemanni in 357; see 240g. See also Stein, *Histoire*, 144. If one fails to see Jerome's lament over losses at Mursa (238d) as a rhetorical exaggeration, the victory here would appear remarkable indeed.

Verbal parallels show that the *Epitome* (47, 2) used Jerome. Ammianus (31, 10, 5-10) records Gratian's assignment of the campaign to one Nannienus and to the Frankish king Mallobaudes. For the number of the Alemanni he gives two reports—forty and seventy thousand in turn. He recounts the slaughter in which the Aleman king Priarius was killed, and which only five thousand of the Alemanni survived.

248g. Florentinus: cf. *Ep.* 4 and 5. See Kelly, *Jerome*, 48-49 on his role in obtaining books for Jerome while the latter was in the Chalcis desert. Bonosus: cf. *Ep.* 3, 4; 6; 7, 3. On Bonosus as a friend of Jerome from childhood and as his companion at school in Rome, see *Ep.* 3, 4-5 and Kelly, *Jerome*, 7-8, 10-11; as Jerome's companion at Trier, *ibid.*, 25, 29; on Bonosus' retirement to a hermit's life off the coast of Dalmatia, *ibid.*, 29. Rufinus: cf. *Apol. c. Rufin.* and *Ep. adv. Rufin.* See Berardino, *Patrology*, 4-6, 88, 100, 133, 210, 247-54, etc. For the controversy between Jerome and Rufinus, see Kelly, *ibid.*, 195-209; on Rufinus' work *Apol. c. Hier.*, see *ibid.*, 234, 249-51, 254, 258. Rufinus was a friend of Jerome early; he founded a monastery at Jerusalem with some connection to the convent of Melania (above), ca. 380. In 397 he returned to Italy, where he lived mainly at Aquileia. In the interim he had become embroiled in the controversy with Jerome due to his own admiration of Origen. Similarly to Jerome, he translated and continued a historical work of Eusebius of Caesarea—in this instance the *Ecclesiastical History*—which he brought down to the year 395.

248h. Goths: see 233c. On the Visigoths' entry into the empire due to the threat of the Huns, see Bury, *Later Roman Empire*, 55-58; Thompson, *Romans and Barbarians*, 38-39; and Lot, *End of the Ancient World*, 190-94.

Theophanes (64, 16 and 34) records the Goths' request for help from Valens after they came under attack by the Huns. Socrates (4, 34) says that the Goths offered themselves as subjects of Rome, and explains that Valens' decision to depend upon barbarians for recruits led to many disasters. Sozomen (6, 37) reflects Socrates on the Goths' admission to the empire and Valens' neglect of the traditional recruitment of the legions. He adds a description of the career of Ulfilas, the Arian Gothic missionary. Philostorgius (9, 17), calling the Goths "Scythians," refers to their crossing of the Rhine under the pretense of friendly relations with Rome. Zosimus (4, 20), like Philostorgius, calls the Goths "Scythians," and likewise records their offer to serve Rome. Then he has it that the disgraceful behavior of Roman commanders was the first cause of subsequent disasters. Ammianus (31, 4, 9) describes Maximus with another general, Lupicinus, as men with stained reputations--"*homines maculosi.*" Similarly to Zosimus, he says (4, 10) "Their treacherous greed was the source of all our evils" (Rolfe trans., 407).

249a. Goths: see 233c.

Sozomen (6, 39) reports that Valens was considered a coward in Constantinople for his procrastination in dealing with the Goths in Thrace. Theophanes (65, 7) likewise has the people of Constantinople's dishonor of Valens as a coward. Zosimus (4, 22) describes the initial successes of Valens' Saracen cavalry against the Goths. Ammianus (31, 5, 9) has the defeat of Lipicinus' army in Thrace, with the capture of Roman standards and the lamentable deaths of the tribunes. He furnishes a very significant military detail--the Goths' use of captured Roman arms.

249b. Valens: see 243e.

Theophanes (65, 7) points to the people's discontent with Valens' delay, as we have seen. According to Socrates (4, 35 and 37), Valens interrupted his exiles of the orthodox after he was informed of the Goths' ravages of Thrace (cf. Jerome's record of Valens' "belated repentance"); he also informs that after Valens' departure from Antioch, the Alexandrians recalled Peter (see 247c above). Sozomen (6, 37) also reports Peter's recall from exile, but he has a different approach to the Emperor's interruption of the persecution; rather than Valens' policy decision, it is simply the result of his preoccupation with the invaders.

249c. "Slaughtered to the last man:" another rhetorical exaggeration as at 238d. Note that in both cases the vanquished emperor was an Arianizer. On the battle of Adrianople, described here, see the following: on negotiations preceding the battle, Thompson, *Romans and Barbarians*, 39-40; for the battle, Bury, *Later Roman Empire*, 58-60; Lot, *End of the Ancient World*, Jones, *Later Roman Empire*, 1, 153-54; Ferrill, *Fall of the Roman Empire*, 60-67 (including a map, 61); W. Goffart, *Barbarians and Romans. A.D. 418-584. The Techniques of Accommodation* (Princeton: Princeton University Press, 1980), 33 (esp. on the Visigoths as "worn down" afterwards by the Romans and by various hardships). On the aftermath of the battle, see Matthews, *Western Aristocracies*, 121-23; Bury, *ibid.*, 60-61; Lot, *ibid.*, 195-96; Jones, *ibid.*, 1, 154; Ferrill, *ibid.*, 64. See also Zosimus (4, 26) and Ammianus (31, 16, 8) on the *magister per Orientem* Julius' orders to massacre the recently recruited Goths serving in Roman garrisons. On Valens' deprivation of a proper burial, *quoque* in the Latin text emphasizes *sepultura.*

Of the primary sources, Socrates (4, 38), Libanius (*Or.* 24, 2) and Ammianus (31, 12, 10-12 and 13, 12-14) include the report that Valens died fighting in the battle itself. Theodoret alone (4, 36) has Valens await the battle's outcome in a village. In their alternate accounts, Socrates and Ammianus also have the story that Valens retreated from the battlefield wounded and took refuge with his followers in a house; this is likewise the report found in Theophanes (65, 17), Philostorgius (9, 17), Sozomen (6, 40), and Zosimus (4, 24), in addition to Jerome. Like Jerome, all the authors except for Libanius, who omits this account entirely, relate that the Goths burned the house afterwards. Theophanes, Philostorgius, Sozomen and Ammianus have it that the Goths did not know the Emperor was inside. *Cons. Const.* (a. 378) simply has it that "from that day the Emperor Valens was never seen again"--"*ex ea die Valens Augustus nusquam apparuit.*"

249d. Jerome undoubtedly arranged these summary statements similarly to the way they now stand in the mss., i.e., separated for emphasis. They divide history into distinct periods for convenience--first, Roman; and then, universal.

250. Cf. Victor of Aquitaine, 7, 25 (*Chron. Min.*, 1, 681), giving the same numbers for the years from the flood to Abraham and for the years from Abraham to the sixth consulship of Valens.

APPENDIX A

HIERONYMI CHRONICON: AD 327-379

EDITED BY R. HELM

*EUSEBIUS' WERKE 5: DIE CHRONIK DES HIERONYMUS*

(GCS 47; BERLIN: AKADEMIE-VERLAG, 1956), 231-250

(313 F)

231

Romanorum

| | | |
|---|---|---|
| | leuit | |
| XVII | *a* Constantius, filius Constantini, Caesar factus | 323 p. Chr. |
| | *b* Licinius Thessalonicae contra ius sacramenti | |
| | priuatus occiditur. | |
| 5 ĪĪCCCXL XVIII | *c* Nazarius rhetor insignis habetur. | 324 |
| CCLXXVI·Olymp· | | |
| XVIIII | *d* Crispus, filius Constantini, et Licinius iunior, Con- | 325 |
| | stantiae Constantini sororis et Licinii filius, cru- | |
| | delissime interficiuntur | |
| 10 XX | *e* Uicennalia Constantini Nicomediae acta et sequen- | 326 |
| | ti anno Romae edita | |
| | *f* Huc usque historiam scribit Eusebius Pamphili marty- | |
| | ris contubernalis. Cui nos ista subiecimus. | |
| XXI | *g* Arnobius rhetor in Africa clarus habetur. Qui | 327 |
| 15 | cum Siccae ad declamandum iuuenes erudiret | |
| | et adhuc ethnicus ad credulitatem somniis com- | |
| | pelleretur neque ab episcopo impetraret fi- | |
| | dem, quam semper inpugnauerat, elucubrauit | |
| | aduersum pristinam religionem luculentissi- | |
| 20 | mos libros et tandem uelut quibusdam obsi- | |
| | dibus pietatis foedus impetrauit. | |
| | *h* Drepanam Bithyniae ciuitatem in honorem mar- | |
| | tyris Luciani ibi conditi Constantinus instaurans | |
| | ex uocabulo matris suae Helenopolim nun- | |
| 25 | cupauit. | |
| | *i* In Antiochia dominicum, quod uocatur aureum, | |

*a* ad CCLXXV Ol. *L*      *b* ut *a L*, ad XVIII *B*      *c* ut *a L*, ad XVII *A*      *d* ad CCLXXVI Ol. *A L*, ad XX *B*      *e* ad XXII *L*

a) † 2 constantius] constantinus *LM*   cesar *L*   *Prosp. 1014 (Chr. m. I 449) (i. J. 324) chron. Gall. a. 511 (Chr. m. I 643, 162)* (a. XVIII) *Marian. Scot. III 339*      b) 3 licinnius *O*   thesalonice *A* thesalonice *L* tesalonice *P* thessalonicae (a) *M*      4 interficitur *L   Prosp. 1016 (Chr. m. I 450) (i. J. 325) lat. imp. (Chr. m. III 422, 6) Oros. VII 28, 20 Marian. Scot. III 339*      c) 5 retor *L* verb. *A* rehthor *M   Marian. Scot. III 340*      d) 7 et ⟨*B*      8 eonstani *O*   sorores *L*   licinnii *O* licini *A P B* verb. *N*   crudelissimae *M*      9 interficitur *O B* verb. *P   Prosp. 1018 (Chr. m. I 450) (i. J. 326) chron. Gall. a. 511 (Chr. m. I 643, 462)* (a. XVIII) *Oros. VII 28, 26 (504, 11) Marian. Scot. III 340*      e) 11 uicenalia *P*   nicomedie·*O A L* comedie *M* comediae *P*      12 rome *L*   aedita *L Prosp. 1020 (Chr. m. I 450) (i. J. 327) Cassiodor. 1056 (Chr. m. II 150) Marian. Scot. III 341* f) *Sam. An.: hic finis chronicorum Eusebii librorum*      12 storiam *L*   scripsit *P*   eusebi *A* esebius verb. *M*   pamphyli *A N* pamfyli *B M* pa *L* pamflii *O Hier. epist. 84, 11, 3 d. vir. ill. 81*      13 contubernales *B*   hinc ieronim' + *P   Prosp. 1022 (Chr. m. I 450) (i. J. 328) Marian. Scot. III 341* g) 14 arnonius *B*   hetor *A* retor *L* rhethor *M*   affrica *P*      15 sicce *L B*   iubenes *L*      16 et ⟨*L* athuc *O* verb. *N*   etnicus verb. *P*   e—ad *A*   compeleretur verb. *N* conpell- *L B M*      17 ep̄so *L* epō *P* inpetraret *L M*      18 inpugnaberat *L* impugnauerat *O P N*   lucubrabit *L* eluc̄rauit *M*      19 religioné *B*      20 ueluti *B P N O* (i + ?)      21 foedus (a. *Rd.* 'fidem) *N*   obsedibus verb. *M*   inpetrabit *L* inpetrauit *M Hier. d. vir. ill. 79 Marian. Scot. III 342* h) 22 ·bythiniae *L* bithiniae *P M*   cibitatem *L*   horem *B*   martiris *L*      23 lucini *L*      24 uo$_t$ (cabulo ⟨*Lücke*⟩) *L* helenopolin *B N* helonopolin *P* helenępolim *M* helenae$_t$ (pol. nunc. ⟨*Lücke*⟩) *L Hier. d. vir. ill. 77   Prosp. 1023 (Chr. m. I 450) (i. J. 328) Bed. 423 (Chr. m. III 231) Marian. Scot. III 342*      i) 26 anthiociam *L* anthiochia *M*

232  (314 F)

Romanorum

aedificari coeptum•

328 p. Chr.  XXII  *a* Constantinus uxorem suam Faustam
interficit•

*b* Donatus agnoscitur, a quo per Africam Donatiani•  5

CCLXXVII·Olymp·

*c* Antiochiae post Tyrannum ·XX· ordinatur episcopus Uitalis. Post quem ·XXI· Filogonius, cui successit ·XXII· Paulinus. Post
quem ·XXIII· Eustathius. Quo in exilium ob  10
fidem truso usque in praesentem diem Arriani ecclesiam optinuerunt, id est Eulalius Eusebius Eufronius Placillus Stefa-

329  XXIII  nus Leontius Eudoxius Meletius Euzoius Dorotheus rursum Meletius. Quorum idcir-  15
co tempora non digessi, quod eos hostes
potius XP̄i quam episcopos iudicem•

*d* Iuuencus presbyter natione Hispanus euan-
gelia heroicis uersibus explicat•

*e* Porphyrius misso ad Constantinum insigni  20
uolumine exilio liberatur•

330  XXIIII  *f* Alexandriae ·XVIIII· ordinatur episcopus
Athanasius•

*g* Dedicatur Constantinopolis omnium paene
urbium nuditate•  25

*h* Metrodorus philosophus agnoscitur•

---

*a* ad XXI *PN*   *c* ad XXIII *BM*   *d* ad XXIIII *O*   *e* ad XXIIII *O*   *f* om. in lac. *L*,
ad XXIII *APN*   *g* ut *f* *L*   *h* ut *f* *L*, ad XXV *B*

1 aedificare *verb. A* coepit *B s. 235* *Marian. Scot. III 342*   a) 3 interfecit *AM* interfini *B*
*Chron. Gall. a. 511 (Chr. m. I 643, 462) Marian. Scot. III 343*   b) 4 affricam *PM Hier. d. uir.
ill. 93 Prosp. 1025 (Chr. m. I 450) (i. J. 329) chron. Gall. a. 511 (Chr. m. I 464) Isidor. iun. 332
(Chr. m. II 465) Marian. Scot. III 343*   c) †7 anthiociae *L* anthiochiae *M* tirannum *L* ordinatur XX uicisimus (uic. *durchstrich.*) ∼ *L*   8 ep̄s *LPN* uitales *B*   10 eustatius *LM*
exilio *L*   11 presentem *M* ecct *L*   12 obtinuerunt *OBM*   13 eufronius eusebius ∼ *A*
placcillus *M* stephanus *PM*   14 melitius *APNB vgl. 241*¹ euzo·i·us *B* euzoius − melitius a.
unteren *Rd. + P*   15 melitius *APNB* qui rum *L*   16 degessi *L* qu̟*ᵗ (Lücke)*, hostes *L*
16/7 potius hostes ∼ *B*   17 proprius *L* episcopus *OA* ep̄s *L* ēp̄os *P s. 241*¹ *Prosp. 1027
(Chr. m. I 451) (i. J. 329) Marian. Scot. III 343/4*   d) 18 prbr *LP* praesbyter *BN* spanus *L*
18/9 euangelicis uersibus *verb. O*   19 eŏicis *L Hier. d. uir. ill. 84 epist. 70, 5, 3 in Matth. 2, 11
Chron. Gall. a. 511 (Chr. m. I 643, 463) Marian. Scot. III 345*   e) 20 porfyrius *OL* porfirius
*BM* porphirius *P* constantinom *verb. B* uo̟ₜ (lum.-lib. ⟨*Lücke*⟩) *L Chron. Gall. a. 511 (Chr. m. I 643)
(a. XXII) Marian. Scot. III 345*   f) ⟨*Lücke*⟩ *L*   22 ep̄s *PN*   23 atanasius *B Prosp.
1030 (Chr. m. I 451) (i. J. 331) chr. Gall. a. 511 (Chr. m. I 643, 467) (a. XXIIII) Marian. Scot. III
346*   g) ⟨*Lücke*⟩ *L*   24 constantinupolis *verb. O* penae *M Chron. Gall. a. 511 (Chr. m. I 643, 466)
(a. XXIII) Cassiodor. 1061 (Chr. m. II 151) Ps.-Isidor. 8 (Chr. m. II 382) (a. XXIII) Oros. VII 28, 27
Marian. Scot. III 346*   h) ⟨*Lücke*⟩ *L*   26 metrodorus *verb. A* medrodorus *B* philosofus *O*
filosofus *B* phylosophus *N* *Marian. Scot. III 346*

Romanorum

XXV  <sup>a</sup> Romae ·XXXII· episcopus ecclesiam tenuit  331 p. Chr.
     Marcus ·mens ·VIII·, post quem ·XXXIII· ordina-
     tus est Iulius ·ann·XVI· mens ·IIII·•
     <sup>b</sup> Edicto Constantini gentilium templa sub-
5    uersa sunt•

XXVI  <sup>c</sup> Romani Gothos in Sarmatarum regione  332
     uicerunt•

CCLXXVIII·Olymp·
  XXVII  <sup>d</sup> Constans, filius Constantini, prouehitur  333
10    ad regnum•
     <sup>e</sup> Pestilentia et fame innumerabilis multitu-
     do in Syria Ciliciaque perit•

IICCCL XXVIII <sup>f</sup> Sarmatae Limigantes dominos suos, qui nunc  334
     Argaragantes uocantur, facta manu in Ro-
15    manum solum expulerunt•
     <sup>g</sup> Calocaerus in Cypro res nouas molitus opprimitur•

XXVIIII  <sup>h</sup> Constantinus cum liberis suis honorificas ad  335
     Antonium litteras mittit•
     <sup>i</sup> Tricennalibus Constantini Dalmatius Caesar  —
20    appellatur•

XXX  <sup>k</sup> Pater rhetor Romae gloriosissime docet•  336
     <sup>l</sup> Nazarii rhetoris filia in eloquentia patri coaequatur•
     <sup>m</sup> Tiberianus uir disertus praefectus praetorio
     Gallias regit•
25    <sup>n</sup> Eustathius Constantinopolitanus presbyter
     agnoscitur, cuius industria in Hierosolymis

 <sup>a</sup> ad XXIIII *A* <sup>c</sup> ad XXV *B* <sup>d</sup> ad CCLXXVIII Ol. *A P N L* <sup>e</sup> ut <sup>d</sup> *L*, ad XXVIII *B*
<sup>f</sup> ad XXX *B* <sup>g</sup> ad XXX *B* <sup>h</sup> ad XXX *B* <sup>i</sup> ad XXX *B* <sup>k</sup> ad XXVIIII *N*

a) 1 episcopos *M* eps *PN* eclesiā *A* 2 men *L* mensibus *A P N B M* octo *A P* VIIII *L*
3 an *B* annis *A P N* annos *L* •XVI *B* m *L* mensibus *A B M* msib; *PN* *Prosp. 1034 (Chr. m.
I 451) (i. J. 333) Marian. Scot. III 349* (m. IX) b) *Prosp. 1035 (Chr. m. I 451) (i. J. 333)
chron. Gall. a. 511 (Chr. m. I 643, 468) Oros. VII 28, 23 = Orig. Constant. imp. 6, 34 (Chr. m. I 11)
Marian. Scot. III 347* c) 6 in] et *B* gentilium templa subuersa sunt *durchstrichen, darüber
regiones uicerunt L* regionem *B* *Prosp. 1036 (Chr. m. I 451) (i. J. 333) chron. Gall. a. 511 (Chr.
m. I 643, 471)* (a. XXV) *Oros. VII 28, 29* d) 9 proueit *L* *Prosp. 1037 (Chr. m. I 451) (i. J. 333)
chron. Gall. a. 511 (Chr. m. I 643, 472)* (a. XXVII) *Marian. Scot. III 348* e) 11 et] e *O M*
famem *L* multitudo *übergeschrieb. O* 12 in ⟨*O* siria *A P M* ciliaq•e (a) *O* cilicia<sup>q:</sup> *L  Marian.
Scot. III 348* f) 13 sarmate *L* sarmataeli *B* dimigantes *L* dimicantes *M* micantes *B* limigantes (a. Rd. ? elimig;) *N* dno *L* suos ⟨*O P* 14 ardaragantes *B* arcaragantes *P* argaragantes
(argarag i. *Ras.*) *N* uocabantur *O* uocatur *verb. M s. P.-W. R.-E. II 429, 9* g) 16 caloche-
rius *M* calocerus (a. Rd. Λ? coloc;) *N* calocerus *Hss.* opprimu *L  Oros. VII 28, 30 = Orig. Constant.
imp. 6, 35 (Chr. m. I 11) Marian. Scot. III 350* (callocerus) h) 17 liueris *L* 18 antoniū +
monachum *M s. 218*<sup>e</sup> *Prosp. 1041 (Chr. m. I 451) (i. J. 336) chron. Gall. a. 511 (Chr. m. I 643, 473)*
(a. XXVIII) *Marian. Scot. III 350* i) 19 dalmaticus *B* 20 appel *L  Prosp. 1043 (Chr.
m. I 451) (i. J. 337) Oros. VII 28, 30 Marian. Scot. III 351* k) 21 pater *Hss.* Patera *Vall. vgl.
Hier. ep. 120 praef. 2 (472, 17 Hilberg) Auson. prof. 5 (58 Schenkl.)* (Attius Patera Pater) *15, 9
(65 Schkl.)* gloriosissim<sub>1</sub> (doc. ⟨<sup>Lücke</sup>⟩ *L  Marian. Scot. III 351* (pater) l) 22 nazari *L* rethoris
*L M N* rhetores *B* filia—patri ⟨<sup>Lücke</sup>⟩ *L* filia eumomius (a. Hd. verb. ei non minus) *M  Schoene Weltchronik 175* patricā equatur (<sup>o</sup>a. Hd.) *M* coequatur *L s. 231*<sup>e</sup> *Prosp. 1044 (Chr. m. I 452)
(i. J. 337) Marian. Scot. III 351* m) 23 tiuerianus *L* uir—regit ⟨<sup>Lücke</sup>⟩ *L  Marian. Scot.
III 351* n) 25 eustatius *M* eustat.—hieros. ⟨<sup>Lücke</sup>⟩ *L*, praesbiter *B P* presbiter *M* preșbyter *N*
26 hierusolimis *B* ierosolymis *P* *Prosp. 1045 (Chr. m. I 452) (i. J. 337) Marian. Scot. III 351*

Romanorum

martyrium constructum est•

CCLXXVIIII·Olvmp·
337 p. Chr.　　　XXXI　　　*a* Constantinus extremo uitae suae tempore ab Eusebio Nicomedensi episcopo bapti-
zatus in Arrianum dogma declinat. A　　　　　　　5
quo usque in praesens tempus ecclesiarum rapinae et totius orbis est secuta discordia•
*b* Constantinus cum bellum pararet in Persas in Acyrone uilla publica iuxta Nicomediam moritur anno aetatis ·LXVI·. Post quem　　　10
tres liberi eius ex Caesaribus Augusti
appellantur•

Romanorum ·XXXV· regnauit Constantinus.
Constantius et Constans
　　　　　　ann ·XXIIII· mens ·V· diebus ·XIII·　　　15
338　　　　I　　　*c* Ablabius praefectus praetorio et multo nobilium occisi•
*d* Sapor rex Persarum Mesopotamia uastata
duobus ferme mensibus Nisibin obsedit•
*e* Dalmatius Caesar, quem patruus Constan-　　20
tinus consortem regni filiis dereliquerat,
factione Constantii patruelis et tumultu
militari interimitur•
*f* Iacobus Nisibenus episcopus agnoscitur. Ad cuius
preces saepe urbs discrimine liberata est•　　　25
339　　　II　　　*g* Ex hoc loco impietas Arriana Constantii regis

　　*a* ad CCLXXVIIII Ol. *L*, num. XXXI om. *A P N*　　　*b* ut *a A P N*　　　*d* ad II *L*　　　*c* ad II *L*
*f* ad II *L*

a) 3 extremo (o *aus* u) *A*　tempore ⟨*L*　　4 nicomediensi *M*　epo P　　5 arryanum *L* arrianorum *A*　dogmate *A* docma *L* domma *B* docmatē (tē *durchstrich*.) *N*　　6 praesenti *O* presens *L*
praesen³ *P N*　eclesiarū *A*　　*Prosp. 1046 (Chr. m. I 452) (i. J. 337) chron. Gall. a. 511 (Chr. m.
I 643, 474) Isidor. iun. 334 (Chr. m. II 466) Marian. Scot. III 352*　　b) 9 aecyrone *L* cyrone *B*
agirone *M*　　11 III *LPN* liueri *L* cesarib: *L* augus, pi *A*　　12 appellatur *verb. A　Prosp.
1048 (Chr.m. I 452) (i. J. 338) Cassiodor. 1069 (Chr. m. II 151) lat. imp. (Chr. m. III 422, 9)
Oros. VII 28, 31 Marian. Scot. III 352*

Rom. 13 regñ *L*　　14 et constantius *A* constantius ⟨*N* (a. *Rd.* A꜏ regnauit c̄stantius cũ
fratrib:)　15 añ *OB* meñ *L* m̄ *P* mensib· *ANB*　dies *L* diebus *M　Prosp. 1049 (Chr. m. I 452)*
(dieb. XII) *chr. Gall. a. 511 (Chr. m. I 643, 475/6)* (a. XXIIII m. V [d. -⟨]) *Cassiodor. 1069 (Chr.
m. II 151)* (d. XXIII) *Ps.-Isidor. 9 (Chr. m. II 382)* (d.-⟨) *Isidor. iun. 335 (Chr. m. II 466)* (m.-d.-⟨)
*Ps.-Isidor. attr. Aug. c. 335 (Chr. m. II 501) Bed. 426 (Chr. m. III 296) exp. temp. Hil. (Chr. m.
III 417, 19)* (d.-⟨) *Oros. VII 29, 1* (m.-d.-⟨) *Marian. Scot. III 352* (a. XXVII [m.-d.-⟨])
c) 16 abladius *A* ablauius *L*　praefecto praeto (o — o *durchstrich*.) us praetorio *O*　multum *verb. L*
nouilium *L*　Marian. Scot. III 353　　d) 18 mesopotamiam *OAB*　　19 opsedit (p *verb.* b) *M*
Marian. Scot. III 353　　e) 20 cesar *L*　quae *L*　　21 filiis suis *L* filii³ suis (³a. *Hd.*) *M*　dere-
liq.ʳᵃᵗ *(a. Hd.*ʳᵃᵗ*) O* derelinquerat *P*　　22 constantini *M　Prosp. 1051 (Chr. m. I 452) (i. J. 339)
Oros. VII 29, 1 (505, 12) Marian. Scot. III 353*　　f) 24 nisibaenus *P* nisibenus (e *verb.* i) *M*
eps̄ *LBP*　　25 praeces *AM B verb. N* p̄ces,p̄ces *L*　saepae *A* epe *L*　lib. est ⟨*Lücke*⟩ *L　Prosp.
1052 (Chr. m. I 452) (i. J. 339) Bed. 427 (Chr. m. III 296) Marian. Scot. III 353*　　g) von regis
ab, am *Rd. beschnitten S*　　26 ex—constantii ⟨*Lücke*⟩ *L* inpietas *BM*

Romanorum

fulta praesidio exiliis carceribus et uari-
is adflictionum modis primum Athanasium,
deinde omnes non suae partis episcopos per-
secuta est•

**5**          **III**          *ᵃ* Constantinus bellum fratri inferens          340 p. Chr.
iuxta Aquileiam Alsae occiditur•

**CCLXXX · Olymp ·**
         **IIII**          *ᵇ* Uario euentu aduersum Francos a Con-          341
stante pugnatur•

**10**                          *ᶜ* Multae Orientis urbes terrae motu horri-
bili consederunt•
*ᵈ* Audeus in Syria Coele clarus habetur. A
quo haeresis Audiana•

         **V**          *ᵉ* Franci a Constante perdomiti et pax cum          342
**15**                          eis facta•
*ᶠ* Hermogenes magister militiae Constantinopoli tractus a populo ob episcopum Pau-
lum, quem regis imperio et Arrianorum
factione pellebat•

**20**                          *ᵍ* Antiochiae dominicum aureum dedicatur•
*ʰ* Macedonius artis plumariae in locum Pau-
li ab Arrianis episcopus subrogatur, a
quo nunc haeresis Macedoniana•
*ⁱ* Paulus crudelitate praefecti Philippi — nam
**25**                          fautor Macedonii partium erat — et Arrianorum insidiis strangulatur•

---

exstat S     *ᵃ* ad II M     *ᵇ* ad CCLXXX Ol. L     *ᶜ* ut *ᵇ* L     *ᵈ* ut *ᵇ* L     *ᵉ* ut *ᵇ* L
*ᶠ* ut *ᵇ* L     *ᵍ* ut *ᵇ* L     *ʰ* ut *ᵇ* L     *ⁱ* ut *ᵇ* L, ad VI B

1 fuit a L   exilii M verb. P   carceri$_t$ , et S     2 afflictionum LMPN   primu$_t$ ,nasium S
anthanasium M     3 omnis L oms PM   partes B par$_t$ ,copos S   episcopus AL epõe P   Prosp.
1054 (Chr. m. I 452) (i. J. 340)   Isidor. iun. 336 (Chr. m. II 466)   Bed. 428 (Chr. m. III 296)   Sulp.
Sev. chron. II 36, 4   Oros. VII 29, 3/4   Marian. Scot. III 354     a) Rd. abgeschnitten S     5 fratrii
ferens L     6 aquiieiam B   Prosp. 1056 (Chr. m. I 452) (i. J. 341)   chron. Gall. a. 511 (Chr. m.
I 644, 477) (a. IIII) Cassiodor. 1073 (Chr. m. II 151) Oros. VII 29, 5 Marian. Scot. III 355
b) wie *ᵃ*) S     8 ualerio Δ   aduersus M s. *ᵉ*)   Chron. Gall. a. 511 (Chr. m. I 644, 478) (a. V) Marian.
Scot. III 355     c) wie *ᵃ* S)     10 multe L   orientis B   templum (durchstrichen) urbaes L
orribili L h$_t$ ,bili S     11 considerunt A consede $\overline{r}$ P con$^{cl}$sederunt $^{(cl}$ a. Hd.) M   Oros. VII 29, 5
Marian. Scot. III 355     d) wie *ᵃ*) S     12 audaeus O   siria PM   clarũ L     13 eresis L
heresis BMP   Prosp. 1058 (Chr. m. I 453) (i. J. 342) Marian. Scot. III 356     e) wie *ᵃ*) S
14/5 cu$_t$ ,eis S s. *ᵇ*)   Cassiodor. 1076 (Chr. m. II 151) Marian. Scot. III 357     f) wie *ᵃ*) S
16 hemogenes A   militaae verb. S miliciae B   magiter verb. M   constantinopoli m L a. Hd. übergeschrieb. O     17 ep$\overline{m}$ P ep$_t$ ,copum S   quaem L     19 factionem L   bellebat M   Prosp. 1061
(Chr. m. I 453) (i. J. 343) Marian. Scot. III 357     g) wie *ᵃ*) S     20 antiocae L   aurem L
dedicat$_t$ S s. 231$^t$ Marian. Scot. III 357     h) wie *ᵃ*) S     21 artes B   art. plum.] statt
ποικιλοτέχνης Scal.     21/2 locum$_t$ ,ab S   pauli $\langle$ᴸ$^ückts)}$ L     22 episcopos B ep$\overline{s}$ P     22/3 sub-
rog. — quo $\langle$ᴸ$^{ückts)}$ L     23 quo$_t$ ,haeresis S   heresis BMP eresim L   macedonior$_t$,$^{(ᴸückts)}$ L
macedonia a. Hd. verb. M s. 241$^h$   Prosp. 1062 (Chr. m. I 453) (i. J. 343) Isidor. iun. 339 (Chr. m.
II 467) Marian. Scot. III 358     i) wie *ᵃ*) S     24 crudilitate A credelitate verb. P   praef. —
26 strang. $\langle$ᴸ$^{ückts)}$ L   filippi SAPB phylippi N     24/5 nam$_t$ ,macedonii S     25 macedoni A et]
ab A     26 insidiis] $_t$is S transgulatur B   Prosp. 1064 (Chr. m. I 453) (i. J. 343) Marian. Scot. III 358

21 Hieronymus

236                                                    (318 F)

Romanorum

348 p. Chr.      VI        ᵃ Maximinus Treuerorum episcopus cla-
                            rus habetur. A quo Athanasius Alexandri-
                            ae episcopus, cum a Constantio quaereretur
344 ĪICCCLX   VII          ad poenam, honorifice susceptus est•
                            ᵇ Sapor Persarum rex X̃P̃ianos persequitur•          5
                            ᶜ Neocaesaria in Ponto subuersa excepta
                            ecclesia et episcopo ceterisque, qui ibi-
                            dem reperti sunt•
              CCLXXXI·Olymp·
345           VIII          ᵈ Titianus uir eloquens praefecturam prae-         10
                            torio aput Gallias administrat•
346           VIIII         ᵉ Athanasius ad Constantis litteras Ale-
                            xandriam regreditur•
                            ᶠ Dyrrachium terrae motu conruit et tri-
                            bus diebus ac noctibus Roma nutauit plu-           15
                            rimaeque Campaniae urbes uexatae•
                            ᵍ Magnis rei publicae expensis in Seleucia Syriae
                            portus effectus•
                            ʰ Rursum Sapor tribus mensibus obsidet Nisibin•
347           X             ⁱ Eusebius Emisenus Arrianae signifer facti-       20
                            onis multa et uaria conscribit•
                            ᵏ Solis facta defectio•                            —
348           XI            ˡ Bellum Persicum nocturnum aput Singaram,
                            in quo haut dubiam uictoriam militum stolidita-
                            te perdidimus. Neque uero ullum Constantio ex      25
                            VIIII· grauissimis proeliis contra Persas bellum fuit ⟨grauius⟩.

exstat S       ᵃ ad VII B       ᵈ ad CCLXXXI Ol. L, num. VIII et VIIII om. B       ᵉ incert. S,
num. VIIII om. A B, ad VIII P N       ᶠ ut ᵉ S A B       ᵍ ut ᵉ S A B       ʰ ut ᵉ S B post ⁱ in fin. pag. A
ⁱ ut ᵉ S, om.in lac. L, ad VIIII P, supra X B       ᵏ ut ᵉ S, ut ⁱ L B P       ˡ ut ᵉ S, ut ⁱ L, ad X A P B

a) Rd. mit Zahlen abgeschnitten S     1 triuerorum O treuirorum B reuirorum L treberorum SN
(a. Rd. Λ? triuirorū) a. Hd. verb. P episcopus verb. S ep̄s LPN     2 hab L⟨O athasius L atanasius P     3 epis L ep̄s PN     4 penam L honorificae O dahinter: in cuius gloriosum recessum
signum tale uisum ē, ut non solum xp̄ianis sed & omnib; iudaeis & gentilibus apud treueris con-
stitutis caelum apertum multis horis uideretur M     Prosp. 1066 (Chr. m. I 453) (i. J. 344) Bed. 429
(Chr. m. III 296) Marian. Scot. III 359       b) wie ᵃ) S     5 rex persarum ～ A verb. N
Prosp. 1068 (Chr. m. I 453) (i. J. 345) Marian. Scot. III 359       c) wie ᵃ) S     6 neocesaria L
7 ecclesiae M ecclaesia verb. N episō L ep̄ō P     8 repti A     Marian. Scot. III 359       d) wie ᵃ) S
10 tatianus M   pra&oro a. Hd. verb. M     11 apud O M PN     Marian. Scot. III 360       e) wie ᵃ) S
12 atanasius P constanti⁸ O litteras a͜͜athenasius (scheint getilgt) alexandriam L     13 regeditur
verb. S Hier. d. vir. ill. 87     Prosp. 1070 (Chr. m. I 453) (i. J. 345) Marian. Scot. III 360
f) wie ᵃ) S     14 dyraccium O dyrracium L dyrratium B terre O M corruit O M PN     15 hac L
romo a. Hd. verb. M natauit A B verb. SN notauit a. Hd. verb. M nutuit L et plurimeq: L
16 campanie LN   Marian. Scot. III 361       g) wie ᵃ) S     17 rei publicae A rei post L rebus
p. PN verb. S     18 porticus B effectus est B Cassiodor. 1081 (Chr. m. II 151) Marian. Scot.
III 362       h) wie ᵃ) S     19 rursus N obsede A nisibin ⟨ᴸᵘᶜᵏᵉ⟩ L s. 234ᶠ Marian. Scot.
III 362       i) wie ᵃ) S ⟨ᴸᵘᶜᵏᵉ⟩ L     20 epemesenus O episē emesenus M emesenus B hemisenus
AN hemiseu̅s S     21 et] e a. Hd. verb. S Hier. d. vir. ill. 91 Marian. Scot. III 362       k) wie ᵃ)
S ⟨ᴸᵘᶜᵏᵉ⟩ L     22 dahinter: XVII kal̄ aū̄g. a. Hd. M Cassiodor. 1083 (Chr. m. II 151) Marian. Scot.
III 363       l) wie ᵃ) S (bis fuit)     23 bellum — 237, 1 nisibis ⟨ᴸᵘᶜᵏᵉ⟩ L     23 apud O M PN
signarā M     23/4 singa͜ⱼm in S     24 haud P M aut verb. haud N millitum B stodilitate B
militum͜ⱼate S     25/6 constan͜ⱼ III S     26 nouem O M A praeliis P M procellis S persas ⟨A
übergeschrieb. S hinter fuit     h) a. unteren Rd. + A ⟨grauius⟩ dett.

Romanorum

    nam ut alia omittam, Nisibis obsessa, Bi-
    zabde et Amida captae sunt.
    *a* XL· Maximus post Macarium Hierosolymarum epi-
    scopus moritur. Post quem ecclesiam Arriani inua-
5     dunt, id est Cyrillus, Eutychius, rursum Cyrillus, [h]I-
    renaeus, tertio Cyrillus, Hilarius, quarto Cyrillus.
    Quorum Cyrillus, cum a Maximo fuisset presby-
    ter ordinatus et post mortem eius ita ei ab Acacio
    episcopo Caesariensi et ceteris Arrianis episcopa-
10     tus promitteretur, si ordinationem Maximi repudi-
    asset, diaconus in ecclesia ministrauit. Ob quam im-
    pietatem sacerdotii mercede pensatus Heraclium,
    quem moriens Maximus in suum locum substitue-
    rat, uaria fraude sollicitans de episcopo in pres-
15     byterum regradauit.

CCLXXXII·Olymp·
  XII     *b* Romanae ecclesiae ·XXXIIII· ordinatur episcopus Li-     349 p. Chr.
    berius. Quo in exilium ob fidem truso omnes cle-
    rici iurauerunt, ut nullum alium susciperent. Ue-
20     rum cum Felix ab Arrianis fuisset in sacerdoti-
    um substitutus, plurimi, peierauerunt et post an-
    num cum Felice eiecti sunt, quia Liberius taedio
    uictus exilii et in haeretica prauitate subscri-
    bens Romam quasi uictor intrauerat.
25   XIII     *c* Magnentio aput Augustodunum arripiente im-     350
    perium Constans haut longe ab Hispania

    *b* ad XI *PN*, ad CCLXXXII Ol. *AL*     *c* ut *b* *L*, ad XII *A*

    1 aliud *M* aliam *A*   nisibi *APNL*   bizande *A* abizabde *B* bezabde *M* bizalde *P*     2 amidae *L*
et]ct *A*  *Oros. VII 29, 6 Marian. Scot. III 363*     a) 3 XL *verb.* XI *P*   maximianus *L*  ma-
charium *BMP* marcum *L*  hierusolymarum *B* hyerosolymarum (*ᵃ. Hd.*) *M* ierosolimarũ *P* epis *A*
eps *P*     5 cirillus *P* euthytius *M* eutichius *PN* et euticius *L* quirillus *B* hirenius *OAPN* hire-
neus *BM* hy••••••reneus *L*   6 tertius *L* quirillus *B* ilarius *L* quirillus *B*   7 quirillus *LB*
fuisse et *L*  praesbyter *BN* prbr *L* presbiter *PM*   8 et ⟨*A* ei] et *B* acaico *M* accacio *P*
9 epõ *APN*  casariensi *A* cesariense *L* `ca&eris *M* epstus *A*   10 maxim *verb.* *A*   11 mini-
strabit *L* qua inpietate *B*   12 sacerdocii *M*   13 quaem *L* substetuerat *A* subsistẹrat *N*
14 epõ *P* epm̃ *L* praesbyterum *BN* praesbiterũ *P*   15 redauit *verb.* *O* regradabit *L* Hier. d.
vir. ill. 112  Prosp. 1074 (Chr. m. I 454) (i. J. 348) Marian. Scot. III 363   b) 17 ect *L* or-
dinatus *L* eps *PN* est *L* liuerius *L*   18 ob] of *L* omnes ⟨*Lücke*⟩ *L*   19 iuraberunt *L* iurauer̃ *P*
20 arr.—in ⟨*Lücke*⟩ *L*  sacerdotio *verb.* *A*   21 sub₍ (stit. — 24 intr. ⟨*Lücke*⟩ *L*  periurauerunt *BM*
peiærauerunt *N* peierauer̃ *P*   22 quia] quoad *B* tedio *O*   23 et ⟨*M* heretica *BP* hereti-
cam *M* prauitatem *M* suscribens *AB* susscribens *a. Hd. verb.* *M* susscr- (sus *aus* sub) *N*
24 qua *verb.* *A* s. 240ˢ Hier. d. vir. ill. 97  Prosp. 1076 (Chr. m. I 454) (i. J. 349) chron. Gall.
a. 511 (Chr. m. I 644, 480) Sulp. Sev. chron. II 39, 7/8 Marian. Scot. III 366, 371   c) 25 magn.—
arrip. ⟨*Lücke*⟩ *L*  apud *OMPN* augustudunum *B* augustodonum *P*   26 aut *L* haud *PN* ᵇaud
(ᵇ *a. Hd.*) *M* spania *L*

21*

**238**

Romanorum

in castro, cui Helenae nomen est, interficitur anno aetatis ·XXX·, quam ob rem turbata re publica Uetranio Mursae, Nepotianus Romae imperatores facti·

*a* Romae populus aduersum Magnentiacos
rebellans ab Heraclida senatore proditur·   5

*b* Nepotiani caput pilo per urbem circum-
latum multaeque proscriptiones nobilium et caedes factae·

351 p. Chr.  XIIII  *c* Uetranioni aput Naissum a Constantio   10
regium insigne detractum

*d* Magnentius Mursae uictus, in quo proelio Romanae uires conciderunt·

*e* Gallus, Constantii patruelis, Caesar factus·

352  XV  *f* Gallus Iudaeos, qui interfectis per noc-   15
tem militibus arma ad rebellandum
inuaserant, oppressit caesis multis hominum milibus usque ad innoxiam aeta-
tem et ciuitates eorum Diocaesariam,
Tiberiadem et Diospolim plurimaque op-   20
pida igni tradidit·

*g* Nonnulli nobilium Antiochiae a Gallo
interfecti·

353  CCLXXXIII·Olymp·
XVI  *i* Iobelaeus
secundum
Hebraeos  *h* Magnentius Lugduni in Palatio propria se   25
manu interficit et Decentius frater eius,

---

*a* ad CCLXXXII Ol. *L*   *b* ut *a* *L*   *c* ad XIII *APN*   *f* ad XIIII *PN*, num. XV om. *B*
*g* om. *M* ut *f* *B*   *i* om. *ALM* ante et post XVI *B*

1 helene *L*   2/3 turbatam remp̄ *O* turbatur p̄ *A* turbata re ·p̄· *M* turbata rp̄ *N*   3 uete-
ranio *M*   murse verb. *O* myrsae *M*   naepontianus verb. *O* nepotiamus *A*   4 impetores verb. *P*
imperatoris *L*   Prosp. 1078 (Chr. m. I 454) (i. J. 350) chron. Gall. a. 511 (Chr. m. 644, 481) (a. XIII)
Cassiodor. 1086 (Chr. m. II 151) (i. J. 350) lat. imp. (Chr. m. III 422, 11) Oros. VII 29, 7|9. 11.
Marian. Scot. III 364   a) 5 aduersus *LBM*   magnentia eos *BM* (a. Hd. ⁿ über eos +)
6 reuellans *L*   ad verb. *O*   heraclidae (m) *O* eraclida *LP* hericlada *M*   Marian. Scot. III 364
b) 8 multeq; *L*   proscribtiones *OB* verb. *N* nouilium *L*   9 cedes *L*   facti verb. *O*   Prosp. 1080
(Chr. m. I 454) (i. J. 351) Marian. Scot. III 364   c) 10 uetranio *L*   apud *OMPN*   naisum
*APNO* (darüber ˢⁱ, aber *i* durchstrichen) constatio *M*   11 regnū (verb. ?) *M*   Prosp. 1081 (Chr.
m. I 454) (i. J. 351) Oros. VII 29, 10 Marian. Scot. III 365   d) 12 myrsae *M*   praelio *LMP*
13 romane *L*   Prosp. 1082 (Chr. m. I 454) (i. J. 351) Oros. VII 29, 12 Marian. Scot. III 365
e) 14 gallius *M*   constii *A* constanti *M*   Prosp. 1084 (Chr. m. I 454) (i. J. 352) chron. Gall. a. 511
(Chr. m. I 644, 482) (a. XV) Oros. VII 29, 14 Marian. Scot. III 365   f) 15 gallos *L* gallius
(i ausradiert?) *M* iudaeis *L*   16 reuellandum *L*   17 inuaserat *L* dahinter milit.—reuell. wiederholt, aber durchstrich. *L* oppraessit *A*   18 innoxiū verb. *O*   19 et ⟨*M* cibitates *L* ciuitatem
*OA* ciuitates eorum (s e aus n) *P* diocesaream *L*   20 plulirimaq; (li durchstrich.) *L*   Marian.
Scot. III 367   g) ⟨*M*   22 nonualli *A* nouilium *L* anthiocie *L⟨O*   23 interfecti sunt *L*
Marian. Scot. III 367   h) 25 magnentius — 26 eius ⟨ᴸᵘᶜᵏˢ⟩ *L*   lugdunii *A*   26 interfecit *M*
et ⟨*B*   i) ⟨*ALM* doppelt *B*   25 iobeleos *O* iobeleus *PN* iubelaeus und iobelaeus *B*
26 hebreos *P* s. 227¹

Romanorum

quem ad tuendas Gallias Caesarem miserat,
aput Senonas laqueo uitam explet•
ᵃ Gennadius forensis orator Romae insignis
habetur•

5  ᵇ Mineruius Burdigalensis rhetor Romae fiorentissime docet•

ĪĪCCC   XVII   ᶜ Gallus Caesar sollicitatus a Constantio pa-    354 p. Chr.
LXX          trueli, cui in suspicionem ob egregiam indo-
lem uenerat, Histriae occiditur•

10  ᵈ Siluanus in Gallia res nouas molitus
XXVIII· die extinctus est•
ᵉ Uictorinus rhetor et Donatus grammaticus
praeceptor meus Romae insignes habentur.
E quibus Uictorinus etiam statuam in foro

15  Traiani meruit•
ᶠ Paulinus et Rodanius Galliarum episcopi
in exilium ob fidem trusi•

XVIII   ᵍ Alcimus et Delfidius rhetores in Aquitani-    355
ca fiorentissime docent•

20  ʰ Donatus, a quo supra Donatianos in Africa
dici memorauimus, Carthagine pellitur.
Quidam sectatores eius etiam montenses
uocant eo, quod ecclesiam Romae primum
in monte habere coeperint•

25  ⁱ Eusebius Uercellensis episcopus et Lucifer ac
Dionysius Caralitanae et Mediolanensis ecclesiae

---

ᵇ om. *M*   ᶜ ad XVI *B*   ᵍ ad XVII *A L B*

1 cesarem *L P*   2 apud *O M P N*   senonas (o *aus* e) *N*   laquaeo *L*   explet (t *aus* x) *L*   *Prosp.
1088 (Chr. m. I 455) (i. J. 355) Oros. VII 29, 13 Marian. Scot. III 368*   a) 3 genadius *L*
foronensis *A* foroensis *P* forensis (a. *Rd.* Λł foroiuliensis) *N*   orator forensis ~ *L*   insignes *B*   ins
hab.] romae fiorentissime docet *M   Marian. Scot. III 368*   b) ⟨*M*   5 burdisalensis *A* bar-
dagalensis *L* burdigallensis *P N*   retor *L*   rome *L   Marian. Scot. III 368*   c) 7 cesar *P*
patruele *M*   8 cuius *N*   ob *(durchstrich.)* in *O*   suspitione *M*   aegregiam *O*   indolorém *L*
9 ueneras *L*   historiae *O* storiae *L*   *Prosp. 1089 (Chr. m. I 455) (i. J. 355) chron. Gall. a. 511 (Chr.
m. I 644, 483) Oros. VII 29, 14 Marian. Scot. III 369*   d) 10 in ⟨*B*   gallias *A* galia *N*
11 XXVIIII *B*   dies *L*   *Oros. VII 29, 41 Marian. Scot. III 369*   e) 12 retor *L* rethor *M* grama-
ticus *A*   13 insignis *L*   14 etiam *(Lücke)* statuam *L*   15 traiano *P* troiani *L   Hier. d.
vir. ill. 101 apol. adv. Rufin. I 16 comm. in Gal. praef.   Aug. conf. VIII 2, 3; 5, 10 Cassiodor. 1092
(Chr. m. II 152) Isidor. iun. 340 (Chr. m. II 467) Marian. Scot. III 369*   f) 16 throdanius *B*
episi *L* epi *P N   s. 241ᵇ   Prosp. 1090 (Chr. m. I 455) (i. J. 355) Sulp. Sev. chron. II 39, 7. 3 Marian.
Scot. III 369*   g) 18 alchimus *O A P N B*   delfidus *L*   retores *O* rethores *L* rethoreˢ *M*   aquitani•ca
(c *aus* a) *B* aquitania *M* aquitaniã (a. *Rd.* ·Λ·Λ· ita) *s. Th. l. L. II 380, 22   Hier. epist. CXX praef. 2
Marian. Scot. III 370*   h) 20 ⟨ᴸᵘᶜᵏᵉ⟩ *L*   supra *s. 232ᵇ* affrica *P M*   21 degi *M*   23 uocant (a. *Rd.* Λł uocant) *N*   24 eccłam *M*   romãe *M   Hier. d. vir. ill. 93 ep. 37, 1   Marian.
Scot. III 370*   i) 25 eusebius — mediol. ⟨ᴸᵘᶜᵏᵉ⟩ *L*   ep̄s *A P N*   26 dyonisius *A* dionisyus *M*
dynisius *verb. N*   cara(a *durch Korr.*)litae (e *durchstrich.*)nae *A* arae (a *durchstrich.*) latanę *M*

Romanorum

episcopi, Pancratius quoque Romanus presbyter et Hilarius diaconus distantibus inter se
ab Arrianis et Constantio damnantur exiliis•
<sup>a</sup> Iulianus frater Galli Mediolanii Caesar ap-
pellatur•                                                           5

356 p. Chr.          XVIIII          <sup>b</sup> Antonius Monachus ·CV· aetatis anno in he-
remo moritur solitus multis ad se ueni-
entibus de Paulo quodam Thebaeo mirae be-
atitudinis uiro referre, cuius nos exitum
breui libello explicuimus•                                          10
<sup>c</sup> Hilarius episcopus Pictauensis factione Satur-
nini Arelatensis episcopi reliquorumque, qui
cum eo erant, Arrianorum ante triennium in Frygiam pulsus libros de nostra religione componit•
<sup>d</sup> Reliquiae apostoli Timothei Constantino-                       15
polim inuectae•
<sup>e</sup> Sarmata, Amatas et Macarius discipuli An-
tonii insignes habentur•
<sup>f</sup> Liberius episcopus Romanus in exilium mittitur•
<sup>g</sup> Magnae Alamannorum copiae aput Argen-                          20
toratum oppidum Galliarum a Caesare
Iuliano oppressae•

CCLXXXIIII·Olymp·
XX.          <sup>h</sup> Saraceni in Monasterium beati Antonii in-
357                           ruentes Sarmatam interficiunt•                           25
<sup>i</sup> Constantio Romam ingresso ossa Andreae

---

<sup>a</sup> ad XVIIII A     <sup>g</sup> in lac. om. L     <sup>h</sup> in lac. om. L

1 ep̄s L epi PN   paneratius B   quoque ⟨L prb A prbr L praesbiter B presbiter P praesby‚byter
(by durchstrichen) N     2 hylarius L hilarus OBPN     3 exibis A s. 242ᵉ 245ᵏ Hier. d. vir. ill.
95. 96. 100   Prosp. 1091 (Chr. m. I 455) (i. J. 355) chron. Gall. a. 511 (Chr. m. I 644, 485) Sulp.
Sev. chr. II 39, 4 Marian. Scot. III 370     a) 4 mediolani LM verb. N casar L   Prosp. 1093
(Chr. m. I 455) (i. J. 356) chron. Gall. a. 511 (Chr. m. I 644, 483) (a. XVIII) Oros. VII 29, 15 Marian.
Scot. III 370     b) 6 antoninus verb. M   anno aetatis ∼APN   aet. ⟨L ann̄ L   here a. Hd.
verb. P     7 solius verb. B     8 quodam] quoq; L thebeo APB teueo L mire L ferrae L
referre (a. Rd. prae) M     9 exitu B   liuello L   Hier. vit. Paul. 7 ff. s. 218ᵉ 233ʰ Hier. d. vir. ill.
88. 135   Prosp. 1095 (Chr. m. I 455) (i. J. 357) (V⟨⟩ Isidor. iun. 341 (Chr. m. II 467) Bed. 430 (Chr.
m. III 296) Marian. Scot. III 371     c) 11 epis L ep̄s PN   pictauiensis L     12 araelatensis L
ep̄s L epi PN     13 trienium A trienniū (ū aus ei) P frigiam ALBM     14 nā L nrā M
conponit LB conposuit M s. 241ᵍ 245ᵉ Hier. d. vir. ill. 100   Prosp. 1096 (Chr. m. I 455) (i. J. 357)
chron. Gall. a. 511 (Chr. m. I 644, 486) Sulp. Sev. chr. II 42, 2 Marian. Scot. III 371     d) 15 reliquae
(a a. Hd. verb. j) M   apti PN   thimothei M   Prosp. 1097 (Chr. m. I 455) (i. J. 357) Bed. 431 (Chr.
m. III 296) Marian. Scot. III 371     e) 17 sarmatas M   amatas ⟨M   macharius LBP disti-
puli N antoni verb. A     18 insignis habetur L s. ᵇ) ʰ) Hier. vit. Paul. 1 Prosp. 1098 (Chr. m. I 455)
(i. J. 357) Marian. Scot. III 371     19 liuerius L ep̄s LPN   in übergeschrieb. O exilio L s. 237ᵇ
Prosp. 1099 (Chr. m. I 455) (i. J. 357) Sulp. Sev. chron. II 39, 7 Marian. Scot. III 371
g) ⟨Lücke⟩ L     20 alammannorum B apud OMPN argentoratoratū verb. A     21 cesare P
22 oppraessae B Cassiodor. 1095 (Chr. m. II 152) Oros. VII 29, 15 (508, 18) Marian. Scot. III 371
h) ⟨Lücke⟩ L     24 sarraceni N monasterii O inraentes A irruentes PN s. ᵉ) Marian. Scot.
III 372     i) 26 constant.-ossa ⟨Lücke⟩ L ossa ⟨A andraeae BA (? oder andraea) andrae L apti N

Romanorum

apostoli et Lucae euangelistae a Constan-
tinopolitanis miro fauore suscepta•

XXI  *a* Nicomedia terrae motu funditus euersa ui-　　　358 p. Chr.
cinis urbibus ex parte uexatis•
5  *b* Paulinus Treuirorum episcopus in Frygia
exulans moritur•
*c* Euanthius eruditissimus grammaticorum Constantinopoli diem obit, in cuius locum ex A-
frica Chrestus adducitur•

10 XXII  *d* Synhodus aput Ariminum et Seleuciam Isau-　　359
riae facta, in qua antiqua patrum fides
decem primum legatorum, dehinc omnium
proditione damnata est•
*e* Honoratus ex praefecto praetorio Galliarum
15  primus Constantinopoli praefectus urbis factus•
*f* Gratianus, qui nunc imperator est, nascitur•
*g* Hilarius cum aput Constantinopolim librum
pro se Constantio porrexisset, ad Gallias
redit•
20  *h* Macedonius Constantinopoli pellitur•
*i* Omnes paene toto orbe ecclesiae sub nomine pa-
cis et regis Arrianorum consortio polluuntur•

XXIII  *k* Constantinopoli ecclesiarum maxima dedicatur•　　360
*l* Meletius Sebastiae Armeniorum episcopus
25  ab Acacio et Georgio episcopis Arrianis
Antiochiam transfertur et post non

---

*b* ad XXII *B*　　*c* ad XXII *B*　　*h* in lac. om. *L*　　*i* in lac. om. *L*, ad XXIII *O* (sed num.
al. m. add.)　　*k* in lac. om. *L*

1 luce euangeliste *L*　euangelistae + reliquiae *A*　constanopolitanis *A*　susceptae *A*　*Hier. d.
vir. ill. 7 ex.　Prosp. 1101 (Chr. m. I 446) (i. J. 358)　Isidor. iun. 342 (Chr. m. II 467)　Bed. 432
(Chr. m. III 296)　Marian. Scot. III 372*　a) 3 terre *L*　*Marian. Scot. III 373*　b) 5 triuerorum *OAPN (a. Rd. Λł* triuiror;) triuirorum *L* treuirorum *B* treuerorum *M*　eps *LP* in ⟨*L* frigia
*APBM s. 239*ᶠ　*Prosp. 1102 (Chr. m. I 446) (i. J. 358)　Marian. Scot. III 373*　c) 7 euan-
tius *OLBM verb. A*　gramaticorum *A* constantinopolim *OLP* -lin *N*　8 obiit *OLMN* affrica *P*
9 chretus *L* charistus *B* charisius *Usener*　ad (as- *PN*) sumitur *APN*　*Marian. Scot. III 373*
d) 10 synodus *OBM* sinodus *LP* sinhodus *N s. 230,* 24　apud *OMPN* hissauriae *N*　13 damna-
tur *O*　*Prosp. 1104 (Chr. m. I 456) (i. J. 359)　Marian. Scot. III 374*　e) 14 prefecto *L*　pre-
torio *M*　15 constantinopolim *L*　urbi *OM*　*Cassiodor. 1099 (Chr. m. II 152)　Marian. Scot. III 374
P.-W. R.-E. VIII 2276, 6*　f) 16 imp *O* ranscitur *A*　*Prosp. 1106 (Chr. m. I 456) (i. J. 360)
Marian. Scot. III 374*　g) 17 cum apud *übergeschrieb. O*　apud *PNM*　libro *verb. M*
19 reddit *M s. 240*ᵉ *Hier. d. vir. ill. 100 adv. Lucifer. 19　Prosp. 1107 (Chr. m. I 456) (i. J. 360)
chron. Gall. a. 511 (Chr. m. I 644, 486)* (a. XXIII)　*Bed. 433 (Chr. m. III 297)　Sulp. Sev. chron. II 45, 3
Marian. Scot. III 374*　h) ⟨*Lücke*⟩ *L*　20 machedonius *M*　constantinopolim *O s. 235*ʰ
*Chron. Gall. a. 511 (Chr. m. I 644, 489)　Marian. Scot. III 374*　i) ⟨*Lücke*⟩ *L*　21 omne *A*
oms *P*　pene *M*　toto paene ~*P*　eclesiae *A*　22 constantio *A*　polluntur *O*　*Prosp. 1108 (Chr.
m. I 456) (i. J. 360)　Marian. Scot. III 374*　k) ⟨*Lücke*⟩ *L*　23 ecclesiā *A* ecclesia *PN*
(*a. Rd. Λł* ecclesiarū m.)　*Marian. Scot. III 375*　l) 24 melet. — *242, 1* temporis ⟨*L*　24 me-
lietus (*a. Rd. Λł* melitius) *N*　arminiorum *B*　eps *APN*　25 acatio *B* actio *M* acio verb. P (c a. Hd.
verb. t)* gergio *verb. N (a. Rd. Λł* gorgonio)　epŝ *P*　26 antiochia *B*　S. 242, 1 interuallos *L* inual-
lum *A*　prbros *L* praesbiteros *B* presbiteris (°*a. Hd.) M* presbiteros *P* presbyteros *N*　2 eodoxio *A*
antecessorē *L* antecesore verb. M*　suo + ppr ñm fidem *L*　3 suscepisse + et noluisset arriani epis com-
municare *L*　suscipisset *B*　4 causam + idcirco exilio damnatus est *L*　fide *AL　Marian. Scot. III 375*

        Romanorum

                        grande temporis interuallum, cum presby-
                        teros, qui ab Eudoxio antecessore suo deposi-
                        ti fuerant, suscepisset, exilii iustissimam
                        causam subita fidei mutatione delusit•
                        ᵃ Gallia per Hilarium Ariminensis perfidiae        5
                        dolos damnat•

CCLXXXV·Olymp·
361 p. Chr.      XXIII       ᵇ Constantius Mopsocrenis inter Ciliciam Cappa-
                        dociamque moritur anno aetatis ·XLV·•
                ·Romanorum ·XXXVI· regnauit Iulianus            10
                        ann ·I· mens. ·VIII·
362          I              ᶜ Iuliano ad idolorum cultum conuerso blanda
                        persecutio fuit inliciens magis quam inpel-
                        lens ad sacrificandum, in qua multi ex no-
                        stris uoluntate propria corruerunt•           15
                        ᵈ Georgio per seditionem populi incenso, qui in
                        locum Athanasii ab Arrianis fuerat ordinatus,
                        Athanasius Alexandriam reuertitur•
                        ᵉ Eusebius et Lucifer de exilio regrediuntur. E qui-
                        bus Lucifer adscitis duobus aliis confessoribus      20
                        Paulinum, Eustathii episcopi presbyterum, qui
                        se numquam haereticorum communione polluerat,
                        rat, in parte catholica Antiochiae episcopum facit•
363          II             ᶠ Prohaeresius sofista Atheniensis lege data, ne
                        XᴾPiani liberalium artium doctores essent,        25
                        cum sibi specialiter Iulianus concederet,

        ᵇ ad CCLXXXV Ol. L      ᶠ ad I P N
        a) 5 ilarium L  perfidie L   Prosp. 1109 (Chr. m. I 456) (i. J. 360) Sulp. Sev. chron. II 45, 5 Marian.
Scot. III 376    b) 8 constantius mopsocrenis ausradiert B  mopsucrenis L  ciliam O ciliciam + & L
capadociāq; N    9 annum L Hier. ep. LX 15, 2   Prosp. 1111 (Chr. m. I 456) (i. J. 361) chron. Gall.
a. 511 (Chr. m. I 644, 488) Cassiodor. 1102 (Chr. m. II 152) (a. aetat. XLVI) lat. imp. (Chr. m. III 422,
14) Marian. Scot. III 379 Oros. VII 29, 17 Iord. Rom. 303    Rom. 10 regnabit L  iulian. ⟨L   11 anno
AB aō O  uno A   mensib· AN B menses O m̄ L P   Prosp. 1112 (Chr. m. I 456) (ann. duob. m. VIII)
chron. Gall. a. 511 (Chr. m. I 644, 490) (ann. II m. VIII) Cassiodor. 1102 (Chr. m. II 152 (m.-⟨) Ps.-Isi-
dor. 9 (Chr. m. II 382) (m.-⟨) Isidor. iun. 343 (Chr. m. II 467) (a. II [m.-⟨]) Ps.-Isidor. altr. Aug. c. 343
(Chr. m. II 501) (a. VI m. VIII) Bed. 434 (Chr. m. III 297) (a. II m. VIII) exp. temp. Hil. (Chr. m. III
417, 20) (a. I m. IIII) lat. imp. (Chr. m. III 422) (a. II [m.-⟨]) lat. Malal. 25 (Chr. m. III 436, 33) (a. VII
[m.-⟨]) Marian. Scot. III 379 (a. II m. VIII) Oros. VII 30, 1 Iord. Rom. 304    c) 12 iulianum L  idolo-
lorum A  cultu L B  conuersum L    13 inligiens (ˡ ᵗ a. Hd.) M inlliciens (verb. ill-) N illiciens P impellens
O P inpellāˢ N    14 nīs L    15 conruerunt L B corrueŕ P  Prosp. 1113 (Chr. m. I 456) (i. J. 361)
Isidor. iun. 344 (Chr. m. II 467) Bed. 435 (Chr. m. III 297) Marian. Scot. III 380 Oros. VII 30, 2
Iord. Rom. 304    d) 16 per i. Ras. M  seducionem B    17 athanasi O athasii L atanasii P
athanasii + qui B  ordinā L  orditatus M    18 athanasius doppelt, verb. O  ath.—reuert. a. unteren
Rd. nachgetrag. M Hier. adv. Lucifer. 19  Prosp. 1115 (Chr. m. I 456) (i. J. 362) Marian. Scot. III 380
e) 19 egrediuntur O regreditur A  e quibus ⟨ᴸᵘᶜᵏᵉ⟩ L    21 paulinum ⟨ᴸᵘᶜᵏᵉ⟩ L  eustatii O M P
eusthatii B N  episcopū A epī L P N  presbyteri A prbm L praesbiterum B presbiterum P M presby-
terū N    22 nunquam N hereticorum Hss.  communione übergeschrieb. O communionē A    23 parte
⟨ᴸᵘᶜᵏᵉ⟩ L  anthiociae L  epīs L episcop. P epm̄ (i. Ras.) N  fuit A factum L  s. 239ᶦ 245ᵏ a. Rd. gor-
gonium dicit de germanicia et ( + et A) cymatium (cymaciū A) de gabala AN B Schoene Weltchronik
176 Hier. adv. Lucifer. 19 d. vir. ill. 95. 96   Prosp. 1116 (Chr. m. I 456) (i. J. 362) Marian. Scot.
III 380    f) 24 proheresio L preheresius Hss.  sophista P  athenienses B  lege — 26 concederet
⟨ᴸᵘᶜᵏᵉ⟩ L    25 liberali••um P  doctores doppelt, verb. P    26 peculiariter B  concideret verb. A

Romanorum
    ut X͞P͞ianus doceret, scholam sponte deseruit•
    <sup>a</sup> Aemilianus ob ararum subuersionem Dorosto-
    ri a uicario incenditur•
    <sup>b</sup> Ecclesia Antiochiae clausa, et grauissima im-
5    minentis persecutionis procella D͞i uolun-
    tate sopita est. Nam Iulianus in Persas pro-
    fectus nostrum post uictoriam dis sangui-
    nem uouerat. Ubi a quodam simulato perfuga
    ad deserta perductus, cum fame et siti apos-
10    statam perdidisset exercitum et inconsul-
    tius a suorum erraret agminibus, ab obuio
    forte hostium equite conto ilia perfossus
    interiit anno aetatis ·XXXII·. Post quem se-
    quenti die Iouianus ex primicerio domesti-
15    corum imperator factus est
   Romanorum ·XXXVII· regnauit Iouianus
        mens ·VIII·

I͞I͞C͞C͞C  I   <sup>c</sup> Iouianus rerum necessitate compulsus Nisi-   364 p. Chr.
L͞X͞X͞X  —   bin et magnam Mesopotamiae partem Sa-
20    pori Persarum regi tradidit•
    <sup>d</sup> Synodus Antiochiae a Melitio et suis facta,
    in qua homousio anomoeoque reiecto medium
    inter haec homoeousion Macedonianum dogma
    uindicauerunt•
25    <sup>e</sup> Iouianus cruditate siue odore prunarum,
    quas nimias adoleri iusserat, Dadastanae

1 xp͞ianos *LBM* xp͞ianus (*a. Rd.* Λ̣ ut xp͞ianos doceret) *N* non doceret *P* •doceret *N* scolam *LBP* deserbit *L* *Prosp. 1117 (Chr. m. I 457) (i. J. 362) Isidor. iun. 344ᵃ (Chr. m. II 467) Marian. Scot. III 381 Aug. d.c.d. XVIII 52 (355,25) conf. VIII 5 (10) Oros. VII 30,3*  a) 2 emillianus *L* emilianus *BMP* oratū *A* dorosthori *LB s. P.- W. R.- E. V 1863,22*  3 a uic. ⟨*Lücke*⟩ *L Martyrolog. Hieronym. XV Kal. Aug. Prosp. 1119 (Chr. m. I 457) (i. J. 363) Marian. Scot. III 381*  b) 4 ecclesiae *B* anthiociae *L* inminentis *OLM*  5 persecutione *L* dei *L* di *Hss.*  7 cum n͞m *L* dis *O* diis *M* ⟨*(Lücke)*⟩ *B* sangunē *A*  8 mouerat *A* a ⟨*A* perfugam *B verb. M*⟩  9 famᵉ *L* siti + idem apostata *L* apostata *P*  10 perdisset *O & übergeschrieb. A* inconsultus *verb. M*  11 a ⟨*B* acminebus (e *verb.* i)*L* obio *L*  12 quite *B verb. L* •equite (a) *M* ilia, ilia *L* perfossos *verb. M Hier. ep. LXX 3, 2 (704, 7)*
14 diei *M* iobianus *O* primocerio *A Hier. ep. LX 15, 2 Prosp. 1121 (Chr. m. I 457) (i. J. 364) Cassio-dor. 1104 (Chr. m. II 152) Isidor. iun. 345ᵃ (Chr. m. II 468) lat. imp. (Chr. m. III 422,18) Marian. Scot. III 381/2 Oros. VII 30, 4—6 Iord. Rom. 304/5 (trecesimo tertio)*  Rom. 16 regnabit *L* iobianus *OL*  17 m̄ *L* mensibus *BMPN* VIIII *M* octo *P Prosp. 1122 (Chr. m. I 457) chron. Gall. a. 511 (Chr. m. I 644, 491) (m. VII) Cassiodor. 1104 (Chr. m. II 152) (i. J. 363) Ps.-Isidor. 9 (Chr. m. II 382) Isi-dor. iun. 346 (Chr. m. II 468 (a. I [m. VIII ]) Ps.-Isidor. attr. Aug. c. 346 (Chr. m. II 501) (m. VII) Bed. 437 (Chr. m. III 297) exp. temp. Hil. (Chr. m. III 417,21) lat. imp. (Chr. m. III 422,19) (m. VII) lat. Malal. (Chr. m. III 436, 34) (m. VII et semis) Marian. Scot. III 382 Oros. VII 31, 1.3 (511, 3. 14) Iord. Rom. 306*  c) 18 iobianus *O* conpulsus *LB verb. MN* nisibi *AB*  19 magnam per ⟨*(Lücke)*⟩po-tamiā & parte *L* sopori *A*  20 regi ⟨*O* tradidi.dit *N Hier. d. loc. Hebr. (Eus. III 1) 5,24 Klostermann Chron. Gall. a. 511 (Chr. m. I 644, 492) Marian. Scot. III 383 Oros. VII 31, 1/2 Iord. Rom. 306*
d) 21 synhodus *N* sinodus *P* antiociam *L* a — 24 uind. ⟨*(Lücke)*⟩ *L* miletio *O* melitio *Hss. s. 232, 14 241, 24*  22 omousium *O* omousio *AB* omousion *PN* anhmoeoq; (*a. Hd.* ᵘˢⁱᵒ) *M* omo eoq (*a. Hd.* dauor an) *P* homoeoque *N* relecto *B*  23 homousion *M* omo euusion *P* omoeousion *OANB* doma *A* machedonianū *M*  24 uindi•cauer̄ *P Prosp. 1124 (Chr. m. I 457) (i. J. 365) (melitio CA me-litic M meletio, ₅V) chron. Gall. a. 511 (Chr. m. I 644, 493) Bed. 438 (Chr. m. III 297) (meletio M¹ R²) Marian. Scot. III 383*  e) 25 iouian. — dadast. ⟨*(Lücke)*⟩ *L* iobianus *O* crudelitate *M* cruditate (*a. Rd.* Λ· crudelitate) *N* pronarū *A*  26 dadastanáe *M* dadastenae *P*

Romanorum

moritur anno aetatis ·XXXIIII·. Post quem
Ualentinianus tribunus scutariorum e Pannonia Cibalensis aput Nicaeam Augustus ap-
pellatus fratrem Ualentem Constantinopoli in communionem regni adsumit•    5

CCLXXXVI·Olymp·

Romanorum ·XXXVIII· regnauit Ualentinianus
et Ualens      ann ·XIIII· mens ·V·*

365 p. Chr.   I     *a* Ualentinianus egregius alias imperator
et Aureliano moribus similis, nisi quod    10
seueritatem eius nimiam et parcitatem
quidam crudelitatem et auaritiam inter-
pretabantur•

*b* Apollinaris Laodicenus episcopus multimo-
da nostrae religionis scripta componit•    15

366   II     *c* Terrae motu per totum orbem facto mare
litus egreditur et Siciliae multarumque in-
sularum urbes innumerabiles populos op-
pressere•

*d* Procopius, qui aput Constantinopolim tyranni-    20
dem inuaserat, aput Frygiam salutarem extinctus et plurimi Procopianae partis caesi atque
proscripti•

*e* Romanae ecclesiae ·XXXV· ordinatur episcopus Damasus et post non multum temporis interuallum Ur-    25
sinus a quibusdam episcopus constitutus Sicininum

---

*a* sin. num. *L*    *b* ut *a L*    *c* ut *a L*    *d* om. in lac. *L*    *e* ut *a L*

1 XXXIII *OLMP* quaem *L*    2 trib. *A* triuunus *L* e] a *M*    3 ciualensis *OLM* cybalen-
sis *B* apud *OMPN* niciam *O* niceam *APNLM* apellatus *A*    4 fratre *B* constantinopolim *O*
constantinupoli verb. *N*    5 adsumit (d verb. s) *MN* assumit *P Hier. ep. LX 15, 3 Prosp. 1125
(Chr. m. I 457) (i. J. 365) Cassiodor. 1106 (Chr. m. II 152) (i. J. 364) lat. imp. (Chr. m. III 422, 21)
Marian. Scot. III 383 Oros. VII 31, 3; 32. 1. 2. 4 Iordan. Rom. 306* (a. XXXIII) *Paul. diac. h. R. 1*

Rom. 7 recnauit *O* reḡ *L* regnaū *P* regna₁nauit *B*    8 annis *ALB* anno (verb. -nis) *M* mensibus *APBM* m̅*O* m̅*L* XV *A*⟨*L Prosp. 1126 (Chr. m. I 457) chron. Gall. a. 511 (Chr. m. I 494) Cassiodor. 1106 (Chr. m. II 152) Ps.-Isidor. 9 (Chr. m. II 382)* (a. XIII [m.-⟨]) *Isidor. iun. 348 (Chr.
m. II 468)* (m.-⟨) *Ps.-Isidor. attr. Aug. c. 348 (Chr. m. II 501) Bed. 440 (Chr. m. III 297)* (a. XI
[m.-⟨]) min. (XIIII [m.-⟨] exp. temp. Hil. (Chr. m. III 417, 22) lat. imp. (Chr. m. III 422, 22. 24)
(a. XI und a. XII) lat. Malal. 25 (Chr. m. III 436, 35) (Valent. a. XVII, Valens a. XIII) Marian.
Scot. III 383* (a. XI m. V) *Oros. VII 32, 1; 33, 1* (Valent. XI, Valens IIII) *Iord. Rom. 307*

a) 9 ualentinus *a. Hd.* verb. *M* alias ⟨*M*    10 et ⟨*M* auriliano *A* nisi *L*    12 quidam + ce-
dere *O* crudelitate *B* interpraetabantur *APNBM* interp̅tabatur *L Marian. Scot. III 384 Iord.
Rom. 307 Paul. diac. h. R. 5*    b) 14 apolinaris *AN* apollinarus *P* ep̅s *LP* laodicaenus *B*
15 nē *L* relegionis *L* scribta *OLB* verb. *N* scriptām *M* conponit *BM Hier. d. vir. ill. 104
Prosp. 1129 (Chr. m. I 457) (i. J. 367) chron. Gall. a. 511 (Chr. m. I 644, 501)* (a. X) *Bed. 441 (Chr.
m. III 298) Marian. Scot. III 384*    c) 16 terre *OLM* motum *O* moto *M* orbe *L* urbem *B*
17 lytus *B* et ⟨*L* sicilia *L* sicyliae *BP*    18 oppraessere *B* oppsere *P Hier. vit. Hilar. 40 comm. 5
in Isai. c. XV Marian. Scot. III 385 Oros. VII 32, 5 Paul. diac. h. R. 2*    d) 20 apud *OMPN*
(d aus t) constantinopolym *A*    21 apud *OMPN* (d aus t) frugiā *A* frigiam *BM*    22 partes *B*
procupianae verb. *M* adque *B*    23 conscripti *A* proscribti *B Prosp. 1131 (Chr. m. I 453)
(i. J. 367) Marian. Scot. III 385 Oros. VII 32, 4 Iord. Rom. 308 Paul. diac. h. R. 2*    e) 24 rom.—
245, 1 suis ⟨^(Lücke) *L* rom••ae (an) *P* eccl. ⟨*P* ep̅s ⟨*P*    25 interualū ·t    26 quib; *M* sicin-
ninum *OM s. O. Richter Topographie d. Stadt Rom* ²*§ 115, 5*

Romanorum

        cum suis inuadit, quo Damasianae partis po-
        pulo confluente crudelissimae interfectio-
        nes diuersi sexus perpetratae.
        <sup>a</sup> Ualens ab Eudoxio Arrianorum episcopo
        baptizatus nostros persequitur.

    III        <sup>b</sup> Gratianus Ualentiniani filius Ambianis       367 p. Chr.
        imperator factus.
        <sup>c</sup> Tanta Constantinopoli est orta tempestas,
        ut mirae magnitudinis decidens grando
        nonnullos hominum interfecerit.
        <sup>d</sup> Aput Atrabatas lana caelo pluuiae mixta
        defluxit.
        <sup>e</sup> Hilarius episcopus Pictauis moritur.

    IIII       <sup>f</sup> Nicaea, quae saepe ante corruerat, terrae      368
        motu funditus euersa.
        <sup>g</sup> Libanius Antiochenus rhetor insignis ha-
        betur.

CCLXXXVII · Olymp·
    V        <sup>h</sup> Agon Constantinopoli a Ualente redditus.    369
        <sup>i</sup> A[i]thanaricus rex Gothorum in $\overline{X}$Pianos per-
        secutione commota plurimos interficit et de
        propriis sedibus in Romanum solum expellit.
        <sup>k</sup> Eusebius Uercellensis episcopus moritur.

    VI       <sup>l</sup> Constantinopoli apostolorum martyri-      370
        um dedicatur.
        <sup>m</sup> Magna fames in Frygia.

<sup>a</sup> sin. num. L, ad III A P   <sup>b</sup> <sup>c</sup> ut <sup>a</sup> L   <sup>e</sup> ut <sup>a</sup> L, ad IIII O N   <sup>f</sup> ad III A   <sup>h</sup> ad CCLXXXVII
Ol. A L   <sup>i</sup> om. in lac. L   <sup>k</sup> ut <sup>i</sup> L, ad VI O   <sup>l</sup> ut <sup>i</sup> L, num. VI om. A B   <sup>m</sup> ut <sup>i</sup> L, ut <sup>i</sup> A B

1 sinuidit *verb.* N  quoda L  partes B   2 interfectionis A   3 diuersis L  sextus L  *Hier.
d. uir. ill. 103*  *Prosp. 1132 (Chr. m. I 458) (i. J. 367) chron. Gall. a. 511 (Chr. m. I 644, 506) Marian.
Scot. III 385*  a) 4 ep̄s L ep̄o PN  5 nōs L  *Prosp. 1133 (Chr. m. I 458) (i. J. 367) chron.
Gall. a. 511 (Chr. m. I 644, 503) Bed. 443 (Chr. m. III 298) Marian. Scot. III 385 Aug. d. c. d.
XVIII 52 (356, 5) Oros. VII 32, 6 Iord. Rom. 308 Paul. Diac. h. R. 3*  b) 6 ualentinianis *verb. O*
7 inperator LM  *Prosp. 1135 (Chr. m. I 458) (i. J. 368) chron. Gall. a. 511 (Chr. m. I 644, 495)*
(a. IIII) *Cassiodor. 1110 (Chr. m. II 152) (i. J. 367) Bed. 444 (Chr. m. III 298)* (a. III) *Marian.
Scot. III 386 Oros. VII 32, 8* (a. III) *Iord. Rom. 309 Paul. Diac. h. R. 1*  c) 8 tanto L  constantinopolim OL  est ⟨L  horta (h a. Hd.) O   9 mire L   10 nonnullus B *verb.* A  interfecit
*verb.* O M  interficeret B  *Marian. Scot. III 386 Paul. Diac. h. R. 2*  d) 11 apud O M P N  atra-
battas O atrabatas (a. Rd. atrabate) N  celo L  pluuie L   12 defluxit (x aus s) M *Cassiodor. IIII
(Chr. m. II 152) (i. J. 367) Marian. Scot. III 386 Oros. VII 32, 8* (a. III) *Paul. Diac. h. R. 2*
e) 13 ep̄s L ep̄s PN  pictabis L pectauis B *verb.* M  s. 240<sup>c</sup>  *Prosp. 1136 (Chr. m. I 458) (i. J. 368)
chron. Gall. a. 511 (Chr. m. I 644, 496) Bed. 447 (Chr. m. III 298) Marian. Scot. III 387 Sulp. Sev.
chron. II 45, 9*  f) 14 nicea LMP  sepe *verb.* O sepae L  antea M  s. 174<sup>d</sup> 198<sup>e</sup> *Ammian.
Marcell. XXII 13, 5*  coruerat *verb.* L conruerat B  terre LM  *Marian. Scot. III 387*
g) 16 liuanius L  antiocenus L antiochenos B  retor L rhethor M  *Marian. Scot. III 387*
h) 19 constantinopolim L  *Marian. Scot. III 388*   i) ⟨<sup>Lücke</sup>⟩ L  ahitanaricus O häithanari-
cus AM ha-i-tanaricus B haitanaricus PN  s. Th. l. L. II 1026  interfecit M  *Prosp. 1140 (Chr. m.
I 458) (i. J. 371)* (athanaricus ⟨a C aithanaricus Hss.) *chron. Gall. a. 511 (Chr. m. I 644, 497)* (a. V)
(athanaricus) *Marian. Scot. III 388* (haitanaricus) *Aug. d. c. d. XVIII 52 Oros. VII 32, 9 Paul.
Diac. h. R. 3* (aithanaricus HV hathanaricus B)  k) ⟨<sup>Lücke</sup>⟩ L  23 ep̄s PN  s. 242<sup>e</sup> *Hier. d. uir.
ill. 96 ex.*  *Prosp. 1141 (Chr. m. I 458) (i. J. 371) Marian. Scot. III 388*  l) ⟨<sup>Lücke</sup>⟩ L  24 apo-
stulorum B  martyrum *verb.* M  *Prosp. 1142 (Chr. m. I 459) (i. J. 371) Bed. 445 (Chr. m. III 298)
Marian. Scot. III 389*   m) ⟨<sup>Lücke</sup>⟩ L   26 famis *verb.* M  frigia P  *Marian. Scot. III 389*

Romanorum

<sup>a</sup> Lucifer Caralitanus episcopus moritur,
qui cum Gregorio episcopo Hispaniarum
et Philone Libyae numquam se Arrianae
miscuit prauitati•

371 p. Chr.　VII　<sup>b</sup> Maximinus praefectus annonae malefi-
cos ab imperatore inuestigare iussus
plurimos Romae nobilium occidit•
<sup>c</sup> Ualentinianus in Brittania, antequam ty-
rannidem inuaderet, oppressus•
<sup>d</sup> Presbyter Sirmii iniquissime decollatur,
quod Octauianum ex proconsule aput se
latitantem prodere noluisset•

372　VIII　<sup>e</sup> Didymus Alexandrinus multa de nostro
dogmate per notarios commentatur. Qui
post quintum natiuitatis suae annum lu-
minibus orbatus elementorum quoque
ignarus fuit•
<sup>f</sup> Probus praefectus Illyrici iniquissimis
tributorum exactionibus ante prouincias
quas regebat, quam a barbaris uasta-
rentur, erasit•

CCLXXXVIII·Olymp·
373　VIIII　<sup>g</sup> Eunomius discipulus Aeti Constantinopoli
agnoscitur, a quo haeresis Eunomiana•
<sup>h</sup> Saxones caesi Deusone in regione Fran-
corum•

---

<sup>a</sup> sin. num. L　<sup>b</sup> ad VI M　<sup>c</sup> ad VII A M　<sup>g</sup> in lac. om. L　<sup>h</sup> ut <sup>g</sup> L

a) 1 lucifer ⟨<sup>Lücke</sup>⟩ L + et L caralitanus (l aus t) L eps LPN 2 epo LP spaniarum L
3 filone OBM lybiae BM lybie L libiae P arriani O 4 prauitae A Hier. d. vir. ill. 95 ex. Prosp.
1143 (Chr. m. I 459) (i. J. 371) Marian. Scot. III 389 b) 5 annone L maleficus BM malifi-
cus L 6 iussus inuestigare ~ O P iussus audire M iussit verb. L 7 nobilium romae ~ N verb. O
nouilium L Marian. Scot. III 390 c) 8 ualentinus O P (a. Hd. darüber <sup>nis</sup>) ualentinianus Hss.
brittania (das erste t durchstrich.) N britannia P brittania verb. britannia M a antequam verb. N über
antequam a. Hd. a maximo O tirannidem L tyrannidam verb. M Marian. Scot. III 390 (ualentinus)
Iord. Rom. 308 (alter ualentinianus) Paul. Diac. h. R. 4 (ualentinus) d) 10 prb L praesbiter B
presbiter PM presbyter N sirmi APLM sermi B syrmi N iniquissimae L decollat (e aus o) P
11 eo quod O octabianum L octouianum N prosule verb. A proconsulae B verb. M proconsulem L
apud O M P N 12 latentē L latentem M Marian. Scot. III 390 e) 13 didimus LP dydymus B dydi-
mus M nō L nostra B 14 dogmatae O docmate L dogmata A notarius L verb. B
15 suae ⟨P 16 elimentorum A B Hier. d. vir. ill. 109 Prosp. 1146 (Chr. m. I 459) (i. J. 372) chron.
Gall. a. 511 (Chr. m. I 644, 498) (a. VII) Marian. Scot. III 391 f) 18 prob. praef. ill.] illyrici equitius comes A P B N (a. Rd. ·Λ· pbus pfectus) s. Schoene Weltchronik 96 ff. Die unnatürliche Wortstellung
erweist die Interpolation prouus L prefectus L illirice L illirici P iniquissimae L iniquissimas
verb. M 19 triuutorum L ante − erasit ⟨<sup>Lücke</sup>⟩ L ante <sup>a</sup> prouintias (<sup>a ci</sup> a. Hd.) M 20 <sup>ante</sup> quā
(a. Hd. <sup>ante</sup>) M rasit M Marian. Scot. III 391 (illiricus equitius comes) g) 23 a-eti BN
(a. Rd. Λt aieti) & in (a. Hd. <sup>arti</sup> vor disc. +) M 24 heresis BMP eunomiani B Prosp. 1148
(Chr. m. I 459) (i. J. 374) chron. Gall. a. 511 (Chr. m. I 644, 499) Marian. Scot. III 392
h) ⟨<sup>Lücke</sup>⟩ L deusonae M deusione (a. Rd. ·Λ· deusone) N fraucorum B cesi P Cassiodor. 1113
(Chr. m. II 152) (i. J. 373) Marian. Scot. III 392 Oros. VII 32, 10 Paul. Diac. h. R. 4

(329 F)

Romanorum

<sup>a</sup> Burgundionum ·LXXX· ferme milia, quod
numquam antea, ad Rhenum descenderunt
<sup>b</sup> Clearchus praefectus urbi Constantinopo-
li agnoscitur. A quo necessaria et diu ex-
5     pectata uotis aqua ciuitati inducitur•
<sup>c</sup> Alexandriae ·XX· ordinatur episcopus Petrus,
qui post Ualentis interitum tam facilis in
recipiendis haereticis fuit, ut nonnullis
suspicionem acceptae pecuniae intulerit•

10 IICCCXC  X     <sup>d</sup> Melanium, nobilissima mulierum Romanorum,     374 p. Chr.
et Marcellini quondam consulis filia, unico
praetore tunc urbano filio derelicto Hieroso-
lymam nauigauit. Ubi tanto uirtutum praecipueque humilitatis miraculo fuit, ut The-
15     clae nomen acceperit
<sup>e</sup> Post Auxenti seram mortem Mediolanii Ambro-
sio episcopo constituto omnis ad fidem rectam
Italia conuertitur•
<sup>f</sup> Aquileienses clerici quasi chorus beatorum ha-
20     bentur•
XI     <sup>g</sup> Quia superiore anno Sarmatae Pannonias ua-     375
stauerant, idem consules permansere•
<sup>h</sup> Ualentinianus subita sanguinis eruptione, quod
Graece apoplexis uocatur, Brigitione moritur.
25     Post quem Gratianus adsumpto in imperium Ualen-
tiniano fratre cum patruo Ualente regnat•

(deest L)    <sup>a</sup> sin. num. L    <sup>b</sup> ut <sup>a</sup> L    <sup>c</sup> ut <sup>a</sup> L    <sup>d</sup> reliqua usque ad pag. 250 om. L, in mg.
inf. add. P    <sup>e</sup> ad XI BN    <sup>f</sup> ad XI BN    <sup>g</sup> ad XII B    <sup>h</sup> ad XII B

a) 1 burgundiorum LBM  quo PN quot. Salm.    2 renum OLB rheneum M  discenderunt B
descendeꞃ P Cassiodor. 1119 (Chr. m. II 153) (i. J. 373) Marian. Scot. III 392 Oros. VII 32, 1 Paul.
Diacon. h. R. 4    b) 3 clearcus LP  prefectus M  urbis LB  constantinopolitanae (tanae
i. Ras.) M  4 agnos. a. Hd. verb. A noscitur (nos vorgeschrieb.) M⟨B  5 ciuitas L Cassiodor. 1120
(Chr. m. II 153) (i. J. 373) Marian. Scot. III 392  c) 6 epꞩ P petrus episcopus ∼ O
8 hereticis LBMP  9 suspicione B suspitione M  accepte L  Marian. Scot. III 392  d) ⟨L
10 melanius OABM (a über u) melaniuꞩ N melanias P melanium He. vgl. Hier. ep. 39, 4 (350, 10
Hilbg.) Texts and Studies VI 2 Butler S. 222 n. 85  femina (durchstrich.) mulierū O nobilissima
(i. Ras.) B    11 et ⟨APN  12 praetor (o aus u) M praetori Vallars.  hierusolimam B hieroso-
limā M ierosolymā P  13 praecipueque M  14 thecle A teclae B theclae (a. Rd. Aꞇ
teclae) N  15 acciperet (i aus e) A acciperet PN acciperit B Hier. ep. 4, 2; 39, 5, 4 Rufin.
apol. 2, 26 (P. L. XXI 605ᵃ) (paruulo filio Romae derelicto) s. Schoene Weltchronik 105 ff. Die Ur-
sprünglichkeit der am Seitenende nachgetragenen Notiz in P wird durch die Beibehaltung der Seitenein-
teilung erwiesen. Marian. Scot. III 393 (unico pretore t. u. f. d.)  e) ⟨L  16 auxenti• (s) P au-
xenti¹ N lambrosio B  17 epō PMN omnes ŌB omꞩ P  18 italiam O ita A conuertetur B s.ᶠ)
Prosp. 1153 (Chr. m. I 459) chron. Gall. a. 511 (Chr. m. I 644, 500) (a. IX) Bed. 446 (Chr. m.
III 298) Marian. Scot. III 394 Paul. Diac. h. R. 13  f) ⟨L  19 aquileiensis O  20 habent + mise-
rabilis presbiter dū aduersū conscientiā furoris sui sacra ficia do offeret (audet offerre verb. a. Hd.)
do audet (d. a. durchstrich.) in mediis p̄cib; eliditur M s. Schoene Weltchronik 156 ff. 224 ff. Prosp.
1154 (Chr. m. I 459) (i. J. 376) Marian. Scot. III 394  g) ⟨L  21 qui A superiori
APNBM uastauerat P  22 idem − perm'ans. ⟨A permanserunt N pmanseꞃ P Prosp. 1152
(Chr. m. I 459) (i. J. 376) Marian. Scot. III 394 Oros. VII 32, 14  h) ⟨L  23 ualentinus
anus verb. M  24 grece BMP brigintione M  25 gratianos B assumpto PN inperium
AN ualentiano N Hier. epist. LX 15, 3 Prosp. 1155 (Chr. m. I 459) (i. J. 376) chron. Gall. a. 511
(Chr. m. I 644, 504) Cassiodor. 1124 (Chr. m. II 153) (i. J. 376) lat. imp. (Chr. m. III 422, 23)
Marian. Scot. III 395 Oros. VII 32, 14/5 Iord. Rom. 309/10 Paul. Diac. h. R. 5

Romanorum

<sup>a</sup> Multi monachorum Nitriae per tribunos
et milites caesi●
<sup>b</sup> Ualens lege data, ut monachi militarent,
nolentes fustibus iussit interfici●

376 p. Chr.     XII          <sup>c</sup> Theodosius, Theodosii postea imperatoris        5
pater, et plurimi nobilium occisi●
<sup>d</sup> Fotinus in Galatia moritur, a quo Fotini-
anorum dogma Iudaicum●
<sup>e</sup> Basilius Caesariensis episcopus Cappado-
ciae clarus habetur. Qui multa conti-             10
nentiae et ingenii bona uno superbiae
malo perdidit●

CCLXXXVIIII·Olymp·
377           XIII          <sup>f</sup> Alamannorum ·XXX· circiter milia aput
Argentariam oppidum Galliarum ab ex-              15
ercitu Gratiani strata●
<sup>g</sup> Florentinus Bonosus et Rufinus insignes
monachi habentur. E quibus Florenti-
nus tam misericors in egentes fuit,
ut uulgo pater pauperum nominatus               20
sit●
<sup>h</sup> Gens Hunnorum Gothos uastat. Qui a
Romanis sine armorum depositione
suscepti per auaritiam Maximi ducis
fame ad rebellandum coacti sunt●               25

    deest L     <sup>a</sup> ad XII B    <sup>b</sup> ad XII B     <sup>c</sup> ad XI A PN     <sup>d</sup> ad XI PN     <sup>f</sup> ad XII APN, ad
XIIII (num. XIII om.) B     <sup>g</sup> post <sup>h</sup> PN, ad XIIII (cf. <sup>f</sup>) B     <sup>h</sup> ante <sup>g</sup> PN, ad XIIII (cf. <sup>f</sup>) B

    a) ⟨L p̓ trib; annos (o verb. j) M        b) ⟨L      3 uales (a. Hd. verb.) O  legēndat M
4 interfeci A   Prosp. 1156 (Chr. m. I 459) (i. J. 376) chr. Gall. a. 511 (Chr. m. I 644, 502) (a. XI)
Bed. 449 (Chr. m. III 298) Marian. Scot. III 396 Oros. VII 33, 1 (515, 11) Iord. Rom. 312 Paul.
Diac. h. R. 8        c) ⟨L     5 theodoxiǫus M  postea übergeschrieb. O  imperatoris (is verb. es) B
6 occiǫsi M   Marian. Scot. III 396 Oros. VII 33, 6/7 (516, 15; 517, 9)        d) ⟨L     7 galatiā M
iudiacum verb. P    Prosp. 1158 (Chr. m. I 460) (i. J. 377) (fotinianum) chron. Gall. a. 511 (Chr. m.
I 644, 505) Isidor. iun. 351 (Chr. m. II 469) Marian. Scot. III 396       e) ⟨L     9 cesariensis M
caesariensis verb. N  eps̄ PNM epis B  cappadotiae M     10 qui — 12 perdidit ⟨A (daß im Original
vorhanden, beweisen die vier leeren Zeilen unten in A) getilgt B + N a. Rd. P  Hier. d. vir. ill. 116
s. Schoene Weltchronik 178  Chron. Gall. a. 511 (Chr. m. I 644, 508) Marian. Scot. III 396
f) ⟨L     14 milio A    apud OM PN     15 argentaria B argentoratum M    Prosp. 1160 (Chr. m.
I 460) (i. J. 378) Cassiodor. 1126 (Chr. m. II 153) (i. J. 377) Marian. Scot. III 397 Oros. VII 33, 8
Iord. Rom. 312        g) ⟨L     17 florentius N     18 e a. Hd. M  flor.] rufinus PN entstanden aus der
Abteilung der Silben wie in A: flo, rentinus durch ·Überspringen des flo,     19 egentis A
20 pater + pater verb. O  Hier. epist. 3. 4. 5  Rufin. apol. 2, 25 (P. L. XXI 605ª) s. Schoene Weltchronik 111 ff.  Marian. Scot. III 397       h) ⟨L     22 hunorum OBM     24 maximi,
(ducis — 250 Ende () O    Prosp. 1161 (Chr. m. I 460) (i. J. 378) chron. Gall. a. 511 (Chr. m. I 644,
509/10) (a. XIII) Bed. 450 (Chr. m. III 298) Marian. Scot. III 397 Oros. VII 33, 10/1 (a. XIII)
Iord. Rom. 313 Paul. Diac. h. R. 10

Romanorum

<sup>a</sup> Superatis in congressione Romanis Gothi
funduntur in Thracia.

XIIII       <sup>b</sup> Ualens de Antiochia exire conpulsus      378 p. Chr.
sera paenitentia nostros de exiliis
5     reuocat.

[XV]      <sup>c</sup> Lacrimabile bellum in Thracia. In quo        [379]
deserente equitum praesidio Romanae      <sup>d</sup> Ab urbe condita
legiones a Gothis cinctae usque ad       usque ad extremum
internecionem caesae sunt. Ipse im-      fiunt anni ·MCXXXI
10     perator Ualens, cum sagitta saucius     hoc modo:
fugeret et ob dolorem nimium saepe       anni ·CCXL
equo laberetur, ad cuiusdam uillulae      sub consulibus
casam deportatus est. Quo persequen-     sub Augustis et Caesa-
tibus barbaris et incensa domo sepul-     ribus   anni ·CCCCXXVII·
15     tura quoque caruit.

---

deest L    <sup>a</sup> ad XIIII (num. XIII om.) B om. O    <sup>b</sup> ad XV B om. O    <sup>c</sup> ad XV APN B
om. O    <sup>d</sup> om. OM

a) ⟨OL     1 in ⟨APN   romani a. Hd. verb. M     2 tratia M    Prosp. 1163 (Chr. m. I 460)
(i. J. 379) Cassiodor. 1127 (Chr. m. II 153) (i. J. 377) Marian. Scot. III 397 Oros. VII 33, 11 Iord.
Rom. 313     b) ⟨OL    3 deo thitia M   compulsus P c̅pulsus M cõ•pulsus (n) N   penitentiae M
poenitentia P     4 exilio B    Prosp. 1164 (Chr. m. I 460) (i. J. 379) Marian. Scot. III 398 Oros.
VII 33, 12 Iord. Rom. 314      c) ⟨OL    6 tracia B trachia M    7 deserentem verb. M
aequitũ M    8 legionis verb. A   a a. Hd. M    9 intertionem M     11 fugiret A verb. M
et + N   dorem verb. A   niminiũ M   sepae M     12 uillolae a. Hd. verb. B     13 caesam verb.
A⟨P   quo (o verb. j) M   Hier. epist. LX 15, 3    Prosp. 1165 (Chr. m. I 460) (i. J. 379) chron. Gall.
a. 511 (Chr. m. I 644, 511) (a. XIIII) Cassiodor. 1129 (Chr. m. II 153) (i. J. 378) lat. imp. (Chr.
m. III 422, 25) Marian. Scot. III 398 Oros. VII 33, 13/5 (a. XV) Iord. Rom. 314 Paul. Diac.
h. R. 11     d) ⟨OLM    7 condit verb. A     8 CCCXXXI B MXXXI verb. N     10 annis A
11 ann̄ N   CCCLXIIII APN      12 ann· N   DXXVI A CCCCXXVIII N CCCCXXIIII B dahinter: M̄CXXXI<sup>II</sup> ·<sub>7</sub> Ab incarnat dn̄i, CCCLXXXI N

Colliguntur omnes anni usque in consulatum Ualentis'·VI· et Ualentiniani iunioris
  iterum Augusti(•)
A ·XV· Tiberii anno et praedicatione D̃ni nostri
  IH̃u XP̃i                   anni ·CCCLI·                              5
A secundo anno Darii regis Persarum, quo
  tempore templum Hierosolymis instau-
  ratum est                anni ·DCCCXCVIIII·
Ab olympiade prima, qua aetate aput He-
  braeos Esaias prophetabat, anni ·M̄CLV·                             10
A Solomone et prima aedificatione tem-
  pli                      anni ·M̄CCCCXI·
A captiuitate Troiae, quo tempore Sampson
  aput Hebraeos erat,      anni ·M̄DLXI·
A Moyse et Cecrope primo rege Atticae                                15
                           anni ·M̄DCCCXC·
Ab Abraham et regno Nini et Semiramidis
                           anni ·M̄MCCCXCV·
Continet omnis canon ab Abraham usque ad
  tempus supra scriptum    ann ·M̄MCCCXCV·                           20
a diluuio autem usque ad Abraham sup-
  putantur                 anni ·DCCCCXLII·
et ab Adam usque ad diluuium  anni ·Ī̄ICCXLII·
Fiunt ab Adam usque ad ·XIIII· Ualentis annum
  id est usque ad consulatum eius ·VI· et Ualen-                     25
  tiniani iterum omnes     anni ·V̄DLXXVIIII·

---

deest *O L*

† *(Epit. Syr. bezieht natürlich alles auf Constantins 20. Regierungsjahr wie Eus.)*     1 colle-
guntur *B* ani *a. Hd. verb. M* in] ad *A* consolatum *A B*     2 VI] ter *B⟨M*     3 augg. *B* aug̃ *M*
4 X *a. Hd. verb. M* predicatione *M* nr̄i *N⟨A P*     5 ihsu *N*     7 hierusolymis *B* ierosolymis *P*
8 DCCC•XLVIIII (L) *M*     9 olimpiadae *M* qua] que *N* apud *P N M* hebreos *M*     10 isaias
*A M* eseias *B* profetabat *B N* ann· *N* mille CLV•• *B* ·I·XLV *N*     11 salomone *A P N M*
& + a *M*     12 miłł CCCXI *B* ᴵCCCCXI *P* CCCCXI *N*     13 quo te *(falsch wiederholt und durch-
gestrich.)* samson *M* samspon *A* samson *P N M*     14 apud *P N M* hebreos *M* mille DLXI *B*
ĪDLVI *N*     15 mose *A P N* cicrope *M* promo *verb. N*     16 mille DCCCCXC *B* ĪDCCCXC *P*
*s. 43, 13*     17 semiramides *B*     18 ĪICCCXV *B* ĪICCCLXLV *M*     19 omnes *B* canonas *N*
20 scribtu *B* anni *A B M* ĪICCCCLXLV *M*     21 autem ⟨*P N* habraham *N* subputantur *P*
22 DCCCCXLV *P*     23 aᾱn *M N* ĪICCXII *N*     24 aᾱn *N*     25 usque] adq. *A* consolatum *M verb. B*     25/6 ualentiniani + iunioris *M*     26 aᾱn *N* ᴵᴵDLXXVIIII (L aus I) *M*
*s. 173 f°*

# AKADEMIE-VERLAG BERLIN

amt.

DIREKTOR

FERNRUF
SAMMELNUMMER
2 00 20

Akademie-Verlag Berlin. Postfach 1233. Berlin. DDR-1086

**Luftpost - Einschreiben**

Herrn
Malcolm Donalson

Winston Avenue 5

Baton Rouge LA
70809

United States

| Ihre Zeichen | Ihre Nachricht vom | Unsere Zeichen | Bestell- und Verlags-Nr. | Tag |
|---|---|---|---|---|
| | 25.9.90 | 50Vt/Za/Pi | | - 9. Nov. 1990 |

Betreff:

**Abdruckgenehmigung - Rudolf Helm, Hieronymus /Chronicon/**

Sehr geehrter Herr Donalson,

Ihr Abdruckersuchen unter dem 25.9.1990 ist uns zugegangen.
Nach Prüfung durch unser Fachlektorat erteilen wir Ihnen
hiermit den Abdruck aus unserem Titel

     Rudolf Helm, Hieronymus /Chronicon/, 1956,
     Akademie-Verlag
     from year (an.) 326 to year 379 A.D.

in dem von Ihnen benannten Umfang für Ihre Dissertation.
Der Abdruck ist vergütungsfrei. Sie wollen bitte, ent-
sprechend den urheberrechtlichen Vorschriften, die
Quellenangabe in Ihrer Publikation vornehmen und uns
2 Werkexemplare übersenden.
Wir wünschen Ihnen bei der Erarbeitung viel Erfolg und
verbleiben

                mit vorzüglicher Hochachtung

        Dr. Bernhard Tesche

# APPENDIX B

## A LIST OF <u>CHRON</u>. NOTICES BY SUBJECTS

An asterisk marks those notices which are applicable to more than one subject. The subjects are listed from that most represented--The Emperor's Character or Deeds--to that least represented--The Philosophers. On the right are the topics of the notices.


The Emperor's Character/Deeds (48 notices)

Constantine
    *231h        restoration and renaming of Drepana as Helenopolis in honor of
                      his mother; honoring a martyr
    232a        execution of his wife Fausta
    *232e       recall of an author from exile
    233b        edict ordering destruction of temples
Constans
    233d        promotion to the throne
Constantine and sons
    *233h       letter to Antony
Constantine
    233i         Dalmatius made Caesar
    *234a       Constantine's baptism by an Arian and lapse into Arianism
                      Constantine and sons
    *234b       preparations for war with Persia; sons promoted
    234 Rom.   reigns and regnal years
Constantine and Constantius
    *234e       promotion and assassination of Dalmatius Caesar; civil war
Constantius
    *234g       support of Arianism; exile and persecution of Athanasius
                      and other orthodox
Constantine II
    *235a       civil war vs. his brother
Constans
    *235b       campaign vs. the Franks
    *235e       defeat of the Franks and establishment of peace
Constantius
    *235f       banishment of orthodox bishop

|  | *236a | persecution of Athanasius |
| Constans | | |
|  | *236e | recall of Athanasius |
| Constantius | | |
|  | *236l | his lack of participation in nine battles vs. the Persians |
| Constans | | |
|  | *237c | in camp at Helena during usurpations of the throne |
| Constantius | | |
|  | *238c | demotion of Vetranio, followed by promotion of |
|  | 238e | Gallus as <u>Caesar</u> |
| Gallus Caesar | | |
|  | 238f | suppression of the Jewish revolt |
|  | 238g | execution of Antiochene nobles |
| Constantius | | |
|  | 239c | assassination of Gallus Caesar |
|  | *239i | exile of orthodox bishops and other clergy in favor of Arians |
|  | 240a | Julian's promotion to <u>Caesar</u> |
| Julian Caesar | | |
|  | 240g | defeat of the Alamanni |
| Constantius | | |
|  | 240i | translation of the relics of Andrew and Luke |
| Gratian | | |
|  | 241f | birth of Gratian |
| Constantius | | |
|  | 241g | recall of Hilary to Gaul |
|  | 241i | partnership with the Arians |
| Julian | | |
|  | 242 Rom. | regnal years |
|  | *242c | idolatry; persecution of Christian |
| Julian/Jovian | | |
|  | *243b | persecution; expedition vs. the Persians; defeat; Jovian's promotion |
|  | 243 Rom. | regnal years |
|  | *243c | surrender of Mesopotamian territory to Persia |
| Valentinian/Valens | | |
|  | *243e | promotion of Valens and Valentinian and as <u>Augusti</u> |
|  | 244 Rom. | regnal years |
| Valentinian | | |
|  | 244a | personal distinction and similarity to Aurelian |
| Valens | | |
|  | *245a | persecution of the orthodox |
| Gratian | | |
|  | 245b | promotion to <u>Augustus</u> |
| Valens | | |
|  | 245h | restoration of public games at Constantinople |
| Valentinian | | |
|  | *246b | ordering of the investigation of criminals at Rome; |

execution of nobles

Gratian, Valentinian II
    \*247h          Gratian promotes Valentinian II to <u>Augustus</u>

Gratian
    \*248f          defeat of the Alamanni at Argentorate
Valens
    \*249b          recall of orthodox from exile
    \*249c          defeat in battle by the Goths; death and lack of burial

## Bishops and Church Order (36 notices)

| | |
|---|---|
| \*231g | bishop in Sicca, unnamed |
| \*232c | orthodox bishops and Arian bishops an Antioch |
| 232f | Athanasius, bishop of Alexandria |
| 233a | Marcus and Julius, bishops of Rome |
| \*234a | Eusebius, bishop of Nicomedia |
| 234f | Iacobus, b. of Nisibis |
| \*234g | orthodox bishops' removal in favor of Arians |
| \*235f | Paulus, b. of Constantinople |
| \*235h | Macedonius, b. of Constantinople |
| \*236a | Maximinus, b. of Treves and Athanasius |
| \*236c | b. of Neocaesaria |
| \*236e | Athanasius |
| \*237a | Maximus, b. of Jerusalem; succession of Arian bishops there |
| \*237b | Liberius, b. of Rome; Felix, Arian b. |
| \*239f | Paulinus and Rodanius, Gallic bishops |
| \*239i | Eusebius, b. of Vercellae; Lucifer, b. of Cagliari; Dionysius of Caralitana; bishops of Milan |
| \*240c | Hilary, b. of Pictavi; Saturnius, b. of Arles |
| \*240f | Liberius, b. of Rome |
| \*241b | Paulinus, b. of Treves |
| \*241d | synods of bishops (Ariminum and Seleucia of Isauria) |
| \*241g | Hilary |
| \*241h | Macedonius |
| \*241l | Arian bishops |
| \*242a | Hilary, and the synod at Ariminum |
| \*242d | Georgius, Arian b. of Alexandria, and Athanasius |
| \*242e | Eusebius, Lucifer, Paulinus, Eustathius, bishops |
| \*243d | synod at Antioch; Meletius <u>et al.</u>, bishops |
| \*244b | Apollinaris, b. of Laodicea |
| 244e | Damasus, b. of Rome; Ursinus, his rival |
| \*245a | Eudoxius, Arian b. |
| 245e | Hilary |
| 245j | Eusebius, b. of Vercellae |
| \*246a | Lucifer (above); Gregory, b. in Spain; Philo, b. in Libya |
| \*247c | Peter, b. of Alexandria |
| \*247e | Auxentius and Ambrose, bishops of Milan |

·

248e       Basil of Caesarea, b. of Cappadocia

## Heresy (26 notices)

232b       Donatism in Africa
*232c      Arianism in Antioch
*234a      Arianism in Antioch, empire-wide
*234g      Arianism in Antioch, empire-wide
235d      Audianism in Coelo-Syria
*235f      Arianism at Constantinople
*235h     Macedonianism at Constantinople
*235i      Arianism/Macedonianism
*236i      Arianism at Emesa
*237a      Arianism at Jerusalem
*237b      Arianism at Rome
239h      Donatism in Africa; the Montensians at Rome
*239i      Arianism, empire-wide
*241d      synods/Arianism
*241h      Macedonius' exile
241i      Arianism, empire-wide
*241l      Arianism at Antioch
*242a      Arianism at the synod of Ariminum
*242d      Arianism at the synod of Alexandria
*242e      heretical communion (Arianism) at Antioch
242l      exile made a mockery by Arianizers
*243d      Macedonianism at Antioch
*245a      Arianism, under Valens
*246a      Arianism, empire-wide
*246g      Eunomianism at Constantinople
*247c      Arian heretics in Alexandria
*247e      Auxentius-Arian bishop's "belated" death
248d      Photinianism in Gaul
*249b      Valens' belated recall of orthodox exiles

## Persecution (20 notices)

*232c      exile of Eustathius
*234g      Constantius vs. orthodox
*235f      Constantius vs. orthodox through the agency of Hermogenes
*235i      strangling of Paulus under prefect Phillippus, a Macedonian
*236a      Constantius seeks to punish Athanasius and the latter is exiled.
*236b      Sapor's persecution of Christians
*237b      Liberius' exile and Arian ascendancy
*239f      exile of orthodox bishops from Gaul
*239i      exile of orthodox bishops and other clergy by the Arians
*240c      exile of orthodox bishops
*240f      exile of Liberius
*241b      death of Paulinus, b. of Treves, in exile

| | |
|---|---|
| *241l | deposition of priests by Eudoxius |
| *242c | Julian's persecution |
| *242e | exiles, confessors |
| *243a | in return for attack on pagan altars, beginning of |
| *243b | Julian's persecution, interrupted |
| *245a | Valens' persecution of the orthodox |
| *245i | Goths' persecution of Christians |
| *248a | execution of monks, under Valens |

## War/Barbarian Peoples (15 notices)

| | |
|---|---|
| 233c | defeat of the Goths in Sarmatian territory |
| 233f | Sarmatians' defeat of the Limigantes or Argaragantes and the arrival of the latter in Roman territory |
| *235b | Constans' unsuccessful campaign vs. the Franks |
| *235e | Constans' defeat of the Franks, and subsequent peace |
| *240g | Julian's defeat of the Alammani at Argentoratum |
| *240h | Saracen attack on Antony's monastery |
| *245i | Athanaric and the Goths' persecution of Christians |
| *246f | barbarian attack on Illyricum |
| 246h | defeat of the Saxons in Frankish territory |
| 247a | descent of 80,000 Burgundians on the Rhine, noted as unprecedented |
| 247g | Sarmatian attack on Pannonia |
| *248f | Gratian's defeat of the Alamanni at Argentorate |
| *248h | Huns' devastation of Gothic lands; Goths' appeal to enter the empire; famine caused by greed of Roman general |
| 249a | Goths' victory over Romans and invasion of Thrace |
| *249c | war with Goths in Thrace; disaster of Adrianople |

## Famous Officials (14 notices)

| | |
|---|---|
| *233m | Tiberianus, praetorian prefect in Gaul |
| 234c | Ablabius, praetorian prefect |
| *235f | Hermogenes, master of the soldiers at Constantinople |
| *235i | Philippus, praetorian prefect |
| *236d | Titianus, praetorian prefect in Gaul |
| *238a | Heraclides, senator at Rome |
| 241e | Honoratus, praetorian prefect in Gaul then first urban prefect at Constantinople |
| *246b | Maximinus, prefect of the grain supply at Rome |
| *246d | proconsul in Sirmium, unnamed |
| *246f | Probus, prefect in Illyricum |
| *247b | Clearchus, urban prefect at Constantinople |
| *247d | Marcellinus, consul; Melania's son, the urban praetor |
| 248c | Theodosius the Elder, general, father of Theodosius I |
| *248h | Maximus, general |

## Famous Rhetors/Orators (11 notices)

| | |
|---|---|
| *231g | Arnobius at Sicca |
| 233k | Pater at Rome |
| 233l | Nazarius and his daughter |
| *233m | Tiberianus in Gaul |
| *236d | Titianus in Gaul |
| 239a | Gennadius at Rome |
| 239b | Minervius of Burgdigala at Rome |
| 239e | Victorinus, rhetor, and Donatus, grammarian, at Rome |
| 239g | Alcimus and Delfidius, rhetors in Aquitania |
| 241c | Evanthius and Chrestus grammarians, at Constantinople |
| 245g | Libanius, rhetor, at Antioch |

## True Faith (11 notices)

| | |
|---|---|
| *231g | "true belief" |
| *232c | Eustatius' "exile for his faith" |
| *239f | Paulinus and Rodanius' "exile for their faith" |
| *240c | "our religion" |
| *241d | Synods condemn "the ancient faith of the fathers" |
| *242a | Gaul undoes the "faithlessness of Ariminum" |
| *244b | "our religion" |
| *245a | "our people" |
| *246e | "our doctrine" |
| *247e | "the right faith" |
| *249b | "our people" |

## Natural Phenomena (11 notices)

| | |
|---|---|
| 233e | pestilence/famine in Syria and Cilicia |
| 235c | earthquake: devastation of many eastern cities |
| *236c | earthquake: destruction of Neucaesaria in Pontus |
| 236f | earthquake: destruction of Dyrrachium, damage in Campania and three-day tremor at Rome |
| 236k | eclipse |
| 241a cities | earthquake: devastation of Nicomedia and damage of neighboring |
| 244c | earthquake: worldwide, esp. Sicily and other islands |
| 245c | deadly hailstorm at Constantinople |
| 245d | rain of wool at Atrabatae |
| 245f | earthquake: ruin of Nicaea |
| 245m | famine in Phrygia |

## Authors and Their Works (10 notices)

| | |
|---|---|
| *231f | Eusebius' Chron. |

| | |
|---|---|
| *231g | Arnobius' "authoritative books" |
| *232d | Iuvencus' "Gospels in epic poetry" |
| *232e | Porphyrius' "excellent book" |
| *236i | Eusebius of Emesa, writer of "many things on a variety of subjects" |
| *240b | Jerome's book on Paul of Thebes |
| *240c | Hilary's "books about our religion" |
| *241g | Hilary's book offered to Constantius |
| *244b | Apollinarius' "great number of works on our religion" |
| *246e | Didymus of Alexandria's "numerous commentaries" |

Usurpers of the Throne (10 notices)

| | |
|---|---|
| 233g | Calocaerus in Cyprus |
| *237c | Magnentius at Augustodunum; Vetranio at Mursa and Nepotianus at Rome |
| *238a | Magnentians' success at Rome |
| 238b | Nepotianus' assassination |
| *238c | Vetranio's demotion at Naissus |
| 238d | Magnentius' defeat at Mursa |
| 238h | Magnentius' suicide at Lugdunum; Decentius' suicide "among the Senones" |
| 239d | Silvanus in Gaul |
| 244d | Procopius at Constantinople; assassination in Phrygia |
| 246c | Valentinian in Britain |

Emperors' Deaths (9 notices)

| | |
|---|---|
| *234b | Constantine, at Ancyra |
| *234e | Dalmatius Caesar, in civil war |
| *235a | Constantine II, at Alsa, in civil war |
| *237c | Constans, at Helena due to usurpers |
| *239c | Gallus Caesar, at Histria, under Constantius' suspicion |
| 242b | Constantius, at Mopsucrene |
| *243b | Julian, vs. Persians |
| *243e | Jovian, at Dadastana |
| *247h | Valentinian, at Brigitio |

Buildings (10 notices)

(A) Secular (4 notices)

| | |
|---|---|
| *231h | restoration of Drepana, renamed Helenopolis |
| 232g | building of Constantinople, at other cities' expense |
| 236g | port at Seleucia |
| *247b | aqueduct at Constantinople |

(B) Church (6 notices)

128

| 231i | the church called "Palace" and "Golden" at Antioch |
| *233n | martyr shrine at Jerusalem |
| 235g | dedication of the Golden Church, Antioch |
| 241k | dedication of Hagia Sophia, Constantinople |
| 244e | fighting in the basilica of Sicininus, Rome |
| *245j | dedication of the martyr shrine of the Apostles, Constantinople, |

## Martyrs/Relics (9 notices)

| *231f | Pamphilus |
| *231h | Lucian |
| *233n | martyr shrine at Jerusalem |
| 240d | Constantinople's reception of the relics of Timothy |
| *240i | translation of the relics of Andrew and Luke to Rome |
| *242d | Georgius, Arian bishop |
| *243a | Aemilianus |
| *245j | martyr shrine at Constantinople |
| *246d | a priest in Sirmium |

## Famous Minor Clergy (8 notices)

| *232d | Iuvencus, priest in Spain |
| *233n | Eustathius, priest in Constantinople |
| *237a | Cyrillus, priest and deacon at Jerusalem, afterwards bishop |
| *239i | Pancratius, Roman priest, and Hilarius, a deacon |
| *242e | Paulinus, priest under Eustathius, afterwards bishop |
| *246d | priest in Sirmium, unnamed; Octavian (status not given) |
| *246g | Eunomius at Constantinople (status not given) |
| 247f | the clergy of Aquileia |

## Monasticism/Monks (8 notices)

| *233h | Antony |
| *240b | Antony, Paul of Thebes |
| 240e | Sarmata, Amatas, Macarius; disciples of Antony |
| *240h | death of Sarmata |
| *247d | Melania at Jerusalem |
| *248a | monks at Nitria |
| 248b | law of Valens requiring monks to serve in the army; capital punishment by clubbing for refusal |
| 248g | Florentinus, Bonosus, Rufinus; distinguished monks |

## Relations with Persia (7 notices)

| *234b | Constantine's perparations for war |
| 234d | Sapor's devastation of Mesopotamia and siege of Nisibis |

| | |
|---|---|
| *236b | Sapor's persecution of Christians |
| 236h | Sapor's second siege of Nisibis |
| *236l | Persian victory at Singara; Constantius' lack of participation in nine battles |
| *243b | Julian's expedition and defeat |
| *243c | surrender of Mesopotamian territory to Sapor by Jovian |

## Philosophers (3 notices)

| | |
|---|---|
| 232h | Metrodorus |
| 242f | Prohaeresius, sophist |
| 248d | Photinus, founder of Photinianism |

# APPENDIX C

## A LIST SUGGESTING JEROME'S MAIN SOURCES AND HIS "ORIGINAL"
## INFORMATION

This list is based upon comparisons of the testimonia and sources in Helm's edition.

"Unknown" indicates either that all of these are later than the Chron. or that there are

none extant. Thus in at least some of these notices we possess Jerome's "original"

contribution, e.g., Chron. 231g on Arnobius' dreams, which are cited in none of our

extant sources. Data in Jerome's notices lacking in other extant sources is listed on

the right.

| Chronicon Notice | Main Source | Jerome's Unique Data |
|---|---|---|
| 231f | unknown | none |
| 231g | unknown | Arnobius' dreams led to his conversion. |
| 231h | The Arian | none |
| 231i | The Arian | none |
| 232a | Eutropius | none |
| 232b | unknown (cf. Optatus 1, 24ff.) | none |
| 232c | unknown (sim. to Theophanes) | none |
| 232d | unknown | none |
| 232e | unknown | none |
| 232f | unknown (sim. to Chron. Pasch.) | none |
| 232g | unknown (sim. to Theoph. and Chron. Pasch.) | none |
| 232h | unknown | none |
| 233a | unknown (sim. to Theoph.) | none |
| 233b | The Arian | Constantine's edict for the desctruction of the temples. |

130

| | | |
|---|---|---|
| | (cf. <u>Cons. Const</u>.) | |
| 233c | unknown | none |
| | (sim. to Theoph.) | |
| 233d | unknown | none |
| | (cf. <u>Cons. Const</u>.) | |
| 233e | The Arian | none |
| 233f | unknown | none |
| | (cf. <u>Cons. Const</u>.) | |
| 233g | The Arian | none |
| 233h | unknown | Constantine's letter to St. Antony. |
| | (sim. to Athanasius <u>Vita Antonii</u>) | |
| 233i | The Arian? | none |
| | (sim. to Theoph. and <u>Chron. Pasch</u>.) | |
| 233k | unknown | The rhetorician Pater at Rome. |
| 233l | unknown | The rhetorician Nazarius and his daughter. |
| 233m | unknown | Tiberianus' rhetoric. |
| 233n | The Arian | none |
| 234a | The Arian | none |
| 234b | Eutropius | The public villa at Ancyra. |
| 234c | The Arian | none |
| 234d | The Arian | none |
| 234e | Eutropius | none |
| 234f | The Arian | none |
| 234g | The Arian? | none |
| | (sim. to Theoph.) | |
| 235a | The Arian?` | The battle at <u>Alsa</u>, near Aquileia. |
| | (sim. to Theoph. <u>Chron. Pasch</u>.) | |
| 235b | unknown | none |
| | (cf. <u>Cons. Const</u>.) | |
| 235c | The Arian | none |
| 235d | unknown | none |
| | (sim. to Epiphanius' <u>Panar. Haer</u>.) | |
| 235e | The Arian? | none |
| | (sim. to Theoph.; cf. to <u>Cons. Const</u>. on the Franks and the peace) | |
| 235y | The Arian? | none |
| | (sim. to Theoph.) | |
| 235g | The Arian | none |
| 235h | The Arian | Macedonius was an embroiderer. |
| | (sim. to Theoph. on Macedonius and Paulus) | |
| 235i | unknown | none |
| | (sim. to Athanasius on | |

|  |  |  |
|---|---|---|
|  | Paulus, Philippus and the Macedonians) |  |
| 236a | The Arian? (sim. to Theoph. on Athanasius' exile and his letter) | none |
| 236b | The Arian | none |
| 236c | The Arian? (sim. to Theoph. on the earthquake and Neocaesaria) | none |
| 236d | unknown | The prefect Titianus' eloquence. |
| 236e | The Arian? (sim. to Theoph. on Constans and Athanasius) | none |
| 236f | The Arian | none |
| 236g | The Arian | none |
| 236h | The Arian | none |
| 236i | The Arian | Eusebius Emisenus as an Arian author. |
| 236k | The Arian | none |
| 236l | Eutropius, Festus (for Bizabde) and Jerome's composition (cf. also Cons. Const.) | none |
| 237a | Jerome's composition (sim. to Theoph. for bishops' names) | none |
| 237b | The Arian? (cf. Philostorgius for parallel events) | none |
| 237c | The Arian | none |
| 238a | unknown | Senator Heraclides betrayed the opponents of Magnentius at Rome. |
| 238b | Eutropius | none |
| 238c | The Arian | none |
| 238d | Eutropius (Victor for 28 days) | none |
| 238e | The Arian | none |
| 238f | The Arian? and Jerome's composition | The towns of Diospolis and Tiberias; the night ambush. |
| 238g | The Arian | none |
| 238h | Eutropius | none |
| 239a | unknown | Gennadius as orator. |
| 239b | unknown | Minervius as rhetorician at Rome. |
| 239c | The Arian | Gallus executed due to his "distinguished talent." |
| 239d | Eutropius | none |

| | | |
|---|---|---|
| 239e | Jerome's composition | Donatus, grammarian and Victorinus the rhetorician. |
| 239f | unknown | none |
| 239g | unknown | Delfidius and Alcimus, rhetoricians of Aquitania. |
| 239h | unknown | none |
| 239i | unknown (cf. Athanasius) | A Roman priest named Pancratius as one of the exiles from Rome. |
| 240a | The Arian | none |
| 240b | Jerome's composition | none |
| 240c | unknown (cf. Jerome, Vita Hilar. PL 9, 184) | none |
| 240d | unknown (cf. Chron. Pasch.) | none |
| 240e | unknown | Sarmata and Amatas, Antony's disciples; their connection with Macarius. |
| 240f | unknown (cf. Athanasius; see Helm, 451) | none |
| 240g | Eutropius | none |
| 240h | unknown | The Saracens' raid on Antony's monastery and and the death of Sarmata. |
| 240i | The Arian? (sim. to Theoph. and Chron. Pasch.) | none |
| 241a | Victor? | none |
| 241b | unknown | none |
| 241c | unknown | Evanthius and Chrestus, grammarians at Constantinople |
| 241d | unknown | none |
| 241e | unknown | none |
| 241f | unknown | none |
| 241g | unknown | Role of Hilary's book in his return from exile. |
| 241h | unknown (sim. to Theoph. and Chron. Pasch.) | none |
| 241i | unknown | none |
| 241k | The Arian | none |
| 2411 | unknown | none |
| 242a | unknown | The key role of Hilary in rejecting the Ariminum Creed in Gaul. |
| 242b | unknown (sim. to Theoph. and Chron. Pasch.) | none |
| 242c | The Arian | none |
| 242d | The Arian | none |
| 242e | unknown | Paulinus, bishop of Antioch. |

| 242f | unknown | none |
| | (cf. Julian Ep. 2, 42; | |
| | Greg. Naz. Or. 4, 6, | |
| | 101; 5, 39) | |
| 243a | The Arian | Reason for Aemilianus' martyrdom |
| 243b | The Arian | none |
| 243c | The Arian | none |
| 243d | unknown | Early account of synod at Antioch |
| | | and its adopion of Macedonian tenants |
| 243e | Eutropius | none |
| 244a | Unknown | none |
| 244b | The Arian? | none |
| | (sim. to Theoph. and | |
| | Chron. Pasch.) | |
| 244c | The Arian | none |
| 244d | unknown | none |
| 244e | unknown | none |
| 245a | unknown | none |
| | (an Arian author?) | |
| 245b | unknown | Ambiani in Gaul as the (cf. to Cons. Const.) |
| | | precise site of Gratian's elevation to |
| | | the throne. |
| 245c | unknown | none |
| | (cf. to Cons. Const.) | |
| 245d | unknown | Miracle of the wool at Atrabatae. |
| 245e | unknown | none |
| 245f | unknown | none |
| | (cf. to Cons. Const.) | |
| 245g | unknown | (Earliest historian to cite the achievements of |
| | | Libanius). |
| 245h | unknown | Valens' reopening of the Constantinople |
| | (cf. to Cons. Const.) | games. |
| 245i | unknown | (Earliest account of |
| | (cf. Ambrose In Luc., 2, 37) | Athanaric's persecution of Christians). |
| 245j | unknown | Eusebius of Vercellae's death. |
| 245m | unknown | none |
| | (cf. Cons. Const.) | |
| 246a | unknown | Lucifer of Cagliari's death; his comparison to |
| | | two other bishops, Gregory in Spain |
| | | and Philo in Libya. |
| 246c | unknown | Jerome has Valentinianus; see note on 246c. |
| | | Ammianus correctly has Valentinus. |
| 246d | unknown | (Earliest record of this execution of the |
| | | unnamed protector of Octavianus.) |
| 246e | unknown | Blindness of Didymus of Alexandria. |
| 246f | unknown | none |
| 246h | unknown | Deuso as the site of the Saxons' defeat. |
| 247a | unknown | The number of Burgundians. |

| | | |
|---|---|---|
| 247b | unknown | none |
| 247c | unknown | none |
| 247d | unknown | none |
| 247e | unknown | none |
| | (cf. to Athanasius *admon*. 75) | |
| 247f | unknown | The <u>reputation</u> of the clergy of Aquileia. |
| 247g | unknown | none |
| 247h | Cf. <u>Cons. Const.</u> | none |
| 248a | unknown | The execution of monks by clubbing for refusal to serve as soldiers. |
| 248b | unknown | none |
| 248c | unknown | none |
| 248d | unknown | none |
| 248e | unknown | none |
| 248f | Unknown | none |
| 248g | unknown | Florentinus, Bonosus, and Rufinus, monks. |
| 248h | unknown | none |
| | (cf. <u>Cons. Const.</u>) | |
| 249a | unknown | none |
| 249b | unknown | none |
| 249c | The Arian | none |
| 249d | Eusebius | none |
| 250 | (ibid.) | none |

# BIBLIOGRAPHY

## Ancient Works

Africanus. *Sextus Julius Africanus. List of the Victors at the Olympic Games.* I. Rutgers, ed. Chicago: Ares Publishers, Inc., 1980, repr. of 1862 ed.

Ambrose. *In Lucan.* C. Schenkl, ed. *CSEL* 32. Vienna: Tempsky, 1902.

Ammianus Marcellinus. *Ammiani Marcellini Rerum Gestarum Libri Qui Supersunt.* C.U. Clark, Ed. Berlin: Wiedmann 1963, repr. of 1917 ed.

_____. *Ammien Marcellin. Historie.* 2 vols. E. Galletier and J. Fontaine, eds. Paris: Société d 'édition, Les belles lettres, 1968.

Anan Isho. *The Paradise or Garden of the Holy Fathers.* E.A.W. Budge, trans. New York: B. Franklin, 1972 repr. of 1907 ed.

Anonymus. *Anonymou Synopsis Chronice.* C. N. Sathas, ed. Bibliotheca Graeca Medii Aevi. Vol. 7. Mesaionikes Bibliothekes. Paris: Jean Maisonneuve, Libraire-éditeur, 1894.

Anonymus Matritensis. *Anonymi Chronographia Syntomos e Codice Matriensi No. 121 (Nunc 4701).* A. Bauer, ed. Leipzig: Teubner, 1909.

Anthologia Latina. *Anthologia Latina sive Poesis Latinae Supplementum.* F. Buecheler and A. Riese, eds. Amsterdam: Adolf M. Hakkert, 1964.

Arnobius. *Adversus Nationes.* A. Reiffersheid, ed. *CSEL* 4. Vienna: Tempsky, 1875.

_____. *Arnobius of Sicca. The Case Against the Pagans.* Newly Translated and Annotated. 2 vols. G. McCracken, trans. *ACW* vols. 7 and 8. New York: Newman Press, 1949.

Athanasius. *Ad Monachos; Apologia de Fuga; Apologia contra Arianos; Apologia ad Constantium.* *PG* 25. J. P. Migne. Paris: 1884.

_____. *Vita Antonii.* *PG* 26. J. P. Migne. Paris: 1857-1866.
Augustine. *De Haeresibus.* *CCSL* 46. *Aureli Augustini Opera.* Pars 13, 2. Turnhout: Typographi Brepols Editores Pontificii, 1969.

Aurelius, Victor. *Aurelius Victor. Livre des Cesars.* P. Dufraigne, ed. Paris: Société d'édition, Les belles lettres, 1975.

_____. *Sexti Aurelii Victoris. Liber de Caesaribus (Praecedunt Origo Gentis Romanae et Liber de Viris Illustribus Urbis Romae Subsequitur Epitome de Caesaribus)*. F. Pichlmayr, ed. Leipzig: Teubner, 1966.

Ausonius. *Decimi Magni Ausonii Burdigalensis Opuscula*. P. Sextus, ed. Leipzig: Teubner, 1978.

Avellana Collectio. *Epistulae Imperatorum Pontificum Aliorum (Inde Ab A. 367 usque ad A. 553 Datae) Avellana Quae Dicitur Collectio*. Pars 1, Prolegomena, Epistulae 1-104. O. Guenther, ed. *CSEL* 35. Vienna: Tempsky, 1895.

Boer, W. den. "Some Remarks on the Beginnings of Christian Historiography," *Studia Patristica* 4 (1959), 348-62.

Barhebraeus, Gregorius. *Gregorii Barhebraei Chronicon Ecclesiasticum Quod e Codice Musei Britannici Descriptum Conjuncta Opera Ediderat, Latinitate Donarunt Annotationibusque Theologicis, Historicis, Geographicis et Archaeologicis Illustrabunt)*. 2 vols. J. Abbeloos and T. Lamy, eds. Louvaine: Peeters, 1872.

Basil. *Saint Basil. The Letters*. R. Deferrari, trans. Cambridge: Harvard University Press, 1972.

Bede. *De Temporum Ratione*. T. Mommsen, ed. *MGH. Chronica Minora* 3. Berlin, Wiedmann, 1892.

Boer, W. den. "Some Remarks on the Beginnings of Christian Historiography," *Studia Patristica* 4 (1959), 348-62.

Camus, P.-M. *Ammien Marcellin. Temoin des courants culturels et religieux à la fin du Ive siécle*. Paris: Société d'Édition "Les belles lettres," 1967.

Cassiodorus. *Historia Tripartita*. T. Mommsen, ed. *MGH. Chronica Minora* 2. 2nd. ed. Berlin: Wiedmann, 1961.

Cedrenus, Georgius. *Synopsis Historion*. I. Bekker, ed. *CSHB*. Bonn: Weber, 1838.

*Chronica Alexandrina. MGH. Chronica Minora* 1. 2nd ed. T. Mommsen, ed. Berlin: Wiedmann, 1961.

*Chronica Italica. MGH. Chronica Minora* 1. 2nd ed. T. Mommsen, ed. Berlin: Wiedmann, 1961.

*Chronicon Paschale*. B. G. Niebuhr, ed. *CSHB*. Bonn: Academia Litterarum Regiae Borussicae, 1832.

*Chronographeion Syntomon*. See Eusebius, *Eusebii Chronicorum*, etc. A. Schoene, ed. Appendix 4.

*Codex Theodosianus*. 2 vols. T. Mommsen, and W. Meyer, eds. Berlin: Wiedmann, 1905.

*Consularia Constantinopolitana*. See Iulius Pollux.

*Corpus Inscriptionum Latinarum*. (*Consilio et auctoriate Academiae Litterarum Regiae Borussicae editum*). Berlin: Reimerum, 1862--.

Epiphanius. *De Mensuris et Ponderibus*. J. P. Migne, ed. *PG* 43. Paris: 1857-1866.

_____. *Panararion Haeresium*. K. Holl, ed. *GCS* 25. Leipzig: Akademie-Verlag, 1915.

_____. *Panararion Haeresium*. *PG* 42. Paris: J. P. Migne, 1863.

Eunapius. *The Fragmentary Classicising Historians of the Later Roman Empire: Eunapius, Olympiodorus, Priscus and Malchus*. 2 vols. Liverpool: Cairns, 1981.

_____. *Philostratus and Eunapius. The Lives of the Sophists*. W. Wright, trans. *LCL*. Cambridge: Harvard University Press, 1952.

Eusebius. *Eusebii Canonum Epitome ex Dionysii Telmaharensis Chronica Petita.* (*Societa Opera Verterunt Notisque Illustraverunt Carolus Siegfried et Henricus Gelzer*). C. Siegfried and H. Goelzer, eds. Leipzig: Teubner, 1884.

_____. *Eusebii Chronicorum Canonum Quae Supersunt.* (*Edidit Alfred Schoene Armeniam Versionem Latine Factam e Libris Mansucriptis Recensuit H. Petermann. Hieronymi Versionem e Libris Manuscriptis Recensuit A. Schoene Syriam Epitomen Latine Factam e Libro Londinensis Recensuit E. Roediger*). A. Schoene, ed. Berlin: Wiedmann, 1866.

_____. *Eusebii Pamphili Caesariensis Episcopi Chronicon Bipartitum.* (*Nunc Primum ex Armeniaco Textu in Latinam Conversum Adnotationibus Auctum Graecis Fragmentis Exornatum*). P.J.B. Aucher, ed. Venice: Typis Coenobii pp. Armenorum in Insula S. Lazari, 1818.

_____. *Eusebii Pamphili Chronici Canones.* (*Latine Vertit, Adauxit, ad Sua Tempora Produxit S. Eusebio Hieronymus*). J. K. Fotheringham, ed. London: H. Milford, 1923.

_____. *Eusebii Pamphili Chronicorum Canonum Libri Duo.* (*Opus ex Haicano Codice a Iohanne Zohrabo Diligenter Expressum et Castigatum Angelus Maius et Iohannes Zohrabus and Primum Coniunctis Cuius Latinitate Donatum Notisque Illustratum Additis Graecis Religuis Ediderunt*). A. Mai and J. Zohrab, eds. Milan: Regiis Typis, 1818.

Eusebius. *Eusebii Pamphili Chronicorum Libri.* (*Scriptorum Veterum Nova Collectio e Vaticanis Codicibus Edita.* v. 8). A. Mai, ed. Rome: 1833. repr. in *PL* 27. Paris: 1854-1864.

_____. *Eusebius. Church History, Life of Constantine the Great and Oration in Praise of Constantine.* P. Schaff and H. Wade, eds. *SL.* 2nd s. Grand Rapids: Wm. B. Eerdmans, 1952.

_____. *Die Chronik des Eusebius aus dem armenischen übersetzt. Eusebius Werke* 5. J. Karst, ed. *GCS* 20. Leipzig: Akademie-Verlag, 1911.

_____. *Die Chronik des Hieronymus. Hieronymi Chronicon. Eusebius Werke* 6. R. Helm, ed. *GCS* 21. Leipzig: Akademie-Verlag, 1956.

_____. *In Praise of Constantine: A Historical Study and New Translation of Eusebius' Tricennial Orations.* H. A. Drake, trans. Berkeley: University of California Press, 1976.

_____. *Oratio de Laudibus Constantini. Eusebius Werke* 1. I. A. Heikel, ed. *GCS* 7. Leipzig: Hinrichs, 1902.

_____. *The Ecclesiastical History.* 2 vols. K. Lake trans. Cambridge: Harvard University Press, 1980.

_____. *Über das Leben des Kaisers Constantin. Eusebius Werke* 1. F. Winkelmann, ed. *GCS* . Berlin: Akademie-Verlag, 1975.

Eutropius. *Eutropii Breviarium ab Urbe Condita.* C. Santini, ed. Leipzig: Teubner, 1979.

Evagrius. *Vita Antonii.* J. P. Migne, ed. *PL* 73. Paris: 1844-1864.

*Excerpta Barbari.* See Eusebius, *Eusebii Chronicorum*, etc. A. Schoene, ed. Appendix 6.

Facundus Hermianensis. *Pro Defensione Trium Capitulorum. PL* 67. J. P. Migne, ed. Paris: 1854-1864.

Festus. *The Breviarium of Festus. A Critical Edition with Historical Commentary.* J. W. Eadie, ed. London: The Athlone Press, 1967.

Filastrius. *Sancti Filastrii Episcopi Brixiensis Diversarum Hereseon Liber.* F. Marx, ed. *CSEL* 38. Vienna: Tempsky, 1898.

*Fragmenta Historicorum Graecorum.* C. Muller, ed. Paris: Didot, 1868.

*Fragmenta Patrum Graecorum: Auctorum Historiae Ecclesiasticae Fragmenta (1814-1815).* G. Leopardi, ed. Florence: Le Monnier, 1976.

Gelasius of Caesarea. *Die Kirchengeschichte des Gelasios von Kaisareia. Byzantinisches Archiv* 6. A. Glas, ed. Leipzig: Hinrichs, 1914.

Gennadius. *De Viris Illustribus.* in *Hieronymus. De Viris Illustribus.* Richardson Texte and Untersuchungen 14. E. C. Richardson, ed. Leipzig: Hinrichs, 1896.

Georgius Monachus. *Chronicon Breve. (Quod ex Variis Chronographis et Expositoribus Decerpsit Concinnavitque). Georgius Monachus Cognomine Hamartolus.* E. de Muralto, ed. *PG* 110. Paris: 1857-1866.

Goulet, R. "Porphyre et la datation de Moise," *Revue de l'histoire des religions* 184 (1977), 137-64.

Gregory Nazianzen. *Orationes. PG* 35-36. J. P. Migne, ed. Paris: 1857-1866.

Grosse, R. *Römische Militärgeschichte von Galienus bis zum Beginn der byzantinischen Themenverfassung.* Berlin, 1920.

Hegemonius. *Hegemonius. Acta Archelai.* C. H. Beeson, ed. *GCS* 16. Leipzig: Akademie-Verlag, 1906.

Hieronymus. *Chronicon.* See Eusebius, *Die Chronik, des Hieronymus.*

_____. "Life of St. Paul, the First Hermit," "The Life of Hilarion of Gaza," and "Life of Malchus," in *FCNT* 15, ed. by R. J. Deferrari. Washington: The Fathers of the Church, Inc., 1952.

_____. *Lettres.* 8 vols. J. Labourt, trans. Paris: Les Belles Lettres, 1949.

_____. *Opera Exegetica.* 8 vols. *CCSL* 72-73, 73A-75A, 76-76A, 77. Turnholt: Brepols, 1959-1970.

_____. *Opera Homiletica,* Pars II. *CCSL* 78. Turnholt: Brepols, 1958.

_____. *Opera Polemica,* Pars I. *CCSL* 79. Turnholt: Brepols,1982.

_____. *Saint Jerome: Letters and Select Works. SL* 6. H. Wace and P. Schaff, eds. New York: Charles Scribner's Sons, 1912.

_____. *Saint Jerome. Dogmatic and Polemical Works.* J. N. Hritzu, trans. Washington: Catholic University of America, 1965.

_____. *Sancti Eusebii Hieronyumi Epistolae*. I. Hilberg, ed. Vienna: F. Tempsky, 1910-1918.

_____. *Select Letters of St. Jerome*. F. A. Wright, trans. Cambridge: Harvard University Press, 1980.

_____. *The Homilies of Saint Jerome*. 2 vols. M. L. Ewald, trans. Washington: Catholic University of America, 1966.

_____. *The Letters of Saint Jerome*. C. C. Mierow, trans. New York: Newman Press, 1963.

*Historia Brittonum (Cum Addendis Nennii)*. T. Mommsen, ed. *MGH Chronica Minora* 3. Berlin: Wiedmann, 1892.

Ioannes Lydus. *Ioannis Lydi de Magistratibus Populi Romani Libri Tres*. R. Wuensch, ed. Stuttgart: Teubner, 1967.

Iulianus. *Orationes*. F. C. Hertlein, ed. Leipzig: Teubner, 1877.

Iulius Pollux. *Julii Pollucis Historia Physica seu Chronicon ab Origine Mundi usque ad Valentis Tempora*. I. Hardt, ed. Munich and Leipzig: Joseph Lindauer, 1792.

Iuvencus. *Evangeliorum Libri*. J. P. Migne, ed. *PL* 19. Paris: 1844-1864.

*Laterculus Heraclianus*. T. Mommsen, ed. *MGH. Chronica Minora* 3. Berlin: Wiedmann, 1892.

Leo Grammaticus. *Chronographia*. I. Bekker, ed. *CSHB*. Bonn: Dindorf, 1842.

_____. *S.P.N. Theophanis Abbatis Agri et Confessoris Chronographia. Cui Accedunt Leonis Grammatici, Auctoris Incerti, Anastasii Bibliothecarii*. G. Henschen, ed. *PG* 108. Paris: 1863.

Libanius. *Libanii Opera*. v. 4. *Orationes 51-64*. R. Foerster, ed. Hildesheim: Georg Olms, 1963.

_____. *Libanius. Selected Works*. 3 vols. A. F. Norman, trans. vol. 1. *The Julianic Orations*. Cambridge: Harvard University Press, 1969.

*Liber Genealogus*. T. Mommsen, ed. *MGH Chronica Minora* 1. Berlin: Wiedmann, 1892.

Malalas. *Chronographia*. L. Weber, ed. *CSHB*. Bonn: Dindorf, 1831.

_____. *s.p.n. Andreae Cretensis Archiepiscopi Opera Quae Reperiri Potuerunt Omnia Accedunt Joannis Malalae Theodori Abucanae Carum Episcopi*. J. P. Migne, ed. *PG* 97. Paris: 1865.

142

_____. *The Chronicle of John Malalas*. E. Jeffries, M. Jeffries and R. Scott, trans. Byzantina Australensia 4. Melbourne: Australian Association of Byzantine Studies, 1986.

Nicephorus Callistus. *Die Kirchengeschichte des Nicephorus Callistus Xanthopulus und ihre Quellen*. G. Gentz and F. Winkelmann, eds. *TU* 98. Berlin: Akademie-Verlag, 1966.

_____. *Nicephori Callisti Xanthopouli Ecclesiasticae Historiae Libri 18*. *(Accedunt Maximi Planudae, Callisti et Ignatii, Callisti Cataphugiotae, Nicephori Monachi, Scripta Varii Argumenti)*. *PG* 145-146. Paris: J. P. Migne, 1865.

_____. *Nicephori Archiepiscopi Constantinopolitani Opuscula Historica*. *(Accedit Ignati Diaconi Vita Nicephori)*. C. de Boor, ed. Roman History Series. New York: Arno Press, Inc., 1975, repr. of Leipzig 1880 ed.

Optatus Milevitanus. *S. Optati Milevitani Libri 7*. *(Recensuit et Commentario Critico Indicesque Instruxit Carolus Ziwsa. Accedunt Decem Monumenta ad Vetera Donatistarum Historiam Pertinentia)*. *CSEL* 26. Vienna: Tempsky, 1893.

*Origo Constantini. Anonymus Valesianus, Teil 1. Text und Kommentar*. I. Konig, ed. Trier: Trierer Historische Forschungen, 1987.

Orosius. *Orosius. Pauli Orosii Historiarum adversum Paganos Libri 7*. C. Zangemeister, ed. Vienna: C. Geroldson Bibliopola Academie, 1882.

Palladius. *The Lausiac History of Palladius*. J. A. Robinson, ed. Texts and Studies Contributing to Biblical and Patristic Literature. v. 6, no. 2. Cambridge: Harvard University Press, 1904.

_____. *The Lausiac History*. R. Meyer, trans. *ACW* 34. New York: Newman Press, 1964.

*Panegyrici Latini*. *(Scriptores Graeci et Latini Consilio Academiae Lynceorum Editi)*. V. Paladini and P. Fedeli, eds. Rome: Typis Officinae Polygraphicae, 1976.

Paulinus Nolanus. *Sancti Pontii Meropii Paulini Nolani Epistulae. Recensuit et Commentario Critico Instruxit Guilelmus de Hartel*. Vienna: Tempsky, 1894.

Philostorgius. *Artemii Passio*. (See *Philostorgius. Kirchengeschichte*).

_____. *Philostorgius. Kirchengeschichte*. 2nd ed. J. Bidez, ed. *GCS* 21. Berlin: Akademie-Verlag, 1972.

_____. See Sozomenus. *The Ecclesiastical History*, etc.

Philostratus. See Eunapius, *Philostratus and Eunapius.*

Photius. *Bibliotheca ex Recensione Immanuelis Bekker.* Berlin: Reimer, 1824-1825.

_____. *Photius. Bibliotheque.* 2 vols. R. Henry, ed. Paris: Société d'édition Les belles lettres, 1977.

Porphyrius. *Publilii Optantiani Porfyrii Carmina.* 2 vols. P. Giovanni, ed. Turin: G. B. Paravia and Co., 1973.

Prosper Tironis. *Epitoma Chronicon.* T. Mommsen, ed. *MGH. Chronica Minora* 1. 2nd ed. Berlin: Wiedmann, 1961.

Rufinus. *Rufinus Kirchengeschichte.* In *Eusebius Werke,* T. Mommsen, ed. *GCS* 9, 2. Leipzig: Hinrichs, 1908.

*The Scriptores Historiae Augustae.* 3 vols. D. Magie trans. *LCL.* Cambridge: Harvard University Press, 1979.

Socrates. *Historia Ecclesiastica. PG* 67. Paris: J. P. Migne, ed., 1864.

_____. *Socrates, Sozomenus: Church Histories.* P. Schaff and H. Wade, eds. *SL.* 2nd s. Grand Rapids: Wm. B. Erdmans, 1952.

Sozomenus. *Church History.* A. C. Zenos, trans. (See Socrates. *Socrates, Sozomenus,* etc.)

_____. *Sozomenus. Kirchengeschichte.* J.Bidez, ed. *GCS* 50. Berlin: Alkademie-Verlag, 1960.

_____. *The Ecclesiastical History of Sozomen . . . also the Ecclesiastical History of Philostorgius as Epitomized by Photius.* E. Walford, trans. London: Henry G. Bohn, 1855.

Suidas. *Lexicon.* A. Adler, ed. 5 vols. Leipzig: Teubner, 1928-1938.

Symmachus. *Symmache: Lettres.* J. P. Callu, trans. Paris: Société d'édition, Les belles lettres, 1972.

Syncellus. *Georgius Syncellus et Nicephorus cp. ex Recensione Gujilielmi Dindorfii.* E. Weber, ed. Bonn: Academia Litterarum Regiae Borussicae, 1829.

Theodoretus. *Haeresium Fabulae.* L. Parmentier, ed. *GCS* 19. Leipzig: Hinrichs, 1911.

_____. *Theodoretus. Kirchengeschichte.* 2nd ed. L. Parmentier and Scheidweiler, eds. *GCS* 44. Berlin: Akademie-Verlag, 1954.

144

Theophanes. *Chronograhia*. 2 vols. C. de Boor, ed. Leipzig: Teubner, 1883.

Theophylactus. *Martyrium Sanctorum Quindecim Illustrium Martyrium. (Qui Imperante Impio Juliano Apostata Tiberiopoli, Quae Strumitza Bulgarice Dicitur. Interprete Bonifacio Finetti.) PG* 126. Paris: J. P. Migne, 1857-1866.

Venantius Fortunatus. *Vita Hilarii*. B. Krusch, ed. *MGH* Auctores Antiquissimi 4, 2. Berlin: Wiedmann, 1885.

Victor Aquitanus. *Cursus Paschalis Annorum DXXXII*. T. Mommsen, ed. *MGH Chronica Minora* 1. 2nd ed. Berlin: Wiedmann, 1961.

Vincentius Lirinensis. *Commonitorium Primum. PL* 50. J. P. Migne, ed. Paris: 1865.

*Vita Athanasii. PG* 25. Paris: J. P. Migne, ed., 1857-1866.

Zonaras. *Ioannou tou Zonara ta Euriskomena Panta. PG* 134. J. P. Migne, ed. Paris: 1957-1866.

Zosimus. *Zosime. Histoire Nouvelle*. 3 vols. Paris: Société d'Édition, Les belles lettres, 1971-1979.

_____. *Zosimus. New History*. R. Ridley, trans. Australian Association for Byzantine Studies. Byzantina Australensia 2. Sydney: University of Sydney, 1982.

## Modern Works

Aegidius, J. P., ed. *Lexikon des Mittel Alters*. v. 2. *Bettlerwesen bis Codex Valencia*. Munich: Artemis Verlag, 1983.

Alfoldi, A., N. Himmelmann-Wildschutz, J. Straub and K. Takenberg, eds. *Antiquitas*. Reiche 3. Abhandlungen zur Vor- und Frugheschichte, zur Klassischen und provinzial-römischen Archäologie und zur Geschichte des Altertums. Band 23. Bonn: Rudolf Habelt, 1978.

_____. *Antiquitas*. Reihe 4. Beitrage zur Historia-Augusta-Forschung unter Mitwirkung von Johannes Straub. Band 2, 3 and 7. Bonn: Rudolf Habelt Verlag, 1964, 1966 and 1970.

_____. "Die verlorene Enmannsche Kaisergeschichte und die *Caesares* des Julianus Apostata," *Bonner H-A Collection* 1966-1967 (Bonn, 1968) v. 4, 1-8.

_____. *The Conflict of Ideas in the Late Roman Empire. The Clash between the Senate and Valentinian I.* I. H. Mattingly, trans. Oxford: Oxford University Press, 1952.

Allen, J. S. *BZ. Author Index of Byzantine Studies.* Washington: Dumbarton Oaks Center for Byzantine Studies, 1986-  .

_____ and I. Sevcenko, eds. *Literature in Various Byzantine Disciplines, 1892-1977.* Washington: Mansell, 1981.

Alonzo-Nunez, J. M. "An Augustan World History: The *Historiae Philippicae* of Pompeius Trogus," *GR* 34 no. 1 (April 1987) 56-72.

_____. "Aurelius Victor et la Peninsule Iberique," *Latomus* 41 (1982) 362-4.

Altaner, B. "Augustinus und Eusebios von Kaisarea. Eine quellenkritische Untersuchung," *BZ* 44 (1951) 1-6.

_____. "Der Einfluss und das Fortleben der griechischen Literatur im Abendland vom die zweite Halfte des 6 - Jahrhunderts," *TR* 48 (1952) 41-50.

_____, and A. Stuiber. *Patrologie, Leben, Schriften und Lehre der Kirchenvater.* Vienna: Herder, 1966.

Anderson, J. C., Jr. "A Topographical Tradition in Fourth Century Chronicles: Domitian's Building Program," *Historia* 32 (1983) 93-105.

Andresen, K. et al., eds. *Lexikon der Alten Welt.* Zurich and Stuttgart: Artemis Verlag, 1965.

Antin, P. "Jérôme, antique et chrétien," *ReAug* 16 (1970) 35-46.

_____. *Recueil sur saint Jérôme.* Collection Latomus 95. Brussels: Latomus. Revue d'études latines, 1968.

Arce, J. "The Inscription of Troesmis (ILS 724) and the First Victories of Constantius II as Caesar," *ZPE* 48 (1982) 245-49.

Ashton, N. G. "The Lamian War. Stat magni nominis umbra," *JHS* 104 (1984) 152-7.

Aubert, R. and E. van Cauwenbergh, eds. *Dictionnaire d'Histoire et de Géographie ecclésiastiques.* Paris: Letouzey et Ane, 1963.

Bagnall, R. S., A. Cameron, S. R. Schwartz and K. A. Worp. *Consuls of the later Roman Empire.* Philological Monographs of the American Philological Association, No. 36. Atlanta: Scholars Press, 1987.

Baker, D., ed. *The Materials Sources and Methods of Ecclesiastical History*. Oxford: Blackwell, 1975.

Baldus, H. R. "Constantius et Constans Augusti. Darstellungen des Kaiserlichen Bruderpaares auf Pragungen der Jahre 340-350 n. Chr.," *JNG* 34 (1984) 77-106.

Baldwin, B. "Literature and Society in the Later Roman Empire," in Gold, *Literary and Artistic Patronage*, below, 67-83.

_____. *Studies on Late Roman and Byzantine History, Literature and Language*. Amsterdam: J. C. Gieben, 1984.

Banchich, T. M. *The Historical Fragments of Eunapius of Sardis*. Diss. State University of New York at Buffalo, 1985.

Bardenhewer, O. *Geschichte der altkirchlichen Literatur*. 5 vols. Freiburg: Herder, 1932.

Bardy, G. "La culture grecque dans l'Occident chrétien au IVᵉ siècle," *RSR* 29 (1939) 5-58.

_____. *La question des langues dans l'Église ancienne*. Paris: Beauchesne, 1948.

_____. *Recherches sur Saint Lucien d'Antioche et son école*. Paris: Gabriel Beauchesne et ses fils, 1936.

Barnes, T. D. *Constantine and Eusebius*. Cambridge: Harvard University Press, 1981.

_____. "Jerome and the Origo Constantini Imperatoris," *Phoenix* (Summer 1989) 158-61.

_____. "The Chronology of Montanism," *JTS* 21 (1970), 403-8.

_____. "The Lost Kaisergeschichte and the Latin Historical Tradition," *BHAC* (1968/69, 1970) 13f.

_____. *Tertullian*. Oxford: Oxford University Press, 1971.

_____. *The Sources of the Historia Augusta*. Collections Latomus 155. Brussels: Latomus, 1978.

_____. "Three Notes on the *Vita Probi*," *CQ* 20 (1970) 189-203.

_____. "Imperial Chronology, A.D. 337-350," Phoenix 34 (1980) 160-66.

_____. *The New Empire of Diocletian and Constantine*. Cambridge: Harvard University Press, 1982.

_____. "Two Victory Titles of Constantius," *ZPE* 52 (1983) 229-35.

Bartelink, G. J. "Hieronymus," in Greschat, ed. *Alte Kirche* II, 145-65.

Bastien, P. "Le monnayage de l'atelier de Lyon: De la reouverture de l'atelier en 318 à la mort de Constantin (318-337)," *Numis. romaine* XIII Wetteren Soc. d'éd. Num. rom. 1982.

Batiffol, P. "Un historiographe anonyme arien du IVe siècle," *RQ* 9 (1895) 57-97.

Baynes, N. "Eusebius and the Christian Empire," *Byzantine Studies and Other Essays*. London: Athlone Press, 1960, 168-72.

_____. *The Historia Augusta: Its Date and Purpose*. Oxford: Oxford University Press, 1926.

_____. "The Death of Julian the Apostate in Christian Legend," *JRS* 27 (1937) 22-29.

Bechtel, E. A. *Sanctae Silviae Peregrinatio: The Text and a Study of the Latinity*. Chicago: The University of Chicago diss., 1902.

Beck, H. G. *Kirche und theologische Literatur im byzantinischen Reich*. Munich: Beck, 1959.

Bellezza, A. "Interpretazione di un passo di Aurelio Vittore (*Caesares* 33, 34) sulla politica imperiale romana del III secolo," *Atti della Accademia Ligure di Scienze e Lettere* 17 (1960) 149-71.

Berardino, A. di. *Patrology*. v. 4. *The Golden Age of Latin Patristic Literature From the Council of Nicea to the Council of Chalcedon*. P. Solari, trans. Westminster, MD: Christian Classics, Inc., 1986.

Bernays, J. *Joseph Justus Scaliger*. New York: Burt Franklin Press, 1965 repr. of 1855 Berlin ed.

Bernouilli, C. A. *Der Schriftstellerkatalog des Hieronymus*. Freiburg and Leipzig: Mohr, 1895.

Berschin, W. *Griechisch-lateinisches Mittelalter. Von Hieronymus zu Nikolaus von Kues*. Bern: Francke, 1980.

Bickel, E. *Diatribe in Senecae Philosophi Fragmenta*, vol. 1. *Fragmenta de Matrimonio*. Leipzig: Teubner, 1915.

Bickerman, E. J. *Chronology of the Ancient World*. London: Thames and Hudson, 1968.

Bidez, J. "Fragments nouveaux de Philostorge sur la Vie de Constantin," *Byzantion* 10 (1935) 403-42.

_____. "L'historien Philostorge," *Mélanges d'histoire offerts à Henri Pirenne*. Brussels: Vromant and Co., 1926, 23-30.

_____. *La vie de l'empereur Julien*. 2nd ed. Paris: Société d'Édition, 1965.

Bird, H. W. "A Note on the *De Caesaribus* 34, 7-8," *CJ* 67 (1988) 360-1.

_____. "A Reconstruction of the Life and Career of S. Aurelius Victor," *CJ* 70 (1975) 49-54.

_____. "A Strong Aggregate of Errors for A.D. 193," *CB* 65 (1989) 3-4, 95-98.

_____. "Aurelius Victor and the Accession of Claudius II," *CJ* 66 (1971) 252-4.

_____. "Eutropius: His Life and Career," *Échos* 32, 1 (1988) 51-60.

_____. "Further Observations on the Dating of Enmann's *Kaisergeschichte*," *CQ* n.s. 23 (1973) 375-7.

_____. *Sextus Aurelius Victor. A Historical Study*. ARCA Classical and Medieval Texts, Papers and Monographs 14. Liverpool: Francis Cairns, 1984.

_____. "The Sources of the *De Caesaribus*," *CQ* n.s. 31 (1981) 457-63.

_____. "Three Fourth Century Issues. A Roman Bureaucrat's Personal Views," *Échos* 20, 3 (Oct. 1976) 91-6.

Blatt, F. "Remarques sur l'histoire des traductions latines," *CM* 1 (1938) 217-42.

Bliase, A. *Dictionnaire Latin-francais des auteurs chrétiens*. Paris: Libraire des Meridiens, 1954.

Blockley, R. C. *Ammianus Marcellinus: A study of His Historiography and Political Thought*. Brussels: Latomus, 1975.

_____. "Constantius, Gallus and Julian as Caesars of Constantius II," *Latomus* 31 (1972) 433-68.

Boehmer, H. "Zur altrömischen Bischofsliste," *ZNW* 7 (1906) 333-9.

Boer, W. den. *Le culte des souverains dans l'empire romain*. Entretiens sur l'antiquité classique, 19. Vandoeuvres-Geneve Fondation Hardt, 1973.

_____. "Rome à travers trois auteurs du quatrieme siècle," *Mnemosyne* 21 (1968) 254-82.

_____. *Some Minor Roman Historians*. Leiden: Brill, 1972.

_____. "Some Remarks on the Beginnings of Christian Historiography," *TU* 79 (1961) 348-62.

Bonfils, G. de. "Alcune riflessioni sulla legislazione di Costanzo II Costante," *Accad. Const. V Conv.* 299-309.

Booth, A. "The Date of Jerome's Birth," *Phoenix* 33 (1971) 346-52.

Boularand, E. "Les débuts d'Arius," *Bulletin de littérature ecclésiastiques* 65 (1964) 178-79.

Bousset, W. *Der Antichrist in der Überlieferung des Judentums des Neuens Testaments und der alten Kirche*. Gottingen: Vandenhoek und Ruprecht, 1895.

Bowder, D. *The Age of Constantine and Julian*. London: 1978.

Bregman, J. *Synesius of Cyrene. Philosopher-Bishop*. Berkeley: University of California Press, 1982.

Brincken, A.-D., von den. *Studien zur lateinische Weltchronik bis in das Zeitalter Ottos von Freising*. Dusseldorf: Michael Triltsch Verlag, 1957.

Brochet, J. *Saint Jérôme et ses enemis*. diss. Paris: 1905.

Brown, P. *Society and the Holy in Late Antiquity*. Berkeley: University of California Press, 1982.

Browning, R. *The Emperor Julian*. Berkeley: University of California Press, 1976.

Bruun, P. "Gloria Romanorum," *Studia Kajanto*. Arctos. Suppl. II. Helsinki, Classical Association of Finland, 1985, 23-31.

Buck, D. F. "Eunapius of Sardis and Theodosius the Great," *Byzantion* 58 (1988) 36-53.

Budischovsky, M.-C. Review of F. Thelamon, *Rufin, Histoire ecclésiastique, Recherches sur la valeur historique de l'Histoire ecclésiastique de Rufin d' Aquilee*. *RH* 528 (1978) 522-5.

Burckhardt, J. *The Age of Constantine the Great*. Trans. by Moses Hadas. Berkeley: University of California Pres, 1983.

Bury, J. B. *History of the Later Roman Empire from the Death of Theodosius I to the Death of Justinian (395-565)*. 2 vols. New York: Dover 1958 repr. of 1923 ed.

_____. *The Invasion of Europe by the Barbarians*. New York: W. W. Norton and Company, Inc., 1967.

Caenegem, R. C. van. *Guide to the Sources of Medieval History*. v. 2. *Europe in the Middle Ages, Selected Studies*. Amsterdam: North-Holland Publishing Co., 1978.

Calder, W. M., III. Review of A. Grafton, *Joseph Scaliger: A Study in the History of Classical Scholarship. I: Textual Criticism and Exegesis*. Oxford: Clarendon Press, 1983.

Calderone, S. "Teologia politica, successione dinastica e consecratio in eta constantiniana," in Boer, W. den, *Le Culte des souverains dans l'empire romain* (above).

Cameron, A.D.E. Review of J. Straub, *Heidnische Geschichtsapologetik in der christlichen Spätantike*. *JRS* 55 (1965) 240.

_____. "Literary Allusions in the Historia Augusta," *Hermes* 92 (1964) 363-77.

_____. "Three Notes on the Historia Augusta," *CR* n.s. 18 (1968) 17-20.

_____ and A. "Christianity and Tradition in the Historiography of the Late Empire," *CQ* n.s. 14 (1964) 316-28.

Carington Smith, J. "Pilate's Wife?" *Antichthon* 18 (1984) 102-7.

Cary, M. and H. H. Scullard. *A History of Rome Down to the Reign of Constantine*. 3rd ed. New York: St. Martin's Press, 1975.

Caspar, E. *Die älteste römische Bischofsliste: Kritische Studien zum Formproblem des eusebianischen Kanons*. Schriften der Konigsberger gelehrte Gesellschaft Geisteswiss. Kl. 2, no. 4. Berlin: Deutsche Verlagsgesellschaft für Politik und Geschichte, 1926.

_____. "Helm, Eusebius Werke VII," *Gottingische gelehrte Anzeigen* 189 (1927) 161-84.

Cassidy, F. P. *Molders of the Medieval Mind*. The Influence of the Fathers of the Church on the Medieval Schoolmen. Port Washington, NJ: Kennikat Press, 1966 repr. of 1944 ed.

Cataudella, M. "Per la cronologia dei rapporti fra cristiano e impero agli inzi del IV secolo," *Siculorum Gymnasium* 20 (1967) 83-110.

Cavallera, F. "The Personality of St. Jerome," *A Monument to St. Jerome*, 13-34. See Murphy below.

_____. *Le Schisme d'Antioche* (ive-ve siecle). Paris: 1905.

_____. *Saint Jérôme: sa vie et son oeuvre.* 2 vols. Specilegium sacrum Lovaninse études et documents, fasc. 1. Louvain: Specilegium sacrum Lovaniense, 1922.

Ceresa-Gastaldo, A. "The Biographical Method of Jerome's 'De Viris Illustribus,'" in *Studia Patristica* 15. Berlin: Akademie-Verlag, 1984, 55-68.

Chadwick, H., ed. *Alexandrian Christianity. Selected Translations of Clement and Origen.* J. E. L. Oulton and H. Chadwick trans. *LCC.* Philadelphia: The Westminster Press, 1954.

Chadwick, H. "The Fall of Eustathius of Antioch," *JThS* 49 (1948) 27-35.

Chalmers, W. R. "Eunapius, Ammianus Marcellinus, and Zosimus on Julian's Persian Expedition," *CQ* 10 (1960) 152-60.

_____. "The Nea Ekdosis of Ammianus Marcellinus, and Zosimus on Julian's Persian Expedition," *CQ* 10 (1960) 165-70.

Chastagnol, A. "Emprunts de l'Histoire Auguste aux *Caesares* d'Aurelius Victor," *RPH* 41 (1967) 85-97.

_____. *La Préfeture urbaine à Rome sous le Bas-Empire.* Paris: 1960.

_____. "La prosopographie, methode de recherche sur l'histoire du Bas-Empire," *Annales* 25 (1970) 1229-35.

_____. "Le probleme de l'*Histoire Auguste*: état de la question," *BHAC* 1963 (1964) 43-71.

_____. *Les fastes de la préfecture de Rome au Bas-Empire.* Etudes prosopographiques 2. Paris: Nouveaux éditions latines, 1962.

_____. *Recherches sur l'Histoire Auguste.* Beitrage zur Historia Augusta Forschungen 6. Bonn: Habelt, 1970.

Chauffin, Y. *Saint Jerome.* Paris: Éditions France-Empire, 1961.

Chestnut, G. F. *First Christian Histories: Eusebius, Socrates, Sozomen, Theodoret and Evagrius.* Theologie Historique 46. Paris: Editions Beauchesne, 1977.

Chibnall, M. *The Ecclesiastical History of Orderic Vitalis.* 6 vols. Oxford: Clarendon Press, 1980.

Chitty, D. J. *The Desert a City*. Oxford: Blackwell, 1966 repr. London and Oxford: Mowbray, 1977.

Christensen, T. "Rufinus of Aquileia and the Historia Ecclesiastica, lib. VIII-IX of Eusebius," *ST* 34 (1980) 129-52.

Clarke, V. K. L. *St. Basil the Great: A study in Monasticism*. Cambridge: 1912.

Clinton, H., *Fasti Romani: The Civil and Literary Chronology of Rome and Constantinople from the Death of Augustus to the Death of Justin II*. 2 vols. New York: Burt Franklin, 1845.

Cochrane, C. N. *Christianity and Classical Culture. A Study of Thought and Action from Augustus to Augustine*. Oxford: Oxford University Press, 1940.

Cohn, A. *Quibus ex Fontibus Sexti Aurelii Victoris et Libri de Caesaribus et Epitomes Undecima Capita Priora Fluxerint*. diss. Berlin: 1884.

Collombet, F. Z. *Histoire civile et religieuse des lettres latines au IVe et au Ve siècle*. Lyons: Perisse, 1839.

_____. *Histoire de Saint Jérôme*. 2 vols. Paris: Paul Mellier, 1844.

_____. *Histoire de Saint Jérôme, Pere de l'Église au IV siècle, ses écrits et ses doctrines*. Paris: 1844.

Conybeare, F. C. "On the Datte of Composition of the Paschal Chronicle," *JTHS* (1901) 288-98.

_____. "The Relationship of the Paschal Chronicle to Malalas," *ByZ* (1902) 395-405.

Cook, S. A., F. E. Adcock, M. P. Charlesworth, and N. H. Baynes, eds. *The Cambridge Ancient History*. Vol. 12. *Imperial Crisis and Recovery A.D. 193-324.*. Cambridge: Harvard University Press, 1965.

Coppola, G. *Il latino di san Girolamo*. Reale Academia delle scienze del' istituto di Bologna. Classe di scienze morali. Bologna: Rendiconto, 1941.

Corbett, P. B. "The *De Caesaribus* Attributed to Aurelius Victor: Points Arising from an Examination of the MSS and of the Teubner Edition of F. Pichlmayr," *Scriptorium* 3 (1949) 254-7.

Courcelle, P. *Late Latin Writers and Their Greek Sources*. H. Wedeck, trans. Cambridge: Harvard University Press, 1969.

Cox, P. *Biography in Late Antiquity. A Quest for the Holy Man*. Berkeley: University of California Press, 1987.

Croke, B. "The Originality of Eusebius' *Chronicle*," *AJPh* 103, 2 (1982) 195-200.

_____. "Porphyry's Anti-Christian Chronology," *JThS* (1983) 168-85.

_____ and A. M. Emmett, eds. *History and Historians in Late Antiquity*. New York: Pergamon, 1983.

Cross, F. L. The Study of St. Athanasius, an Inaugural Lecture Delivered Before the University of Oxford on 1 December 1944. Oxford: Clarendon Press, 1945.

Crump, C. G. and E. F. Jacob, eds. *The Legacy of the Middle Ages*. Oxford: Clarendon Press, 1962.

Cruttwell, C. T. *A Literary History of Christianity Including the Fathers and the Chief Heretical Writers of the Ante-Nicene Period*. 2 vols. New York: Ams Press, 1971 repr. of 1983 ed.

Cuendet, G. "Ciceron et saint Jerome Traducteurs," *REL* 11 (1933) 380-400.

Cutts, E. L. *Saint Jerome*. 4th ed. New York: London Society for Promoting Christian Knowledge, 1897.

Dagron, G., and D. Feissel. "Inscriptions inedites du musee d'Antioche [Antakya] *Travaux et Memoires* Centre de recherche d'histoire et de civilisation byzantines 9 (1985) 421-61.

Dagron, G. *Naissance d'une capitale: Constantinople et ses institutions de 330 a 451*. Paris: Bibliothèque Byzantine, études VII, 1974.

Damsholt, T. "Zur Benutzung von dem *Breviarium* des Eutrop in der Historia Augusta," *CM* 25 (1964) 138-50.

Damste, P. H. "Ad S. Aurelius Victor," *Mnemosyne* 45 (1917) 367ff.

Deferrari, R. J. Saint Basil. The Letters. 4 vols. Cambridge: Harvard University Press, 1972.

Dekkers, E. "Les traductions grecques des écrits patristiques latines," *SE* 5 (1953) 193-233.

Demandt, A. *De Fall Roms. Die Auflösung des römischen Reiches im Urteil der Nachwelt*. Munich: C. H. Beck, 1984.

Demougeot, E. *La formation de l'Europe et les invasions barbares: Des origins germaniques à l'lavènement de Diocletien*. Paris: 1979.

DieKamp, F. "Gelasius von Caesarea in Palestina," *OCA* 117 (1938) 16-32.

154

Dilleman, L. "Ammien Marcellin," *Syria* 38 (1961) 87-158.

Dimaio, M. "Smoke in the Wind: Zonaras' Use of Philostorgius, Zosimus, John of Antioch, and John of Rhodes in His Narrative on the Neo-Flavian Emperors," *Byzantion* 58 (1988) 230-55.

Doignon, J. Hilaire de Poitiers avannt l'exil; recherches sur la naissance l'enseignement et l'épreuve d'une foi episcopale au milieu du IV e siècle. Paris: 1971.

_____. "Tradition classique et tradition chrétienne dans l'histoiriographie d'Hilaire de Poitiers au carrefour des IVe - Ve siècles," *Caesarodunum* 15 (1980) 215-26.

Dolger, F. et al. *Reallexikon für Antike und Christentum Sachwörterbuch zur Auseinandersetzung des Christentums mit der antiken welt*. Stuttgart: Anton Hiersemann, 1957.

_____. "Das Kaiserjahr der Byzantiner," *SbM* 1 (1949) 18-20.

Downey, G. *Antioch in the Age of Theodosius*. 1st ed. Norman: University of Oklahoma, 1962.

_____. *A Study of the Comites Orientis and the Consulares Syriae*. Diss. Princeton University, 1939.

Drinkwater, J. F. "The Pagan Underground, Constantius II's Secret Service and the Usurpation of Julian the Apostate," in C. Deroux, III. *Studies in Latin Literature and Roman History*. Brussels: Latomus, 1983.

Duckett, E. S. *Latin Writers of the Fifth Century*. New York: H. Holt, 1930.

Dufraigne, P. *Aurelius Victor: Livre des Cesars*. Paris: Société d'édition, Les belles lettres, 1975.

Dvornik, F. *The Idea of Apostolicity in Byzantine and the Legend of the Apostle Andrew*. Cambridge: Harvard University Press, 1958.

Eadie, J. and J. Ober. *The Craft of the Ancient Historian: Essays in Honor of Chester G. Starr*. Lanham, MD: University Press of America, 1985.

Ebeling, P. *Quaestiones Eutropianae*. diss. Halle: 1881.

Echols, E. C. *Sextus Aurelius Victor. Brief Imperial Lives*. Exeter, NH: Knight House, 1962.

Eiswirth, R. *Hieronymus' Stellung zu Literatur und Kunst*. Klassische-philologische studien. Heft 16. Wiesbaden: O. Harrassowitz, 1955.

Eklund, S. *The Periphrastic, Completive and Finite Use of the Present Participle in Latin with Special Regard to Translations of Christian Texts in Greek up to 600 A.D.* Uppsala: Universitet, 1970.

Elia, S. d'. *Studi sulla tradizione manoscritta di Aurelio Vittore, I: La tradizione diretta.* Naples: Napoli Libraria Scientifica, 1965.

Ellspermann, G. L. *The Attitude of the Early Christian Latin Writers toward Pagan Literature and Learning.* Catholic University of America Patristic Studies 82. Washington: Catholic University of America Press, 1949.

Eltester, W. "Die Kirchen Antiochias im IV Jh." *ZNTW* 36 (1937) 251-86.

Enmann, A. "Eine verlorene Geschichte der römischen Kaiser und das Buch *De Viris Illustribus Urbis Romae*," *Philologus* suppl. bd. 4 (1884) 337-501.

Ensslin, W. "Philogonios" *RE* 19 (1938) 2483.

_____. "Zur Geschichtschreibung und Weltanschaung des Ammianus Marcellinus," *Klio* 16 (1923) 472.

Ernout, A. and A. Meillet. *Dictionnaire étymologique de la langue latine. Histoire de mots.* 4th ed. Paris: Librairie C. Klincksieck, 1959.

Favez, C. *Saint Jérôme peint par lui-meme.* Brussels: Latomus. Revue d' études latines, 1958.

Fears, J. R. *Princeps a Diis Electus: The Divine Election of the Emperor as a Political Concept at Rome.* Rome: American Academy at Rome, 1977.

Feder, A. *Studien zum Schriftstellerkatalog des heiliges Hieronymus.* Freiburg: Herder and Co., 1927.

Ferrill, A. *The Fall of the Roman Empire. The Military Explanation.* London: Thames and Hudson, 1986.

Ferrua, A. *Epigrammata Damasiana.* Rome: 1942.

Festugiere, A.-J. *Les moines d'Orient, IV, 1: Enquête sur les moines d' Egypte.* Paris: 1964.

Fischer, B., J. Gribomont, H.F.D. Sparks and W. Thiele, eds. *Biblia Sacra iuxta Vulgatam Versionem.* Stuttgart: Wurtembergische Bibelanstalt, 1969.

Fliche, A., and V. Martin. *Histoire de l'église, depuis les origines jusque à nos jours, sous la direction de A. Fliche et. V. Martin.* Paris: 1946ff.

Fotheringham, J. K. "On the List of Thalassocracies in Eusebius," *JHS* 27 (1907) 75-89.

_____. *The Bodleian Manuscript of Jerome's Version of the Chronicle of Eusebius Reproduced in Collotype.* Oxford: Clarendon Press, 1905.

Fox, M. M. *The Life and Times of Basil the Great.* 1939.

Frank, R. I. *Scholae Palatinae. The Palace Guards of the Later Roman Empire.* Rome: American Academy in Rome, 1969.

Frend, W.H.C. Athanasius as an Egyptian Christian Leader in the Fourth Century" Ch. 16 in *Religion Popular and Unpopular.* London: Variorum Books, 1976.

_____. *The Rise of Christianity.* Philadelphia: Fortress Press, 1984.

Fritz, K. von. *Die Griechische Geschichtsschreibung* 1. 2 vols. Berlin: de Gruyter, 1967.

Fuhrmann, M. "Die Romidee der Spatantike," *HZ* 207 (1968) 529-61.

Galdi, M. *L'epitome nella litteratura latina.* Naples: P. Federico and G. Ardia, 1922.

Garrido, G. E. "Observaciones sobre un emperador cristiano Fl. Jul. Constante." *Lucentum* 3 (1984) 261-78.

Geanakoplos, D. J. Church Building and "Caesaropapism," A.D. 312-565," *GRBS* 7 (1966) 167-86.

Giunta, F. "Idazio ed i barbari," *Annuario de estudios medievales* 1 1964) 491-94.

Gelzer, H. *Étude lexicographique et grammaticale de la latinité de saint Jérôme.* Paris: Librairie Hachette et Cie, 1884.

Gelzer, H. *Sextus Iulius Africanus und die byzantinische Chronographie.* 2 parts. New York: Burt Franklin 1967 repr. of Leipzig 1885 ed.

Gensel, W. "Eutropius," *RE* 6 (1907) 1521-7.

Geppert, F. *Die Quellen des Kirchenhistorikers Socrates Scholasticus. SGT* 3, 4. Leipzig: Lippert and Co., 1898.

Gerth, K. "Die sogenannte zweite sophistik (mit Ausschluss der roman-und christ-lichen Schriftsteller," *Bursian* 272 (1941) 250-2.

Gigon, O. *Die antike Kultur und das Christentum.* Darmstadt: Gutersloh Mohn, 1966.

Gildersleeve, B. L. and G. Lodge. *Gildersleeve's Latin Grammar.* 3rd ed. New York: St. Martin's Press, 1971.

Girardet, K. M. "Constance II, Athanase e l' édit d'Arles (353)," *Politique et theologie,* ed. Kannengiesser, 63-92.

_____. "Kaiser Constantius II als 'Episcopus episcoporum," und das Herrscher-bild des Kirchlichen Widerstandes," *Historia* 26 (1977) 95-128.

Glas, A. "Die Kirchengeschichte des Gelasios von Kaisareia, die Vorlage für die beiden letzten Bücher der Kirchengeschichte Rufins," *BA* 6 (1914) 32-73.

Glover, T. R. *Life and Letters in the Fourth Century.* Cambridge: Harvard University Press, 1901.

Gold, B. K., ed. *Literary and Artistic Patronage in Ancient Rome. Literature and Artistic Patronage in Ancient Rome.* Austin: University of Texas Press, 1982.

Good, G. *Harvard Studies in Classical Philology* 74 (1970).

Gorce, D. "Saint Jérôme et son environment artistique et liturgique," *CC* 36 (1974) 150-78.

_____. *Vie de Sainte Melanie.* Sources chrétiennes. 1962.

Grafton, A. *Joseph Scaliger: A Study in the History of Classical Scholarship. I: Textual Criticism and Exegesis.* Oxford: Clarendon Prss, 1983.

_____. "Joseph Scaliger and Historical Chronology: The Rise and Fall of a Dis-cipline," *HT* 14 (1975) 156-85.

Grant, R. M. *Eusebius as Church Historian.* Oxford: Clarendon Press, 1980.

Gregg, R. C. and D. E. Groh. *Early Arianism. A View of Salvation.* Philadelphia: Fortress Press, 1981.

Greschat, M., ed. *Gestalten der Kirchengeschichte.* vols. *Alte Kirche* II. Stuttgart: Verlag W. Kohlhammer, 1984.

Grisart, A. "*La Chronique* de s. Jérôme. Le lieu et la date de sa composition," *Helikon* 1 (1962) 248-58.

Groh, D. "The Rise of Christian Palestine: Eusebian Formulae," Paper presented for the annual meeting of the Society of Biblical Literature. American Academy of Religion, 1979.

158

Grumel, V. "L'annee du monde dans la chronographie de Theophane," *EO* 33 (1934) 396-408.

_____. "Les premieres eres mondiales," *REB* 10 (1952) 93-108.

Grutzmacher, G. *Hieronymus. Eine biographische Studie zur alten Kirchenges-chichte.* 3 vols. B and 1. *Sein Leben und seine Schriften bis zum Jahre 395.* Berlin: Scientia Verlag Aalen 1969 repr. of 1901 Leipzig ed.

_____. *Hieronymus.* Band 2. *Sein Leben und seine Schriften von 385 bis 400.*

Gustafsson, B. "Eusebius' Principles in Handling His Sources as Found in His Church History," *TU* 79 (1961) 429-41.

Gutschmid, A. von. "De Temporum notis quibus Eusebius utitur in Chronicis Canonibus." Leipzig: *Kleine Schriften* 1, 1889 repr. of 1868 ed., 448-82.

_____. "Uber Schoenes Ausgabe der Chronik des Eusebius." Leipzig: *Kleine Schriften* 1, 1889, 417-47.

_____. "Untersuchungen uber die syrische Epitome der eusebischen Canones." Leipzig: *Kleine Schriften* 1, 1889, 483-529.

Gwatkin, H. *Studies of Arianism: Chiefly Referring to the Character and Chronol-ogy of the Reaction Which Followed the Council of M Nicaea.* New York: AMS Press 1978 repr. of 1882 ed.

Haehling, R. von. *Die Religionzugehörigkeit der hohen Amtstrager des römischen Reiches seit Constantins I. Alleinherrschaft bis zum Ende der theodosianischen Dynastie.* Bonn: Rudolf Habelt Verlag, 1978. *Antiquitas.* Reihe 3 (serie in 4to): Abhandlungen zur vor-und Fruhgeschichte, zur klassischen und provinzial-romischen Archaologie und zur Geschichte des Altertums. A. Alfoldi, N. Himmelmann-Wildschutz, J. Straub and K. Tackenberg, eds. Band 23.

Hagendahl, H. *Latin Fathers and the Classics.* Studia Graeca et Latina Gothoburgensia 6. Goteborg: Acta Universitatis Gothoburgensis, 1958.

_____. *Von Tertullian zu Cassiodor. Die profane literarische Tradition in dem lateinischen christlichen Schrifttum.* Studia Graeca et Latina Gothoburgensia 44. Goteburg: Acta Universitatis Gothoburgensis, 1983.

Hamblenne, P. "La longevité de Jérôme Prosper avait-il raison?" Latomus 28 (1969) 1081-1119.

Hardy, E. R., ed. *Christology of the Later Fathers.* E. R. Hardy and C. C. Richardson trans. *LCC.* Philadelphia: The Westminster Press, 1954.

Harnack, A. *Geschichte der altchristliche Literatur bis Eusebius*. 2 vols. 2nd ed. Leipzig: J. C. Hinrichs, 1958.

_____. *Militia Christi. The Christian Religion and the Military in the First Three Centuries*. D. M. Gracie, trans. Philadelphia: Fortress Press, 1981.

_____. "Das Monchtum, seine Ideale und seine Gesschichte," *RA* 1 (1906) 103-12.

_____. "Sokrates und die alte Kirche," *RA* 1 (1906) 27-48.

Hartke, W. *De Saeculi Quarti Exeuntis Historiarum Scriptoribus Quaestiones*. Leipzig: diss., 1932.

_____. *Geschichte und Politik im spatantike Rom; Untersuchungen uber die Scriptores Historiae Augustae*. Aalen: Scientia Verlag, 1962.

Helm, R. "De Eusebii in Chronicorum Libro Auctoribus," *Eranos* 22 (1924) 1-40.

_____. "Die Liste der Thalassokratien in der Chronik des Eusebius," *Hermes* 61 (1926) 241-63.

_____. "Die neuesten Hypothosen zu Eusebius' (Hieronymus') Chronik," *SPA* phil.-hist. kl. 21 (1929) 359, 371-408.

_____. "Eusebius' Chronik und ihre Tabellenform," *Abhandlungen der Berliner Akademie*, phil.-hist. kl. no. 4 (1923). Berlin: 1924.

_____. "Hieronymus und Eutrop," *RhM* (1927) 138-70.

_____. "Hieronymus' Zusatze in Eusebius' Chronik und ihr Wert für die Literaturgeschichte," *PS* 21 no. 2 (1929) Berlin.

Hebermann, G. C. et al., eds. *The Catholic Encyclopedia. An International Work of Reference on the Constitution, Doctrine, Discipline and History of the Catholic Church*. vol. 8, "Jerome." New York: The Glenmary Society, 1913-1940.

Henry, M. "Le temoignage de Libanius et les phenomenes sismiques du ive siècle de nôtre ere. Essai d'interpretation," *Phoenix* 39 (1985) 36-61.

Herron, M. C. *A Study of the Clausulae in the Writings of St. Jerome*. Washington: The Catholic University of America, 1937.

Hertling, L., and Kirschbaum, E. *The Roman Catacombs and Their Martyrs*. M. J. Costelloe, trans. Milwaukee: The Bruce Publishing Co., 1956.

Hoberg, G. *De Sancti Hieronymi Ratione Interpretandi*. diss. Munster: 1886.

160

Hoffmann, M. *Der Dialog bei den christlichen Schriftstellern des ersten vier Jahrhunderte.* Berlin: Akademie Verlag, 1966.

Hohl, E. "Bericht über die Literatur zu den S.H.A. fur die Jahre 1916-1923," *Bursian* 200 (1924) 167-210.

_____. "Bericht über die Literatur zu den S.H.A. fur die Johre 1924-35," *Bursian* 256 (1937) 127-56.

_____. "Die *Historia Augusta* und die *Caesares* des Aurelius Victor," *Historia* 4 (1955) 220-8.

_____. "Die Ursprung des *Historia Augusta*," *Hermes* 55 (1920) 296-310.

_____. "Über das Problem der *Historia* Augusta," *WS* 71 (1958) 132-52.

_____. "Zur *Historia-Augusta*-Forschung," *Klio* 27 (1934) 149-64.

Holdsworth, C. and T. P. Wiseman, eds. *The Inheritance of Historiography 350-900.* Exeter Studies in History 12. Exeter: University of Exeter, 1986.

Honigmann, E. "Gelase de Cesaree et Rufin d'Aquilee," *BCL* 40 (1954) 122-61.

Hoss, K. *Studien über das Schriften und die Theologie der Athanasius auf Grund einer Echtheitsuntersuchung von Athanasius contra gentes und de incarnatione.* Freiburg: 1899.

Hunger, H. *Die hochsprachliche profane Literatur der Byzantion.* 2 vols. Band 1. *Philosophie, Rhetorik, Epistolographie, Geschichts, Geographie.* Munich: Beck, 1978.

Hunt, E. D. "From Dalmatia to the Holy Land. Jerome and the World of Late Antiquity," Review of J.N.D. Kelly, *Jerome: His Life, Writings and Controversies. JRS* 67 (1977) 166-71.

Huxley, G. L. Textual Topics in the *Chronicle* of Eusebius," *Byzantinische Zeitschrift*, 1984.

Janin, R. *Constantinople byzantine.* 2nd ed. Paris: 1964.

Jay, P. *Jérôme et sa exegese.* Paris: 1985.

_____. "Sur la date de naissance de s. Jérôme," *RELA* 51 (1973) 262-80.

Jeep, L. "Aurelii Victoris de *Caesaribus* et l'*Epitome de Caesaribus*," *RF* 1 (1873) 505-18.

_____. "Quellenuntersuchungen zu den griechischen Kirchenhistorikern," *Jahresbericht für klassischen Philologie.* Suppl. Band 14 (1885) 58-63.

Jeffreys, R.  "The Attitudes of Byzantine Chroniclers Towards Ancient History,"
   *Byzantion* 49 (1979) 199-238.

Jeffreys, R.  "The Date of Messalla's Death," *CQ* 35 (1985) 140-8.

Joannou, P. P.  *La legislation imperiale et la christianisation de l'empire romaine
   (311-476)*. Rome: *Orientalia christiana anglecta*, 192, 1972.

Johnson, S.  *Later Roman Britain*. London: Paladin Grafton Books, 1982.

Jones, A.H.M.  *Constantine and the Conversion of Europe*. New York: Collier
   Books, 1962.

_____. *The Later Roman Empire, 284-602: A Social, Economic and Administra-
   tive Survey*. 2 vols. Baltimore: Johns Hopkins University Press, 1986.

_____, J. R. Martindale and J. Morris. *The Prosopography of the Later Roman
   Empire 1, 260-395*. Cambridge: Harvard University Press, 1971.

_____, J. R. Martindale and J. Morris. *Prosopography of the Later Roman
   Empire. I: 260-395*. Cambridge: 1971.

Jullian, C.  *De protectoribus et domesticorum Augustorum*. Paris, 1883.

Kaegi, W. E.  *Byzantium and the Decline of Rome*. Princeton: Princeton University
   Press, 1968.

Kaimio, J.  *The Romans and the Greek Language*. Humanae Litterae 64. Helsinki:
   Soc. Sc. Fennica, 1979.

Kellner, W.  *Libertas und Christogramm. Motivegeschichtliche Untersuchungen zur
   Münzpragung des Kaisers Magnentius (350-353)*. Karlsruhe: 1968.

Kelly, J.N.D.  *Early Christian Doctrines*. New York: Harper and Row, Publishers,
   1960.

_____. *Jerome*. New York: Harper and Row, 1975.

_____. *The Oxford Dictionary of Popes*. Oxford: Oxford University Press,
   1986.

Kelly, M. J.  *Life and Times as Revealed in the Writings of St. Jerome Exclusive of
   His Letters*. Catholic University of America Patristic Studies 70. Washington: Catholic University of America, 1949.

Kent, R. G.  "The Latin Language in the IVth Century," *TAPhA* 50 (1919) 91-100.

Keseling, P. "Die Chronik des Eusebius in der syrischen Überlieferung," *Oriens Christianus*, 3rd sen. I (1927), 23-48.

_____. "Die 'Chronik' des Eusebius in der syrischen Überlieferung," *OC* 1 (1926) 23-48, 223-41 and 2 (1927) 33-56.

Klauser, T. "Die Hagia Sophia," *Jahrbuch für Antike und Christentum* 13 (1970) 107-18.

_____., ed. *Reallexikon für Antike und Christentum*. Band 6. Stuttgart: Anton Hiersemann, 1966.

Klein, R. *Constantius II und die christliche Kirche*. Darmstadt: Wissenscshaftliche Buchgesellschaft, 1977.

Klotz, A. "Die Quellen Ammianus in der Darstellung von Julians Perserzug," *RhM* 71 (1916) 461-506.

Koep, L. "Chronologie, Christliche," *Reallexicon für Antike und Christentum* 3 (1957), 50-59.

König, I. Origo Constantini. Anonymus Valesianus. Teil 1. Text und Kommentar. Trier: Trierer Historische Forschungen 11, 1987.

Kraus, S. "The Jew in the Works of the Church Fathers. VI: Jerome," *JQR* 6 (1894) 225-61.

Krautheimer, R. *Three Christian Capitals. Topography and Politics*. Berkeley: University of California Press, 1983.

Krumbacher, K. *Geschichte der byzantinischen Literatur von Justinian bis zum Ende des oströmischen Reiches (527-1453)*. 2nd ed. New York: Burt Franklin, 1958.

Labriolle, P. de. *Histoire de la littérature latine chrétienne*. 3rd ed. 2 vols. Paris: Société d'édition, Les belles lettres, 1947.

_____. *History and Literature of Christianity*. H. Wilson, trans. New York: Alfred A. Knopf, 1925.

_____. "Le songe de s. Jérôme," *Miscellanea Geronimiana*. Rome: 1920, 217-39.

Lacroix, G. *L'historien au moyen age*. Conference Albert-le-grand, 1966. Montreal: Institut d'etudes medievales, Librarie J. Vrin, 1971.

Laistner, M. L. *Christianity and Pagan Culture in the Later Roman Empire*. The J. W. Richard Lectures in History 1950-1951. Ithaca: Cornell University Press, 1951.

_____. "The Study of St. Jerome in The Middle Ages," *A Monument to St. Jerome*, 235-56. See Murphy below.

_____. "Some Reflections on Latin Historical Writings in the Fifth Century," *CP* 35 (1940) 241-58.

Lamb, H. *Constantinople, Birth of an Empire*. New York: Alfred A. Knopf, 1957.

Lammert, F. "Die Angaben des Kirchenvaters Hieronymus über vulgares Latein," *Philologus* 75 (1919) 395-413.

Lancel, S. "Aux origines du Donatisme et du movement des circoncellions," *Cahiers tunisiennes* 15 (1967) 183-88.

Laquer, R. "Die beiden Fassungen des sog. Toleranzedikte von Mailand," *EPITYMBION*. Reichenberg: Heinrich Swoboda, 1927, 132-41.

_____. *Eusebius als Historiker seiner Zeit*. Berlin and Leipzig: Walter de Gruyter and Co., 1929.

_____. "Synkellos," *RE* 55 (1932) 1387-1410.

Lawlor, H. J. *Eusebiana*. Oxford: Oxford University Press, 1912.

_____, N. H. Baynes and G. W. Richardson. "The Chronology of Eusebius," *CQ* 19 (1925) 94-100.

Lebon, J. "Pour une edition critique de Saint Athanase," *Revue d'histoire ecclesiastique* 21 (1925) 324-30.

Lehmann, P. "Die heilige Einfalt," *Historische Jahrbuch* 58 (1938) 327-31.

Lerner, R. "Refreshment of the Saints: The Time after Antichrist as a Station for Earthly Progress in Medieval Thought," *Traditio* 32 1976) 97-144.

Lewis, A.-M. "Latin Translations of Greek Literature: The Testimony of Latin Authors," *L'AC* 55 (1986) 163-74.

Liebeschuetz, J. H. W. *Antioch: City and Imperial Administration in the Later Roman Empire*. Oxford: 1972.

Lippold, A. "Der Kaiser Maximinus Thrax und der romische Senat," *Antiquitas*. Reihe 4, Band 2 (1964) 73-89 (*BHAC* 1963).

Lofstedt, E. *Late Latin*. Cambridge: Harvard University Press, 1959.

_____. *Philologischer Kommentar zur Peregrinatio Aetheriae. Untersuchungen zur Geschichte der lateinischen Sprache.* 2nd ed. Uppsala: Almquist and Wiksell, 1936 repr. of 1911 ed.

_____. *Roman Literary Portraits.* P. M. Fraser, trans. Oxford: Clarendon Press, 1958.

_____. *Syntactica: Studien und Beitrage zur historischen syntax des lateins.* Lund: Gleerup, 1956.

Lommatzch, E. "Literarische Bewegungen in Rom im vierten und funften Jahrhundert n. Chr.," *ZL* 15 (1904) 177-92.

Loofs, F. *Paulinus von Samosata: eine Untersuchung zur altkirchlichen Literatur und Dogmengeschichte.* Leipzig: 1924. Texte und Untesuchungen Bd. 44, Heft 5.

Lot, F. *The End of the Ancient World and the Beginning of the Middle Ages.* Trans. by P. and M. Leon and ed. by G. Downey. New York: Harper and Row, Publishers, 1961.

Lounsbury, R. C. *The Arts of Suetonius: An Introduction.* New York: Peter Lang, 1987.

Luebeck, A. *Hieronymus Quos Noverit Scriptores et ex Quibus Hauserit.* Leipzig: Teubner, 1872.

MacMullen, R. *Constantine.* New York: Harper and Row, Publishers, 1971.

Malcovati, E. "I breviari storici del IV secolo," *CF* 1 (1942) 23-65.

Mango, C. *Le Developpment urbain de Constantinople (lVe-Vlle siecles).* Travaux et Memoires Monographies 2, Paris: 1985.

Markus, R. A. "Chronicle and Theology: Prosper of Aquitaine," in Holdsworth and Wiseman, 1986.

Matthews, J. *Western Aristocracies and Imperial Court A.D. 364-425.* Oxford: Clarendon Press, 1975.

McGuire, M. R. "The Decline of Knowledge of Greek in the West from c. 150 to the Death of Cassiodorus. A Reexamination of the Phenomenon from the Viewpoint of Cultural Assimilation," *CF* 13, no. 1 (1959) 3-25.

Markus, R. A. *Church History and Early Church Historians. The Materials, Sources and Methods of Ecclesiastical History.* D. Baker, ed. Oxford: Oxford University Press, 1975, 1-17.

Martimort, A. G. *Deaconesses. An Historical Study.* San Francisco: Ignatius Press, 1982.

Maximilianus, M. *Geschichte der lateinischen Literatur des Mittelalters.* 3 vols. Munich: Beck, 1911-1913.

Meeks, W. A., and R. L. Wilken. *Jews and Christians in Antioch in the First Four Centuries of the Christian Era.* Missoula, Montana: Scholars Press, 1978.

Meershoek, G.Q.A. *Le latin biblique d'apres Saint Jérôme.* Nymwegen-Utrecht: Dekker and Van de Vegt, 1966.

Meijering, E. P. *Orthodoxy and Platonism in Athanasius: Synthesis or Antithesis?* Leiden: E. J. Brill, 1968.

Meinhold, P. *Geschichte der Kirchlichen Historiographie,* 2 vols. Munich: Alber, 1967.

Mendels, D. "Greek and Roman History in the *Bibliotheca* of Photius - A Note," *Byzantion* 56 (1986) 196-206.         —

Mercati, G. "A Study of the Paschal Chronicle," *JThS 7 (1906) 397-412.*

Meyer, E. *Forschungen zur alten Geschichte.* 2 vols. Halle: M. Niemeyer, 1892-1899.m

Mierow, C. C. *St. Jerome, the Sage of Bethlehem.* Milwaukee: Bruce Publishing Co., 1959.

Mohrmann, C. *Etudes sur le Latin des chretiens.* v. 2. Latin  chrétien et medieval. Rome: Edizioni distoria e letteratura, 1961.

_____. "Le Latin commun et le latin des chrétiens," VCHr (1947) 1-12.

_____. "Quelques observations linguistiques à propos de la nouvelle version latine de Psauter," VChr (1947) 114-28 and 168f.

_____. "Quelques traits characteristiques du latin des chrétiens," *Bibbia, Letteratura cristiana antica; Studi & Testi* 121. *Miscellanea Mercati, 1.* Citta del Vaticano: Biblioteca apostolica Vaticana, 1946, 437-66.

Momigliano, A. *The Conflict between Paganism and Christianity in the Fourth Century A.D.* Oxford: Clarendon Press, 1963.

_____. "The Historians of the Classical World and Their Audiences: Some Suggestions," *ASP Classe di lettere e filosofia* ser. 3, 8, 1 (1978) 61-75.

Mommsen, T. "Das römische Militärwesen seit Diocletian," *Hermes* 24 (1889), 195-276.

_____. "Die alteste Handschrift der Chronik des Hieronymus," *Hermes* 24 (1889) 383-401.

Monceaux, P. *Saint Jérôme. Sa jeunesse, l'étudiant et l'ermite.* Paris: Grasset, 1932.

_____. "Saint Jérôme au desert de Syrie," *Revue des Deux Mondes* 58 (1930) 155-7.

Moreau, J. "Constantius II," *JAC* 2 (1959) 178ff.

Morris, J. "The Chronicle of Eusebius: Irish Fragments," *Bulletin of the Institute of Classical Studies* 19 (1972) 80-93.

Morrison, E. F. *St. Basil and His Rule: A Study in Early Monasticism.* Oxford: 1912.

Mosshammer, A. A. "Lucca Bibl. Capit. 490 and the Manuscript Tradition of Hieronymus' (Eusebius') Chronicle," *CS* 8 1975, 203-40.

_____. *The Chronicle of Eusebius and Greek Chronographic Tradition.* Lewisburg: Bucknell University Press, 1979.

_____. "Two Fragments of Jerome's Chronicle," *RhM* 1234 (1981) 66-80.

Mras, K. "Nachwort zu den beiden letzten Ausgaben der Chronik des Hieronymus," *WS* 46 (1928) 200-15.

_____. "Ein Fund bei Eusebius," *WS* 47 (1929) 39-42.

Muckle, J. T. "The de officiis ministrorum of St. Ambrose. An Example of the Process of the Christianization of the Latin Language," *Medieval Study* 1 (1939) 63-80.

Murphy, F. X. *A Monument to St. Jerome. Essays on Some Aspects of his Life, Works and Influence.* New York: Sheed and Ward, 1952.

_____. *Rufinus of Aquileia (345-411). His Life and Works.* n.s. 6. Washington: Catholic University of America, 1945.

Nathanson, B. G. "Jews, Christians and the Gallus Revolt in Fourth Century Palestine," *BA* 49 no. 1 (March 1986) 26-36.

Nautin, P. Études de chronologie hieronymienne," *REAug* (1972) 209-18.

_____. "Hieronymus," *Theologische Realenzyklopädie*. Berlin: Walter de Gruyter, 1986, Band XV, 306-7.

_____. La date du De viris inlustribus de Jérôme," *RHE* (1961) 33-35.

_____. "La liste des oeuvres de Jérôme dans le *De viris inlustribus*," *Orpheus* 5 (1984) 319-34.

_____. "Le premier échange épistolare entre Jérôme et Damase: lettres reeles ou fictives?" *ZPT* 30 (1983) 331-4.

_____. "La date du *De Viris Illustribus* de Jérôme, de la mort de Cyrille de Jerusalem et de celle de Gregoire de Nazianze," *RHE* 56 (1961) 33-35.

Neri, V. "Ammiano Marcellino e l'elezione di Valentiniano," *Rivista Storica dell' Antichita* 15 (1985) 153-82.

Niebuhr, B. G. "Historischer Gewinn aus der armenischen Übersetzung der Chronik des Eusebius," Leipzig: *Kleine Schriften* 1, 1889 repr. of 1820-1821 ed.

Nixon, C.E.V. *An Historiographical Study of the 'Caesars' of Sextus Aurelius Victor*. diss. Ann Arbor, MI: 1971.

Noble, A. N. *Indices Verborum Omnium Quae in Sexti Aurelii Victoris Libro 'de Caesaribus' et Incerti Auctoris 'Epitome de Caesaribus' Reperiuntur*. diss. Columbus, OH: 1938.

Nolan, J. G. *Jerome and Jovinian*. Washington: The Catholic University of America Press, 1956.

Opelt, I. "Hieronymus' Leistung als Litteraturhistoriker in der Schrift *De viris illustribus*," *Orpheus* n.s. 1 (1980) 52-75.

_____. *Roma Aeterna. Études sur le patriotisme romain dans l'occident latin a l'époque des grandes invasions*. Rome: Institut Suisse de Rome, 1967.

Opitz, H. G. *Untersuchungen zur Überlieferung der Schriften des Athanasius* (Arbeiten zur Kirchengeschichte, 23). Berlin and Leipzig: de Gruyter, 1935.

Opitz, T. "Quaestionum de Sexto Aurelio Victore Capita Tria," *SPL* 2, 1 (1872) 199-270.

Oulton, J.E.L. "Rufinus' Translation of the Church History of Eusebius," *JTS* 30 (1929) 150-74.

Palangue, J. R. "St. Jerome and the Barbarians," *A Monument to Saint Jerome*, 171-200. See Murphy above.

Paschoud, F. *Cinq études sur Zosime.* Paris: Les Belles Lettres, 1975.

————. "L'eglise dans l'empire romain," Actes VIIᵉ *Congres de Federation internationale des associations d'études classiiques.* Budapest: Harmatta J.-Budapest Akademiai Kiado, 1984, 2, 197-207.

Patzig, E. *"Über einige Quellen des Zonaras,"* BZ 6 (1897) 324-9.

Paucker, K. *De Latinitate Hieronymi.* Berlin: S. Calvary and Associates, 1880.

Pease, A. S. "The Attitude of Jerome Towards Pagan Literature," *TAPA* 50 (1919) 150-67.

Pelikan, J. *The Christian Tradition. A History of the Development of Doctrine.* v. 1. The Emergence of the Catholic Tradition (100-600). Chicago: The University of Chicago Press, 1971.

————. *The Excellent Empire. The Fall of Rome and the Triumph of the Church.* New York: Harper and Row, 1987. Ch. 4 "History as Divine Apocalypse," 43-52.

Penella, R. J. "A Lowly Born Historian of the Roman Empire: Some Observations on Aurelius Victor and his *De Caesaribus,"* Thought 55 (1980) 122ff.

Penna, A. *Principi e carattere dell' esegesi di santo Gerolamo.* Rome: Pontificio istituto biblico, 1950.

————. *Santo Gerolamo.* Turin and Rome: Pontificio instituto biblico, 1949.

Pernoud, R. and M. *Saint Jerome.* R. Sheed, trans. New York: Macmillan, 1962.

Peter, H. W. *Die geschichtliche Litteratur über die römische Kaiserzeit bis Theodosius I und ihre Quelle.* Hildesheim: G. Olms 1967 repr. of 1897 ed.

Peterson, J. M. *The Dialogues of Gregory the Great in Their Late Antique Background.* Studies and Texts 69. Liverpool: Liverpool University Press, 1984.

Pickman, E. M. *The Mind of Latin Christendom.* Oxford: Oxford University Press, 1937.

Piganiol, A. *L'empire chrétienne, 325-395.* Paris: Presses Universitaries de France (Histoire romaine, vol. 4), 1947.

Pighi, G. B. "Ammianus Marcellinus," *RAC* 1 (1950) 386-94.

Pricoco, S. "Motivi polemici e prospettive classicistiche nel *De viris inlustribus,"* SG 32 (1979) 69-99.

_____. "Some Historical Remarks on Rufinus' *Historia Ecclesiastica* (H.E. IV, 2, 1-5)," *RSA* 11 (1981) 123-8.

Quain, E. A. "St. Jerome As a Humanist," *A Monument to St. Jerome*, 203-32. See Murphy above.

Quasten, J. *Patrology. Vol. III. The Golden Age of Greek Patristic Literature from the Council of Nicea to the Council of Chalcedon*. Westminster, Md.: The Newman Press, 1963.

Quinn, K. *Catullus. The Poems*. London: Macmillan, 1973.

Ricciotti, G. *Julian the Apostate*. M. J. Costelloe, trans. Milwaukee: The Bruce Publishing Co., 1960.

Ridley, R. T. "Eunapius and Zosimus," *Helikon* 9-10 (1969-1970) 574-92.

Rowell, H. T. *Ammianus Marcellinus, Soldier-Historian of the Late Roman Empire*. Cincinnati: The University of Cincinnati, 1964.

Ryan, G. J. and R. P. Casey. *The 'De Incarnatione' of Athanasius*. Studies and Documents XIV. Philadelphia: University of Pennsylvania Press, 1945-46.

Sabbah, G. *La methode d'Ammien Marcellin. Recherches sur la construction du discours historique dans les 'Res Gestae'*. Paris: Les belleslettres, 1978.

Samuel, A. E. *Greek and Roman Chronology*. Munich: Beck, 1972.

Sanders, H. A., ed. *Roman Historical Sources and Institutions*. New York: Macmillan Co., 1904.

Sandys, J. E. *A History of Classical Scholarship*. v. 1. *From the Sixth Century B.C. to the End of the Middle Ages*. 3rd ed. New York: Hafner Publishing Co., 1967.

Sasel, J. "The Struggle Between Magnentius and Constantius II for Italy and Ilyricum," *Ziva Antika* 21 (1971) 205-16.

Scaliger, J. *Thesaurus Temporum*. 2nd ed. Osnabruck: Zeller, 1968 repr. of 1658 Amsterdam posthumous ed.

Schamp, J. "Gelase ou Rufin: un fait nouveau sur les fragments oublies de Gelase de Cesaree (CPG No. 3521)," *Byzantion* 57 (1987) 360-90.

Schanz, M., ed. *Geschichte des römische Litteratur bis zum Gesetzgebungswerk des Kaisers Justinian*. v. 4. *Litteratur von Constantinus bis zum Gesetzgebungswerke Justinians*. 2 vols. Munich: Iwan von Muller's Handbuch, 1914-1935.

Schlumberger, J. *Die 'Epitome de Caesaribus': Unterschuchungen zur heidnischen Geschichtsschreibung des 4. Jahrhunderts n. Chr.* Vestigia 18. Munich: Beck, 1974.

Schmidt, P. L. "S. Aurelius Victor, *Historiae Abbreviatae*," *RE* Supplementband 15. Munich: 1978, 1660-71.

Schneemelcher, W. "Athanasius von Alexandrien als Theologe und als Kirchenpolitiker," *ZNW* 43 (1950/51) 242-56.

Schoene, A. *Die Weltchronik des Eusebius in ihrer Bearbeitung durch Hieronymus.* Berlin: Wiedmann, 1900.

Schoo, G. *Die Quellen des Kirchenhistorikers Sozomenos.* Neue Studien zur Geschichte der Theologie und die Kirche 11. Berlin: Trowitsch, 1911.

Schwartz, E. "Die Königslisten des Eratosthenes und Kastor mit Excursen über die Interpolationen bei Africanus und Eusebios." *AKG.*

_____. "A propos des donnees chronographiques de l'Histoire Auguste," *Antiquitas.* Reihe 4, Band 3 (1966) 197-210 (*BHAC* 1964-65).

_____. "Chronicon Paschale," *RE* 3 (1899) 2460-77.

_____. "Eusebius," *RE* 6 (1907) 1370-1439.

Schwartz, J. "A propos d'une notice de la chronologie de Jerome," *Historia Augusta Colloquium* (1977-1978) 225-32.

Seager, R. *Ammianus Marcellinus. Seven Studies in His Language.* Columbia: University of Missouri Press, 1986.

Seeck, O. "Chronica Constantinopolitana," *RE* 3, 2 (1899) 2454-9.

_____. *Die Briefe des Libanius.* Hildesheim: Georg Olms, 1966.

_____. "Festus," *RE* 6, 2 (1909) 2257-8.

_____. "Studien zur Geschichte Diocletians und Constantins," *Fleckeisens Neven Jahrbuch für Philologie* 139 (1889) 611ff.

_____. "Panodorus," *RE* 36 (1958) 631-35.

_____. "Studien zur Geschichte Diocletians und Constantins," *Fleckeisens Neven Jahrbuch für Philologie*, 139 (1889), 611 ff.

_____. "Zur Chronologie und Quellenkritik des Ammianus Marcellinus," *Hermes* 41 (1906) 481-539.

Sellers, R. V. *Eustathius of Antioch and His Place in the Early History of Christian Doctrine*. Cambridge: 1928.

Setton, K. M. *The Christian Attitude Towards the Emperor in the Fourth Century*. New York: Columbia University Press, 1941.

Sevcenko, I. and J. S. Allen, eds. *Literature in Various Byzantine Disciplines, 18992-1977*. Washington: Mansell, for Dumbarton Oaks Center for Byzantine Studies, 1981.

Siegmund, A. *Die Überlieferung der griechischen Literatur in der lateinische Kirche bis zum XII Jahrhundert*. Munich: Pasing, 1949.

Simonetti, M. "Saint Ambroise et saint Jérôme, lecteurs de Philon," *Aufstieg und Niedergang der römischen Welt: Geschichte und Kultur Roms in Spiegel der neuern Forsschung*. Ed. by H. Temporini and W. Haase. Berlin: Walter D. Guyter, 1984, vol. 2, 21, 1, 731-59.

Sirinelli, J. *Les vues historiques d'Eusebe de Cesaree durant la periode preniceenne*. Publications de la section de langues et de littératures 10. Paris: University of Dakar, 1961.

Soren, D. "The Day the World Ended at Kourion. Reconstructing an Ancient Earthquate," *National Geographic* 174, no. 1 (July 1988), 30-53.

Souter, A., ed. *A Glossary of Later Latin to 600 A.D.* Oxford: Clarendon Press, 1949.

Spellar, L. A. "A New Light on the Photinians," *JTS* n.s. 34, 1 (1983) 99-113.

Spittler, L. T. "Historia critica Chronici Eusebiani," *CSR* Phil.-hist. class. 8 (1785-1786) 39-67.

Stead, G. C. *Divine Substance*. New York and London: Oxford University Press, 1977.

Stein, E. *Histoire du Bas-Empire: De l'État romain à l'État byzantin, 284-476*. French edition by J.-R. Palanque. Amsterdam: Adolf M. Hakkert, 1968.

Steinmann, J. *Saint Jerome and His Times*. R. Matthews, trans. University of Notre Dame: Fides Publishers, 1959.

Stevenson, J. *Studies in Eusebius*. Cambridge: Harvard University Press, 1929.

Storch, R. H. "The Eusebian Constantine," *CH* 40 (1971) 145-55.

Straub, J. *Heidnische Geschichtsapologetik in der christlichen Spätantike*. Untersuchungen über Zeit und Tendenz der Hist.-Aug. Antiquitas Reihe 4: Beitrage zur Hist.-Aug.--Forschungen. Band 1. Bonn: R. Habelt, 1963.

_____. *Regeneratio Imperii. Aufsatze über Roms Kaisertum und Reich im Spiegel der heidnischen und christlichen Publizistik*. Darmstadt: Wissenschaftliche Buchgesellschaft, 1972.

_____. *Studien zu den Historia Augusta*. Dissertationes Bernenses serr. 1, fasc. 4. Bern: A. Francke, 1952.

Sugano, K. *Das Rombilds des Hieronymus*. Europäischen Hochschulschriften. Reihe 15. Klassischen Sprachen und Literaturen. Band 25. Frankfurt-am-Main: Peter Lang, 1983.

Sundermeier, A. *Quaestiones Chronographicae Eusebiii et Hieronymi Chronica Spectantes*. Kiel: diss., 1896.

Swain, J. W. *Edward Gibbon the Historian*. London: Macmillan, 1966.

_____. "The Theory of the Four Monarchies. Opposition History under the Roman Empire," *CP* 35 (1940) 1-21.

Sychowski, S. *Hieronymus als Litterarhistoriker, eine quellenkritische Untersuchung der Schrift des heiliges Hieronymus 'de viris illustribus'*. *KS* 2, 2. Munster: Heinrich Schoningh, 1894.

Syme, R. *Ammianus and the Historia Augusta*. Oxford: Oxford University Press, 1968.

_____. *Emperors and Biography*. Oxford: Oxford University Press, 1971.

_____. "Ignotus, The Good Biographer," *Antiquitas*. Reiche 4, Band 4 (1964) 131-53 (*BHAC* 1963).

_____. "The Bogus Names in the Hist.-Aug.," *Antiquitas*. Reihe 4, Band 2 (1964) 257-72 (*BHAC* 1963).

Szymanski, L. *The Translation Procedure of Epiphanius-Cassiodorus in the Historia Tripartita, Books I and II*. Catholic University of America Studies in Medieval and Renaissance Literature 24. Washington: Catholic University of America Press, 1963.

Testard, M. *Jérôme, l'Apôtre savant et pauvre du patriciat romain*. Paris: Société d'Édition. Les belles lettres, 1969.

Thelamon, F. *Païens et chrétiens au IV^e siècle*. L'apport de l''Histoire ecclésiastique de Rufin d'Aquilee. Paris: Études Augustiniennes, 1981.

_____. "Recherches sur la valeur historique del' 'Histoire ecclésiastique' de Rufin d'Aquilee," *ReH* 102 (1978) 522-5.

*Thesaurus Linguae Latinae. (Ex Concilio Academiarum Quinque Germanicarum Berolinsensis, Gottingensis, Lipsiensis, Monacensis, Vindobonensis).* Leipzig: Teubner, 1900----.

Thompson, E. A. "Ammianus Marcellinus," in T. A.Dorey, ed., *Latin Historians.* New York: Basic Books, Inc., 1966.

_____. "The Historical Methods of Ammianus Marcellinus," *Hermathena* 59 (1942) 44-66.

_____. *The Historical Work of Ammianus Marcellinus.* Groningen: Bouma's Boekuis N.V. Publishers, 1969.

_____. *Romans and Barbarians. The Decline of the Western Empire.* Madison: University of Wisconsin Press, 1982.

Topfer, B. *Das Kommende Reich des Friedens.* Berlin: Akademie Verlag, 1964.

Traube, L., ed. *Hieronymi Chronicorum Codicis Floriacensis Fragmenta Leidensia, Parisina Vaticana.* Codices Graeci et Latini Photographice Depicti, Supplementum 1. Leiden: A. W. Sijthoff, 1902.

Treadgold, W. T. *The Nature of the Bibliotheca of Photius.* Washington: Dumbarten Oaks Center for Byzantine Studies, 1980.

Trieber, C. "Die Idee der vier Weltreiche," *Hermes* 27 (1892) 321-44.

Turner, C. H. "The Early Episcopal Lists," *JTS* 1 (1899-1900) 181-200, 529-53.

_____. "The Early Episcopal Lists," *JTS* 18 (1916-1917) 103-34.

Villain, M. "Rufin d'Aquilee et l''histoire ecclesiastique d'Eusebe," *RSA* 33 (1946) 164-210.

Vogt, J. *Ammianus Marcellinus als erzählender Geschichtsschreiber der Spätzeit.* Wiesbaden: Akademie der Wissenschaften und der Literatur in Mainz, 1963.

Wachsmuth, C. *Einleitung in der Studium der alten Geschichte.* Leipzig: S. Hirzel, 1895.

Wallace-Hadrill, D. S. *Christian Antioch: A Study of Early Christian Thought in the East.* New York: Cambridge University Press, 1982.

_____. *Eusebius of Caesarea.* London: A. R. Mowbray, 1960.

_____. "The Eusebian Chronicle: The Extent and Date of Composition of its Early Editions," *JTS* n.s. 6 (1955) 248-53.

Wattenbach, W. and F.-J. Schmale. *Deutschlands Geschichtsquellen im Mittelaltern.* v. 1. *Vom Tode Kaiser Heinrichs V bis zum Ende des Interregnum.* Darmstadt: Wissenschaftliche Buchgesellschaft, 1976.

Weber, W. "Constantinische Deckenmalde aus dem römische Palast unter dem Trierer Dom," *Museumsführer Bischofl. Dom- & Diozesanmus.* Trier: 1984.

Westermann, A., ed. *Biographi Graeci Minores.* Amsterdam: A. M. Hakkert, 1964 repr. of 1845 ed.

Widmer, W. "Felicium temporum reparatio," *Festschift für H. F. Haefele,* ed. by A. Reinle. Sigmaringen Thorbecke. 1985, 11-16.

Wiesen, D. S. *St. Jerome As a Satirist. A Study in Christian Latin Thought and Letters.* Ithaca: Cornell University Press, 1964.

Wilken, R. "The Restoration of Israel in Biblical Prophecy. Christian and Jewish Responses in the Early Byzantine Period," in J. Neusner and E. Frerichs, *"To See Ourselves as Others See Us." Christians, Jews, "Others" in Late Antiquity.* Chico: Scholars Press, 1985, 443-71.

Wilken, R. L. *The Christians As the Romans Saw Them.* New Haven: Yale University Press, 1984.

Williams, S. *Diocletian and the Roman Recovery.* New York: Methuen, Inc., 1985.

Winkelmann, F. "Charakter und Bedeutung der Kirchengeschichte des Gelasios von Kaisareia," *BF* 1 (1966) 346-85.

_____. "Das Problem der Rekonstruktion der 'Historia ecclesiastica' des Gelasius von Caesarea," *FF* 38, 10 (1964) 311-14.

_____. "Die Quellen der 'Historia Ecclesiastica' des Gelasius von Cyzicus (nach 475)," *Byzantinoslavica* 27 (1966) 104-30.

_____. "Spätantike lateinische Übersetzungen der christlichen griechischen Literatur," *ThLZ* 95 (1967) 229-40.

_____. *Untersuchungen zur Kirchengeschichte des Gelasios von Kaisareia.* Sitzungsberichte der deutschen Akademie der Wissenschaften zu Berlin. Klasse für Sprache, Literatur und Kunst 1965 no. 3. Berlin: Akademie-Verlag, 1966.

Winter, P. *Der literarische Charakter der 'Vita beati Hilarionis' des Hieronymus.* Zittau: Druck von R. M. Nachf, 1904.

Wölfflin, E. "Aurelius Victor," *RhM* 29 (1874) 282-308.

_____. "Epitome," *ALLG* 12 (1902) 333.

_____. "Zur Latinität der Epitome Caesarum," *ALLG* 12 (1902) 445-53.

Zeiller, J. "Saint Jerome et les Goths," *Miscellanea Geronimiana*. Rome: Tipografia poliglotta Vaticana, 1920, 123-30.

Ziegler, J. *Zur religiösen Haltung der Gegenkaiser im 4. Jh. n. Chr.* Kalmunz, 1970.

_____. "Die alteste Handschrift der Chronik des Hieronymus," *Hermes* 24 (1889) 383-401.

_____. "Die armenischen Handschriften der Chronik des Eusebius," *Hermes* 30 (1895) 321-38.

_____. "Über die Quellen der Chronik des Hieronuymus," *GS* 7 (1909) 606ff. repr. of 1850 Abhandlungen der philologisch-historischer Classe der Königlichen Gesellsschaft de Wissenschaften 1, 1850, 669-93.

_____. "Zu den *Caesares* des Aurelius Victor," *SKPA* 2 (1884) 951-58.

_____. "Zu den oxforder Hieronymus-Handschrift," *Hermes* 24 (1889) 649.

Ziegler, K. Z. and W. Sontheimer, eds. *Der Kleine Pauly. Lexikon der Antike auf der Grundlage von Pauly's Realenencyclopädie der classischen Wissenschaft.* Stuttgart: Alfred Druckenmuller Verlag, 1964, vols. 1-2.

Zischucke, C. F. "Die Römische Münztatte Trier. Von der Münzreform der Bronzeprägung unter Constans und Constantius II 346/348 n. Chr. bis zu ihrer Schliessung im 5. Jh." *Kl. numism. R. der Trierer Munzfunde V.* Trier. Petermanchen-Verlag, 1982.

Zöckler, O. *Hieronymus. Sein Leben und Wirken aus Seinen Schriften dargestellt.* Gotha: Verlag von Friedrich Andreas Berthes, 1865.

Zwierlein, O. "Der Fall Roms im Spiegel der Kirchenväter," *ZPE* 32 (1978) 45-80.

DDS

## BIOGRAPHICAL SKETCH

Malcolm Donalson earned his B.A. and M.A. in Classics at Florida State University before pursuing the Ph.D. in Humanities. He has published articles in several publications including *Classics Chronicle*, *The Classical Outlook*, and *The Classical Journal*. He has taught Latin, mythology, history and humanities courses at the following: Marianna High School, Marianna, Florida (1974-1984); Florida State University (1984-1989); Episcopal High School, Baton Rouge, Louisiana (1989-1990); and currently, McKinley and Istrouma Magnet Schools, Baton Rouge.